BEST CAREERS FOR VETERANS

Transitioning to Civilian Life

LEARNINGEXPRESS ®

NEW YORK

BEST CAREERS FOR VETERANS

Transitioning to Civilian Life

Library of Congress Cataloging-in-Publication Data
Best careers for veterans.—1st ed.

   p. cm.
 ISBN: 978-1-57685-670-3
  1. Veterans—Employment—United States. 2. Veterans—Vocational guidance—United States. 3. Career changes—United States—Handbooks, manuals, etc. 4. Job hunting—United States—Handbooks, manuals, etc. 5. Résumés (Employment)—United States—Handbooks, manuals, etc. UB357. B476 2009

 331.702086'970973—dc22   2008050609

Printed in the United States of America

For more information or to place an order, contact LearningExpress.

2 Rector Street
26th Floor
New York, NY 10006

Or visit www.learnatest.com

ABOUT THE AUTHOR

Olivia M. Cloud is a researcher, writer, and editor living in Nashville, Tennessee. She has devoted nearly three decades to the publishing industry and is the owner of Guardian Angel Communications Services.

She is the author of six books, among them *Roadmaps for Living* (National Baptist Publishing Board, 1999), *Life Challenges for Teens* (Mega Corporation, 2000), *Testify!* (Mega Corporation, 2002), and *Rules of the Road: More Roadmaps for Living* (Mega Corporation, 2004).

She has contributed writing and research to many other important works including *I'll Find a Way or Make One: A Tribute to Historically Black Colleges and Universities* (Amistad/HarperCollins, 2004). She was also the editor of *Joy to the World: Inspirational Christmas Meditations from America's Preachers* (Atria Books/Simon & Shuster, 2006).

TABLE OF CONTENTS

• • • • • •

Section II: Best Careers for Veterans 207

Whether you decide to market your current military skills or choose a new employment direction, you will want a career that gives you job satisfaction and provides a reasonable amount of job security.

Chapter Six: Finding Your Right Career 209

• • • • • •

Section III: Resources and Information 263

Knowledge is power. Having a full understanding of your rights and resources will equip you for the transition, journey, and settlement into civilian life.

Chapter Seven: Working USERRA 265

BEST CAREERS FOR VETERANS

Transitioning to Civilian Life

INTRODUCTION

Joining the military is a pretty simple process—just about as easy as signing on the designated line. But separating from military service can be a complex and involved process for a variety of reasons. Depending on how long you've been in the military, transitioning to civilian life can be a challenge in many ways, some predictable and some totally unexpected.

Foremost on the minds of the majority of transitioning servicemembers is what they will do when they get out. Some soldiers returning home to the United States are finding they still have a fight on their hands, but this time it's for jobs. You've likely heard a few horror stories, talked to some disgruntled veterans, and may be wondering if you can make it once you get out. There's a lot to consider, and only you can decide what's best for you.

Despite good economic performance and job growth in certain employment areas, federal labor statistics show nearly one-in-five veterans between the ages of 20 and 24 are unemployed, a number three times the national average. Luiz Arrango joined the Navy in 2000. After serving as an aviation machinist mate for four years, he returned to his Chicago neighborhood at age 24 and found himself struggling to locate career options that offered the same challenge. Eventually, he did find a good job, but Luiz believes a major obstacle for him was the employer's lack of understanding of how the skills he acquired in the Navy matched their open positions.

"My military background definitely proved to be an asset," Luiz says. "While employers did recognize that being in the military involves hard work and results, it was difficult for them to see why an aviation machinist was the right fit for their job."

Obstacles in career planning can also affect veterans who are more seasoned in the civilian workforce. Paula Reese, a 37-year-old Milwaukee native who has served in the National Guard for 18 years, was deployed to Kuwait in 2004. Prior to her departure, she worked as an operations manager for a large business. When she returned home one year later, she was rehired by her employer with the same seniority and pay, but in a different position. Paula was unhappy with the new position and left to search for a new job. After six months with no real prospects, she realized her predicament. "It can be difficult to pinpoint military-friendly employers who are willing to take a gamble on an employee who can be deployed at any time and who will make available the same opportunities when that servicemember returns," she says of her experience.

The military is an amazing and life-changing experience for practically every servicemember. It is a great career opportunity, but it can be difficult when transitioning back to the civilian world. However, there is definitely some good news worth considering—many companies are eager and willing to hire veterans. The following reasons are cited by the U.S. Department of Labor to demonstrate why employers are looking to hire veterans.

Integrity—Veterans know what it means to do an honest day's work. Prospective employers can take advantage of a track record of integrity, one that often includes security clearances. This integrity translates into qualities of sincerity and trustworthiness.

Leadership—The military trains people to lead by example, as well as through direction, delegation, motivation, and inspiration. Veterans understand the practical ways to manage behaviors for results, even in the most trying circumstances. They also know the dynamics of leadership as part of both hierarchical and peer structures.

Accelerated learning curve—Veterans have the proven ability to learn new skills and concepts. In addition, they enter the workforce with identifiable and transferable skills that are proven in real-world situations. This type of strong background can enhance an organization's productivity.

Technology and Globalization—Their experiences in the service have made many veterans aware of international and technical trends pertinent to business and industry. Vets can bring the kind of global outlook and technological savvy that businesses of any size need to succeed.

Teamwork—Veterans understand that genuine teamwork grows out of a responsibility to one's colleagues. Military duties involve a blend of individual and group productivity. They also necessitate a perception of how groups of all sizes relate to each other and reach an overarching objective.

Awareness of health and safety standards—Thanks to extensive training, veterans are aware of health and safety protocols, both for themselves and the welfare of others. Individually, they represent a drug-free workforce that is sensitive to maintaining personal health and fitness. On a corporate level, their awareness and conscientiousness translate into protection of employees, property, and materials.

Experience with diversity and inclusion—Veterans have learned to work side-by-side with a diverse pool of individuals (i.e., race, gender, geographic origin, ethnic background, religion, or economic status, as well as mental, physical, and attitudinal capabilities). They have the sensitivity to cooperate with many different types of individuals.

Performance under pressure—Veterans understand the rigors of tight schedules and limited resources. They have developed the capacity to accomplish priorities on time, in spite of tremendous stress. They understand the critical importance of staying with a task until done right.

Respect for protocol and procedures—Through their military service, veterans have gained a unique perspective on the value of accountability. They can grasp their place within an organizational framework and become responsible for subordinates' actions to higher supervisory levels. They know how policies and procedures serve to strengthen an organization.

Triumph over adversity—In meeting the challenges of military service, veterans have likely proven their determination in mission-critical situations that demand flexibility, stamina, and endurance. Some will have overcome personal disabilities through strength and determination.

Educated Workforce—According to CareerCommandPost.com, the website for the Military Transition Group, more than 95% of all military personnel have high school diplomas, over 35% have some college experience, and 25% have college degrees. In addition, all military personnel have received specialized professional or technical training and continue to take courses to advance their skills and expertise.

Military-friendly companies acknowledge that recruiting veterans is a smart business choice. Military personnel represent some of the best-trained candidates in the job market. Veteran employees offer a unique blend of leadership and teamwork skills, as well as integrity, technology proficiency, and the ability to perform under pressure. In other words, it's worth the risk for employers.

Many employers appreciate your service and sacrifice, even if they don't understand it right away. Many companies are still looking for the characteristics and skills you gained as an experienced soldier, sailor, pilot, or marine.

Best Careers for Veterans contains a wealth of resources and information based on research, expert recommendations, and the experiences of real-life veterans. While their names have been changed, the stories and experiences highlighted in this book are from real people who, like you, served their country and found a way to have a life beyond the military.

By planning early for your transition, you can tap into the many resources available to help veterans. There's a lot of information that can often be confusing and sometimes even conflicting. This book pulls it all together, including an occasional VET VIP (Very Important Pointer), to help you focus on information that is critical to your transition success. At the end of each chapter you will find several REF pages that contain valuable reference information to help you in the transition process.

You are coming to the end of one of the most honorable acts of humanity—serving your country in the Armed Forces. Now that you have decided to trade your fatigues for civilian work clothes, do all you can to ensure a smooth transition for a successful and fulfilling life beyond the military. Once you have made the decision to leave, don't look back. Keep looking ahead, knowing that your military service has given you a great jump-off point for a successful future.

Your career transition may be a piece of cake or you may hit a few bumps in the road. If you don't lock into the kind of career you want right away, don't get discouraged. If you put the same energy and enthusiasm into your transition that you gave to your service responsibilities, you will succeed.

SECTION I

Starting Over: Getting a New Start Post-Service

• CHAPTER ONE: Finding Yourself—Out of Uniform

There is a lot to consider in making the transition to civilian life, but hundreds of thousands of veterans have done it successfully, and so will you! Planning early for your transition and tapping into the right resources will make all the difference.

• CHAPTER TWO: The Military *Is* School: An Accelerated Course!

You deserve credit for your military service, and not just a pat on the back. Your service time could earn you college credit. Plus, your ability to communicate the training and experience you received and link them to the requirements of the job you desire may be the key to landing your next position.

• CHAPTER THREE: Creating Your Post-Military Resume

It's true that most civilian employers won't understand the significance of your military training and skills—unless you know how to translate them into a language an employer can understand. All you need is a few ideas for reworking your resume to maximize your chances of getting the job you want.

• CHAPTER FOUR: Mastering the Interview Process

Whether being interviewed by a patriot or a pacifist, interviews for veterans can be challenging. Doing a little prep work before the interview will help you counter preconceived and incorrect notions.

• CHAPTER FIVE: Networking—Using Your Military Connections

Let the people you met in the armed services and the people they know help you find your next career. You already have the network in place; now, make it a part of your strategy for finding the job that you want.

What Other Vets Are Saying...

Don't wait until the last month or two—start planning before you have one year left in the service.

I started my Coast Guard career as an enlisted member in the mid-1970s. I attended Electronics Technician School and earned the proper certification and a number of promotions.

Since my military retirement, I've been a realtor with a local real estate agency and I own a small business with my wife. I got interested in real estate after we bought our home. After watching our agent work, I thought: "I can do what the realtor did." Now I'm doing just that. I especially enjoy helping fellow veterans find new homes.

Retirement was difficult at first because of the relocation, no guaranteed job, and three mouths to feed. My kids adjusted pretty well—a lot quicker than my wife and I did. Since the initial transition, we've all adjusted to civilian life.

My military experience honed my interpersonal skills. I also learned what it was like to work for a "good" and "bad" supervisor. I tried my best to emulate the positive leaders. I miss the friendship and camaraderie of military life, but I keep in touch with former colleagues thanks to e-mail, phone calls, and occasional visits.

I didn't use any career services, military or civilian, prior to my retirement. I was so busy with my Coast Guard job that I failed to attend all those helpful programs. If I had it to do again, I'd focus less on my current job and more on my future career.

To someone leaving the military, I would advise them to write down goals, and develop a plan to achieve those goals. Don't wait until the last month or two—start planning before you have one year left in the service.

T. J.
Coast Guard, Retired

CHAPTER ONE

FINDING YOURSELF— OUT OF UNIFORM

Leaving the Military?

There really is life after military service! Although there's a lot to consider, it's still possible to enjoy a successful career out of uniform. Truthfully, though, a big part of the transition process can involve stress—including good stress. Even doing something that's exciting and pleasurable can produce stress. Perhaps you have been in the military for a number of years and you are now making the transition back to civilian life. Understanding and coping with stress are essential skills you will need to get through this challenging time.

People leave the military for different reasons, but the process is typically the same.

Desireé's Desire

Desireé, a 26-year-old Air Force captain, had enjoyed her four years of service, but she decided it was time to leave. At the time of her decision, her husband Stephen, an F-16 pilot in the Air Force, was deployed to the Middle East. At the same time, Desireé left for a deployment to South America. Prior to that, she had an overseas tour in Afghanistan that lasted six months.

"It was becoming increasingly hard for Stephen and I to be able to spend good amounts of quality time together," Desireé says of their overlapping deployments.

Desiree loves the Air Force, which does have a program designed to help couples serving at the same time; however, its needs ultimately come first, a fact that helped shape her decision to move on.

"I wanted a little more control in my life—our lives," Desireé says.

As soon as you put away your uniform and become a civilian, you will enter a work world with different rules, cultures, and expectations. This move likely will be the biggest transition of your life.

Leaving military service means leaving behind a certain level of stability and familiarity. On the other hand, transitioning out of military service marks the beginning of a new, uncharted career path. As soon as you put away your uniform and become a civilian, you will enter a world with different rules, cultures, and expectations. This move will likely be the biggest transition of your life.

For those leaving the military today, the transition to civilian life can be just as difficult as the transition made when entering the military, and frequently more so. The transition process is even more difficult for the many men and women who leave the military without taking the time to properly prepare for such a major life shift. For disabled veterans, the adjustment can be more complex and frustrating since the costs for required special services and medical attention are constantly rising and jobs may be increasingly scarce.

No matter what the circumstances of your departure from the military, you should not wait until the last minute to start your job search.

Kevin's Key Decision

Kevin Marcum was 21 years old, single, and barely making a living in New Jersey when he decided to join the Air Force in 1980. He trained to become an aircraft mechanic, traveled the world from base to base, and rose to the rank of master sergeant.

By all appearances, Kevin was a career military— someone who would not leave to take a civilian job. He served tours in several countries, including Afghanistan. His sense of belonging and purpose, cultivated in military life, were elevated even more.

"I was in charge of the flight line," he says. "Those planes made it up in the air—those ground troops expected those planes in the air."

But after 20 years of marriage and two teenaged children, Kevin decided that 25 years as an aircraft mechanic in the Air Force was enough. He made a wise decision to prepare to leave the military well before his separation date. Kevin said he knew plenty of people who, after 20 years or so in the military, decided to retire and find a civilian job without preparing well in advance. He was advised to start planning two years before his retirement.

Whatever your rank or length of service, it is important to recognize that you have invested yourself in the armed services and have grown accustomed to the military's unique lifestyle.

What's Your Story?

Your reasons for departure may be quite different from Desireé's or Kevin's. Regardless of your reasons, however, it is important to know what to expect before you leave. Whatever your rank or length of service, it is important to recognize that you have invested yourself in the armed services and have grown accustomed to the military's unique lifestyle. Whether you are separating after four years of service or retiring after 20 or more years, you will need to plan both personally and professionally for this major life transition.

It has been estimated that about 250,000 people part with the military every year, including retirees and those who have fulfilled their contract with the military and chosen to move on. Some who leave are war veterans who have tired of multiple deployments to the Middle East and want out. Others are military members who don't want to keep moving their families around to various bases in the United States and overseas. Even though he had achieved the rank of major, Samuel decided to leave the Army because he and his family were tired of moving every two years. Plus, his wife wanted to finally have a career of her own, something that was impossible to do as long as Samuel held on to his military career.

Why is planning for departure so important? It can be very difficult to move from a structured environment like the military where self-sacrificing is the norm. The civilian sector is different than the military environment. There is a sea of opportunities in the civilian sector and it's largely up to you to handle the many options available. If you plan ahead of time, your transition need not be traumatic.

How do you make this adjustment smoothly, efficiently, and successfully? One of the first and most important steps is to take a good honest look at yourself and assess how and where you would like to be employed. Employers will highly value your military experience, provided you target the type of job you are seeking, identify the skills and expertise you want to use, and market your strengths.

Earl's Experience

"My transition experience was a good one, mainly because I did a lot of research and planning before leaving the Air Force," says Earl, a U.S. Navy retiree.

Earl retired from the Navy with the goal of using his training and management experience to become a human resources specialist. He explains, "About a year before my retirement date, I earned a Human Performance Improvement Certificate through an online education program and joined local chapters of HR professional organizations for networking purposes. When I retired from the military, I took a month off to transition into civilian life." After three months of job searching, Earl was hired by a great company to deliver their high-performance assessment training programs to organizations. "It's a great job for me and the skills I learned in the military," he says.

How can you manage your military transition so that your adjustment time is minimal and has the least amount of discomfort and strain? By recognizing the factors that play a role in this life-affecting change, you can significantly increase the likelihood of a successful transition experience. This chapter will emphasize things to consider when making the transition, testimonials from those who have made the transition, and resources to make your transition process simpler.

Leaving the military doesn't have to mean a loss of your identity.

Leaving Can Affect Your Identity

You worked hard to earn your rank—whether that of a captain, sergeant, or petty officer. If you were on active duty, but dressed out of uniform, and someone asked what you did for a living, you probably replied, "I'm in the Army, Air Force, Navy, Coast Guard, or Marines." But when you become a civilian and enter a world that may have little regard for military service or rank, as it relates to your employability, who are you? After leaving the service, you may feel like you're just another civilian walking the streets.

Changing careers can be a stressful undertaking, and probably even more so for those leaving military service after many years. Some servicemembers may have worked for 30 years to achieve a rank or grade, but upon leaving the Armed Forces, they leave it behind— and with it, a large portion of their identity. But leaving the military doesn't have to mean a loss of your identity.

Instead, think of it as an adventure. You're gaining an entirely new sense of self.

A career servicemember who entered at age 18 or 22 still has a lot of living to do, even after 30 years of service. Re-entry into civilian life at around age 40 or 50 means there's time to establish a whole new career; therefore, finding a new identity is important.

When a transition is approached as an opportunity to grow, you will have already taken a giant step toward reestablishing your identity.

Some people find it easier than others to adopt new identities. It's a simple fact that some people are more flexible than others, but don't let this get in your way. The transition process from military to civilian life can be traumatic and stressful, but it can also open the door to a variety of possibilities. When a transition is approached as an opportunity to grow, you will have already taken a giant step toward reestablishing your identity.

Steps to a Successful Transition

Have you thought about what type of work you want to do after you leave military service or where you want to live? Do you know how much you need to earn to ensure that you and your family maintain a decent quality of life? You might think you can be happy with any job as long as it pays enough. Or, that living in the place where you've always wanted can compensate for a lack of good career opportunities. The truth is that the type of work you do, how much you earn, and where you live are all equal factors in achieving career satisfaction.

One of the many skills you gained while in the military was targeting an objective. No matter what you were planning to acquire or accomplish, the first step in every military mission includes targeting the objective. Now, the objective is your career. It's time to apply what you've learned to your job search.

Start focusing on your career objective by thinking about your personal interests and aspirations. Ask yourself the following questions. Where do you want to be five or ten years from now? Do you want to work with addicts, children, animals, or heavy machinery? Or, would you like to be in an office, at a desk, involved in sales or editorial work of some sort? Is your present job the type of work you would like to continue doing? Do you want to start your own company? If so, what will it take to establish your business? You can begin to find the answers by creating a list of things you'd like your civilian career to include.

> *Start focusing on your career objective by thinking about your personal interests and aspirations.*

What Are Your Skills?

While you were on active duty, you gained excellent skills that are usable in the civilian workplace. The military probably sent you to school or provided on-the-job training. So, how will you use these skills and knowledge to transition to your new life? Review your work history and identify the tasks you enjoyed performing, as well as the ones you hated. Don't worry about job titles right now. There are a number of online resources that can help transfer your Military Occupational Specialty (MOS) or Military Occupational Classification (MOC) into civilian terminology (e.g., HireVetsFirst.gov, Military.com, and online.onetcenter.org). Additionally, a simple online search, using the keywords *military skills translation*, will yield several sites, such as www.veteranemployment.com, which focus on assisting veterans and employers.

What Are Your Work Preferences?

Think about your job responsibilities and how you feel about them. Do you enjoy working with your hands? Are you comfortable supervising others? Does working as a team member appeal to you or do your prefer to work on your own?

Your career in the military provided a wonderful opportunity to establish and understand your personal work values. Think about your military assignments and the conditions under which you have worked. Do you prefer working in an office or outdoors? Have you decided that you never want to operate a vehicle for a living? Upon leaving military service, have you made a vow never to do anything outdoors again? Do you prefer a routine or enjoy the excitement of a varied work environment?

Understanding your work preferences contributes to your job satisfaction, as do any strong ethical feelings you may have. For example, would you work at a job you hate if it paid enough money? You may think that only the money matters, but personal satisfaction in your work is vital to a satisfying life. Some people will never feel comfortable selling insurance, driving a tractor-trailer, or sitting behind a desk all day. Understanding your work preferences can positively impact your long-range career decisions and overall career satisfaction.

What Are Your Qualifications?

Whether you plan to continue working in your current career field or look for a different type of position, you should assess whether you are qualified for the job you're considering. If you don't know whether you have the right qualifications, conduct some research. You can learn more about job qualifications by reading want ads, talking to people who have similar jobs, or conducting online research. Discussing occupation choices with your state's employment office can be helpful.

If the type of work you're considering requires certification or licensure, you can find out more about requirements from the Credentialing Opportunities On-Line (COOL) website at www.cool.army.mil.

Where Will You Live?

Whatever dictates your location preferences, you should make sure they don't conflict with your occupational preferences. Consider whether you can find work in your chosen field and location. For example, a career in aquatics might be difficult if you're living in Nevada, and you might go broke establishing a snow-plowing business in Florida.

For most of us, where we live is important. Maybe you want or need to live near your family or your spouse's family. Perhaps you're divorced but want to settle in a place where you can see your children more frequently. Maybe your children have special needs that require certain schools, healthcare facilities, or support services. Or, perhaps your spouse has career aspirations that will impact where you choose to live.

How Much Money Do You Need?

Working at a job you hate just for the money is a drag, but so is working at a job you love that doesn't pay enough money. Before diving headfirst into a new career, make sure you can afford to do the kind of work you want to do. Research salaries and cost of living for your dream job in the location where you want to live. The cost of living changes with location, sometimes dramatically. You may be able to make a living doing what you want if you live in Birmingham, Alabama, but not in Los Angeles, California.

Whether you are single or have a family, the bottom line is that you need to earn enough money to meet your financial and family obligations. The same apartment may cost $600 a month in one city and $1,000 in another. To help you be realistic as you explore career objectives, create a budget worksheet that compares your current monthly expenses to what those expenditures would be in different locations.

What's Realistic?

Setting a realistic objective requires taking an honest look at yourself, your abilities, and your circumstances. Don't lie to yourself or make important decisions without doing thorough research first. If you have a family, find out what is important to them. This is a major, life-impacting decision that can affect everyone's happiness and sense of well-being. Your successful career transition requires that your objective is realistic and satisfies your needs and goals, as well as those of your family members.

Sample Budget Worksheet

MILITARY INCOME

Basic Monthly Pay	$ _____
Basic Allowance for Housing (BAH)	$ _____
Basic Allowance for Subsistence (BAS)	$ _____
Family Separation Allowance (FSA)	$ _____
Flight Pay	$ _____
Foreign Language Proficiency Pay	$ _____
Hazardous Duty Pay	$ _____
Hostile Fire Pay/Imminent Danger Pay	$ _____
Medical/Dental Pay	$ _____
Sea Pay/Submarine Pay/Diving Pay	$ _____
Other (Explain)	$ _____
Other (Explain)	$ _____
TOTAL MILITARY PAY/ALLOWANCES	$ _____

MILITARY PAY DEDUCTIONS

Federal Income Tax (FITW)	$ _____
Social Security Tax (FICA)	$ _____
State Income Tax For: _____	$ _____
Local Income Tax For: _____	$ _____
Allotment To: _____	$ _____
Allotment To: _____	$ _____
Allotment To: _____	$ _____
Allotment To: _____	$ _____
Combined Federal Campaign:	$ _____
Other (Explain): _____	$ _____
Other (Explain): _____	$ _____
Other (Explain): _____	$ _____
TOTAL MILITARY PAY DEDUCTIONS	$ _____

NOTE: *This worksheet reflects expenses that are most likely to change once you leave the military. However, both your military and civilian budget should include allowances for investments/savings, credit card payments and other revolving debt, pets, entertainment and miscellaneouse expenses (personal grooming, gifts, donations, toiletries, etc.).*

MONTHLY CIVILIAN INCOME NEEDED	$ _____

HOUSING

Mortgage or Rent	$ _____
Homeowners/Renters Insurance	$ _____
Property Taxes	$ _____
Home Repairs/Maintenance/Fees	$ _____
Home Improvements	$ _____
TOTAL HOUSING COSTS	$ _____

UTILITIES

Electricity	$ _____
Water/Sewer	$ _____
Natural Gas or Oil	$ _____
Telephone (Land Line, Cell)	$ _____
TOTAL UTILITY COSTS	$ _____

FOOD

Groceries	$ _____
Restaurant/Lunch/Snacks	$ _____
TOTAL FOOD COSTS	$ _____

FAMILY OBLIGATIONS

Child Support	$ _____
Alimony	$ _____
Day Care	$ _____
Other _____	$ _____
TOTAL FAMILY OBLIGATIONS	**$ _____**

MEDICAL EXPENSES

Insurance (medical/dental/vision)	$ _____
Non-reimbursed Expenses/Copays	$ _____
Fitness (health club/pilates/yoga)	$ _____
Other _____	$ _____
TOTAL MEDICAL EXPENSES	**$ _____**

TRANSPORTATION EXPENSES

Car Payments	$ _____
Gasoline	$ _____
Auto Repairs/Maintenance	$ _____
Insurance	$ _____
Other _____	$ _____
TOTAL TRANSPORTATION EXPENSES	**$ _____**

Understanding Your Abilities

A major step in your successful transition into civilian life involves a realistic understanding of your talents, skills, and abilities, and how these attributes relate to business and industry. The good news is that the traits you developed during your military service are beneficial to commercial enterprises because they are held to high standards of performance and operations.

Employers want people who can fit within the company culture and get the job done. Whether or not an employer recognizes these qualities in you depends on how effectively you show yourself to be the perfect match for the job. Showing how your skills, education, training, experience, and work ethic fit the company's requirements starts with an extensive inventory.

In the military, a person who demonstrates outstanding leadership qualities is targeted for intense training and development. The person may be assigned to managing a troop, then to an assignment in human resources, and later to a position involving policy-making and strategic planning. The intent is to develop a top-notch, trained officer who can function in a large, structured organization. Because of the size, structure, and nature of doing business in the military, this individual has great potential for success in operations management in almost any industry. Depending on his or her length of service, the veteran applicant could immediately transition into first-line supervision or senior-level management. The challenge is not the skills you possess, but rather the ability to correlate the different assignments you've had to private sector roles, such as financial planning and analysis, operations management, purchasing, human resource management, systems administration, and administrative support.

Skills represent either natural abilities or things you have learned, and fall into the following three categories.

● **VET VIP**

According to MilitaryHire.com, in a poll taken among employment agency staffers, recruiting professionals agreed that military personnel make excellent leaders. Once given a specific task, they are decisive, resourceful, and tremendous team players—and they perform well under pressure.

1. Self-management skills—the way you manage yourself on the job (e.g., dependable, resourceful, etc.)

2. Functional skills—knowledge/abilities that you use on the job or have used in previous jobs (e.g., operate equipment, supervise, analyze, etc.)

3. Technical skills—specific skills required to perform a described task (e.g., computer programming, accounting, sales, etc.)

Newspaper and Internet job listings can help determine what package of skills employers are looking for in an employee. Be honest in your assessment of your own skills and make sure you understand the terminology used by employers. Using a computer to enter data into a file control system does not mean you have experience as a computer programmer. If you don't have what it takes, reevaluate your objective or begin to look for ways to acquire the skills you need to get the job you want.

Experience

Former military personnel can offer a great deal of experience and dedication to prospective corporate employers. Yet, their capabilities are often discounted if they adhere to a formal military-style resume. With some analysis and innovation, individuals making the transition from military to civilian careers can effectively position themselves as the well-qualified, capable candidates they are.

From your written materials to the first telephone contact, and through the stages of the interview, as a military applicant, you need to practically reinvent yourself in order to be competitive in the market you have selected.

Your time in the military gave you excellent experience, but it may be difficult to compare this military experience to civilian job experience. Forget about military job titles or occupational codes. Instead, look at what you did. Your Verification of Military

With some analysis and innovation, individuals making the transition from military to civilian careers can effectively position themselves as the well-qualified, capable candidates they are.

Experience and Training (VMET) document is a great place to start. (Refer to page 17 to see a sample VMET document. To get your official verification document, visit the VMET website at www.dmdc.osd.mil/vmet. Note: This site can only be accessed from a government computer network.)

As with any specialized field, military applicants need to prepare their resumes and cover letters in lay terms and strategize how they will position and market themselves throughout the process. The last thing you want as an applicant is for the recruiter or potential employer to focus on your military rank or title. Rather, target your resume and your attention on the professional capabilities you will bring to the company.

Stay away from the traditional textbook format and style. In most cases, military experience is best handled in a modified, functional resume, because it highlights work experience in professional categories as opposed to chronological achievements by job title or rank. A functional resume has an up-front objective that explains the applicant's skills and experience, as well as other outstanding areas of expertise.

When composing your resume, statements following your career objective should categorize your experience, particularly in commercial areas such as management, operations, and human resources expertise. This format allows you to neatly tie together all the pieces of your military experience into a continuous, comprehensive story that comes across clearly and directly. This helps seemingly fragmented assignments to read as parts of one position, showing progressively more duties and responsibilities along the way. (For more information about resumes and job interviews, go to Chapter Three: Building Your Post-Military Resume.)

Employers prefer proven performers, and with your solid military experience, you are a proven performer!

Employers prefer proven performers, and with your solid military experience, you are a proven performer!

Make sure you know what employers are looking for in comparison to your military work experience.

Employers want to hire applicants who have the requisite skills and experience. Keep in mind, though, that what you gained in the military—a positive attitude, physical fitness, dedication, genuine enthusiasm, and the discipline of showing up every day for work—can do a lot to shift the balance in your favor.

Training and Education

Employers usually use specific training and education requirements as a means of determining an applicant's ability to do a job. Find out what employers are looking for and determine if you meet those criteria. Remember, your military training may qualify you for a particular job. Your VMET document or DD Form 2586 [Figure 1] is a helpful resource you can use to start your training and education inventory. If you still don't have what it takes, talk with an academic or vocational counselor at a college, technical institute, or local state employment office to find out how to acquire the training you need.

Certification and Licenses

Regardless of your training, education, or experience, some employers will require that you hold a specific certificate or license. For example, most municipalities will require that you are a certified Emergency Medical Technician (EMT) before offering you a position. Employers will normally require a local license or certificate. The fact that you have a Virginia teaching certificate may not be sufficient to allow you to teach in Montana. Make sure you understand the licensure and certification requirements for your job objective. You can learn more about licensure and certification requirements by visiting the COOL website or CareerInfoNet at www.acinet.org.

● **VET VIP**

Check out this COOL (Credentialing Opportunities On-Line) web site if the type of work you're considering requires certification or a license — (www.cool. army.mil)

FIGURE 1: DD Form 2566, Verification of Military Experience and Training

<table>
<tr><td colspan="3" align="center">VERIFICATION OF MILITARY EXPERIENCE AND TRAINING</td></tr>
<tr><td>1. LAST NAME - FIRST NAME - MIDDLE NAME</td><td>2. SOCIAL SECURITY NUMBER</td><td>3. PAY GRADE</td></tr>
<tr><td>4. MILITARY SERVICE AND COMPONENT</td><td>5. DATE OF INFORMATION
(YYYYMMDD)</td><td>6. YEAR(S) IN SERVICE</td></tr>
</table>

7. EXPERIENCE AND TRAINING HISTORY *(In reverse chronological order)* AND RELATED INFORMATION

DD FORM 2586, APR 2007   PREVIOUS EDITION IS OBSOLETE.

Work Style and Ethic

Once you demonstrate yourself as the perfect match for the job, consider your work style or ethic. Some employers are looking for candidates who will work well as part of a team. Others want self-starters who need little or no supervision. But, all employers want employees who are punctual, dependable, capable, and free of alcohol or drug dependency.

Know what the employer is looking for and then determine if you fit the bill. Do you have what they want? Are you willing to work irregular and long hours or do you want a set weekly work schedule? Are you prepared to risk a salary on commission rather than a fixed income? Employers are good at figuring people out—they have to be. But even if you're camouflaging certain things during the interview process, they'll find out who you really are and what you can do soon after you start work.

Handling Your Transition Process

The experiences of thousands of servicemembers who have separated from the military suggest that the transition process is likely to be stressful for you and your family. Previous transitioners have found several important tactics in dealing with the stress related to separation from the military. The Department of Defense (DoD) offers the following general suggestions to transitioners.

Get going. Transitioning into civilian life is your own responsibility; no one can do it for you. It's best to simply dive in, work through the letting go process, and not procrastinate.

Sell yourself. You have a great product to sell—you! This is no time to be modest about your accomplishments.

Transitioning into civilian life is your own responsibility; no one can do it for you. It's best to simply dive in, work through the letting go process, and not procrastinate.

Most likely, no one will come to hunt you down to give you a job. First, they have to know you are available for work. Once you let them know, you will find many people who will help you.

Work your plan. Work at planning your transition as if it were a job, because until you get a job, transition planning is your job. Don't spend every waking hour working on it; you will burn out. Take time for yourself and your family.

Lighten up. This is probably the most important piece of advice. Do not lose your sense of humor. An upbeat disposition will see you through. Conversely, a tense and anxious demeanor may give potential employers cause for concern.

Keep your family involved. Your family has a large stake in your transition and is experiencing many of the same feelings, worries, and uncertainties as you. Do not keep your plans to yourself; get your family involved in this process. It's their life, too. Let them in on your plans and ask for their input throughout.

Volunteer. Consider doing volunteer work. Your charitable actions will help others, assist you in getting to know the community beyond the military, and enhance your networking capability.

Consider a course in managing change. A change-management course should be taken before stress appears, or at the first signs of stress, to help offset its effects.

Do not keep your plans to yourself; get your family involved in this process. It affects their lives, too. Let them in on your plans and ask for their input throughout.

Embracing Your New Identity

Some people find it easier than others to adopt new identities. Transition can be traumatic and stressful, but it also opens up a whole range of possibilities. If you approach your transition as an opportunity to grow, you will have already taken a giant step toward reestablishing your identity.

It's not always easy. Some veterans have a more difficult time than others, as you'll see in the following statements from three frustrated veterans.

"Well, it's been three months total. I had a slew of offers for temporary [three to six months] IT work in the general area. Those darned insurance companies won't leave me alone and I've gotten inquiries and answered some questions for a few different companies but it doesn't look like I'll be hired anytime soon." J. (female, honorably discharged)

• • • • • •

"Been retired ten years, have wandered from job to job, and never satisfied. Tried my darndest to get the Navy to call me back, of course no luck. My advice is if you are thinking about leaving military service, think hard. The outside world is full of chaos and unemployment, think hard." E. (male, honorably discharged)

• • • • • •

"As I like to say, vets don't need parades. They need jobs—well-paying jobs reflective of the skills and experience they represent. Every time a veteran remains unemployed or homeless because he or she loses a job or can't find a job—that's a failure of our government. Yet, our government will blame veterans for their own fate. If we're going to maintain a well-qualified armed service, then we're going to have to face up to the issue of transition assistance that results in gainful employment of a veteran. If my story went public, it would certainly detract many of our fellow Americans from joining the military." K. (male, honorably discharged)

Sound familiar? If not, then maybe someone you know has expressed these or similar frustrations. Truthfully, there are a lot of disappointed vets who feel let down and left out, despite the laundry list of agencies and laws established to help make the transition process easier. However, many veterans have successfully evolved from military service to civilian employment, including some very famous personalities.

Famous people are not the only ones who successfully transition from military service; many ordinary men and women have been able to make the shift with little frustration or anxiety. The most successful transitions are those who have taken advantage of every opportunity out there for veterans.

A Look at Some Famous Vets

Many of veterans have successfully evolved from military service to civilian employment, including some famous personalities. Take a look:

Alan Alda, (actor, director, and screenwriter)
Former Army Reserve Gunner

Tony Bennett (singer)
Former Private, U.S. Army

George H.W. Bush (41st United States President)
Former Naval Aviator Lieutenant (JG), U.S. Navy

Drew Carey (comedian and actor)
Former U.S Marine

Johnny Carson (television host of The Tonight Show)
Former Ensign, U.S. Navy

Bill Cosby (actor)
Former Hospital Corpsman, U.S. Navy

Clint Eastwood (actor and director)
Former Instructor, U.S. Army

Jocelyn Elders (former surgeon general)
Former Second Lieutenant, Army Medical Specialist Corps

Malcolm Forbes (publisher)
Former Staff Sergeant, U.S. Army

R. Buckminster Fuller (inventor and engineer)
Former Ensign, U.S. Navy

Rocky Marciano (heavyweight boxing champion)
Former Enlisted, U.S. Army

Chuck Norris (actor and martial arts champion)
Former Air Policeman, U.S. Air Force

Orville Richard Burrell, a.k.a. **Shaggy** (reggae musician)
Former U.S. Marine

Fred W. Smith (CEO of FedEx®)
Former Commissioned Officer, U.S. Marine Corps

George Steinbrenner (baseball executive and businessman)
Former General's Aide, U.S. Air Force

Dave Thomas (founder and CEO of Wendy's® restaurants)
Former Staff Sergeant, U.S. Army

Montel Williams (former talk show host, actor, and motivational speaker)
Former Lieutenant, Naval Security Fleet Support Division

A QUICK LOOK AT TRANSITION HELPS AND BENEFITS FOR VETERANS

Transition Bulletin Board

The Transition Bulletin Board (TBB) is an electronic bulletin board accessible at more than 330 transition offices. It displays want ads, business opportunities, a calendar of events (job fairs and Transition Assistance Program workshops), and information about veterans' organizations, products, services, education and training opportunities, etc. DoD personnel and their spouses should contact their local installation transition offices for more information.

America's Job Bank

This Department of Labor (DoL) resource lists thousands of jobs and points of contact across the country. This information, as well as additional local-state employment information, is available at 1,700 job-service offices located nationwide.

Job Service

The local job-service office (state employment service office) provides employment assistance. Contact your local installation transition officer or the veterans' representative to determine if job-service assistance is available on base or in your local community.

Job Fairs

The DoD sponsors annual job fairs in Europe and the Far East to assist servicemembers, DoD civilian employees, and spouses stationed overseas whose location hinders their ability to job search. Many bases in the United States also sponsor job fairs. Contact your local transition office for more information.

Retirement Programs

Most installations offer seminars and workshops in addition to those provided by the transition offices to assist service members through the retirement process.

Temporary Early Retirement

Military services may offer early retirement to qualifying members. The pay formula is 2.5% of the base pay for each year of completed service, reduced by 1% for each year short of 20 years. Early retirees who take public and community service jobs from validated public and community service program employers may earn additional retirement credits at age 62. Eligible military members are those with 15 to 19 years of active service. Contact your military personnel office or military service headquarters personnel office. Benefit: Additional opportunity to enroll in the Montgomery GI Bill (MGIB). Must meet requirements and contribute $1,200 prior to separation.

Household Goods Storage

This government provision offers the following benefits: (1) six months of storage for voluntary separatees and one year of storage for eligible involuntary; (2) a Voluntary Separation Incentive (VSI) package and Special Separation Benefit (SSB) for separatees; (3) travel to home-of-record (moving costs), provided the member has under eight years of service; and (4) travel to home-of-selection (moving costs) provided the member has eight or more years of service.

Transition Health Benefits

The Civilian Health and Medical Program of the Uniformed Services (CHAMPUS) provides care at a military medical facility for 60 days for servicemembers (SMs) and their dependents with under six years of service; and 120 days for SMs with at least six years of service. Eligibility: SMs (and their families) who are involuntarily separated or are VSI or SSB recipients. Option available to purchase a Continued Health Care Benefit Program (CHCBP) for up to 18 months. Preexisting conditions coverage is provided for those eligible members if CHCBP is purchased.

Conversion Health Benefits

A conversion health policy is available through Mutual of Omaha for all separatees not eligible for the Transition Health Benefits.

Commissary and Exchange Privileges

These privileges are available for two years after separation. Eligibility: VSI, SSB, and involuntary separatees. Contact your local military personnel office.

Moral, Welfare, and Recreational (MWR) Privileges

Two years after separation (at revenue-generating facilities only), excluding childcare. Eligibility: VSI, SSB, and involuntary separatees. Contact your local military personnel office.

Quarters Extension

Family housing (space available), for up to 180 days. Rental rate equates to VHA and BAQ for that locality. Eligibility: VSI, SSB, and involuntary separatees. Contact your local military personnel or housing office.

Transition Permissive TDY (TPTDY)

Ten days (all separatees). Ten days or 30 days excess leave for involuntary, VSI, or SSB separatees. Last permanent change of station entitlement to look for job or home. Stationed within the Continental United States (CONUS), 20 days; 30 days if domicile is outside the CONUS.

Continued Enrollment in DoD Schools

For 12th graders, if the 11th grade was completed prior to the member's separation. Eligibility: VSI, SSB, and involuntary separatees. Contact your local DoD high school.

Non-Appropriated Fund Hiring Preference

One-time hiring preference (including dependents) in Non-Appropriated Fund (NAF) activities, such as commissaries, exchanges, and clubs. Eligibility: VSI, SSB, and involuntary separatees. Contact your local MWR or NAF personnel office for more information.

Guard or Reserve, Unit Affiliation Reference

Priority placement on applications made within one year after separation. Eligibility: Certain involuntary separatees, VSI, and SSB. Contact your local military personnel, Reserve, or Guard office for more information.

Troops to Teachers

This program provides stipends to assist separatees in obtaining certifications as elementary and secondary schoolteachers or teachers' aides. In addition, this program also awards grants to local educational agencies that receive Chapter One funds and have schools with a concentration of low-income families and shortages of teachers and teachers' aides (with emphasis in areas of math and science). Eligibility requirements: A bachelor's degree is required for teacher placement and an associate's degree for teacher aide placement. Military personnel separating after six years of service, DoD and Department of Energy civilians, and displaced scientists and engineers of defense contractors who have lost their jobs because of defense spending reductions are also eligible.

Transition Assistance Program (TAP)

The Department of Veterans Affairs (VA) maintains an active Transition Assistance Program and Disabled Transition Assistance Program (TAP/DTAP) throughout the United States and around the world. Since the implementation of TAP/DTAP, through original (P.L. 101-237) and expanded (P.L. 101-510) legislation, the VA has provided benefit information to separating servicemembers and their families.

The VA encourages all separating servicemembers to contact their respective transition centers to determine when the VA Transition Assistance Briefings (TAB) are scheduled. TABs provide information help make

• VET VIP

Contact the Defense Activity for Non-Traditional Education Support (DANTES) at 1-800-452-6616, ext. 6617 for more information.

the transition to civilian life easier by identifying many of the VA benefits available to you.

You can find the locations of TAB sites through the Department of Defense transition website, www.dodtransportal.dod.mil. Click on the "At Your Service" link and then on the "Military Services Transition Assistance locations" link to locate the center nearest you.

Because of the massive amount of information available, more is discussed in this chapter regarding the Transition Assistance Program.

Transition Health Benefits

CHAMPUS or care at a military medical facility for 60 days for SMs and their dependents for SMs with under six years of service; and 120 days for SMs with at least six years of service. Eligibility: SMs (and their families) who are involuntarily separated or are VSI or SSB recipients. Option available to purchase a conversion health policy (CHCBP) for up to 18 months. Preexisting conditions coverage is provided for those eligible members if CHCBP is purchased.

Transition Permissive TDY (TPTDY)

Provides ten days or 30 days excess leave for involuntary, Voluntary Separation Incentive, or Special Separation Benefit separatees. This is the last permanent change of station entitlement to look for a job or home for those stationed within the continental United States (CONUS). Servicemember is allowed 20 days to 30 days if domicile is outside the CONUS.

TAP Pre-Separation Guide

Returning to civilian life is an exciting time, one full of hope for what the next chapter of your life may bring. But a major life transition, such as leaving the military, can also be a complex undertaking. You have many steps to take and many questions to get answered. Transition assistance staff, personnel office staff, relocation specialists, education counselors, and many others can help offer sound advice. But only you and your family can make the critical decisions regarding your future. So, where should you start?

The DoD's *Pre-separation Guide* will help you work through the sections listed on DD Form 2648, *Pre-separation Counseling Checklist*. The checklist allows you to indicate the benefit and services for which you would like to receive additional counseling as you prepare your Individual Transition Plan

(ITP). In cases where the transition counselor cannot answer questions, you will be referred to subject matter experts that will provide the information you need. As you work through each element of the guide, take advantage of opportunities to request the specific resources that are appropriate for you.

If you are uncertain about your future plans, now is the time to obtain all the assistance and information available to you. Professional guidance and counseling are available at your transition assistance office, as are workshops, publications, information resources, automated resources, and government programs. Take advantage of each resource that pertains to your unique situation. It is your transition plan. Others can assist and offer guidance, but ultimately, it is your responsibility and your life.

TAP was designed by the Department of Defense to smooth the transition process for military personnel (and family members) leaving active duty. It is a partnership with the Departments of Labor and Veterans Affairs, and consists of the following components.

SOURCE:
Transition Assistance Online (www.taonline.com)

● **VET VIP**

Independent research has found that on average, servicemembers participating in the Transition Assistance Program find their first post-military job three weeks sooner than those who do not participate in TAP.

TAP INTO T.A.P.

TAP was designed by the Department of Defense to smooth the transition process for military personnel (and family members) leaving active duty. It is a partnership with the Departments of Labor and Veterans Affairs, and consists of the following components.

Full-Time Active Duty Servicemembers

1. **DoD Pre-Separation Counseling:** A thorough review of transition services, benefits, and resources begins your transition process. It is recommended that you make an appointment with your transition office about 12 months before your known separation date (retiring servicemembers can make appointments 24 months prior to their retirement date).

2. **Department of Labor Employment Workshops:** During this two-and-a-half-day workshop, you will learn how to write a resume and cover letter, obtain information on skills assessment and job search techniques, and learn other important information about career and job services available through DoL.

3. **VA Benefits Briefing:** In this four-hour session, you'll learn about VA benefits you may be entitled to, including the Montgomery GI Bill,

healthcare, VA counseling, home loan programs, and more.

4. **Disabled Transition Assistance Program:** If you have a service-connected disability (or think that you may), you must attend this two-hour briefing. You will learn about eligibility for Chapter 31, Vocational Rehabilitation and Employment Service benefits by VA, and more.

Once you have completed the four workshops above, you are eligible for one-on-one counseling and employment assistance training through your service.

Demobilizing Guard and Reserve

DoD Pre-Separation Counseling: During demobilization, and prior to release from active duty, servicemembers returning from Operation Iraqi Freedom (OIF) and Operation Enduring Freedom (OEF) can receive two hours of pre-separation counseling.

Department of Labor Uniformed Services Employment and Reemployment Rights Act (USERRA) Briefing: You are eligible to receive a USERRA briefing prior to your release from active duty. Once home, you can contact the DoL Career One-Stop Center in your community to receive further employment assistance.

VA Benefits Briefing

Prior to release from active duty, you are eligible to receive a VA Benefits Briefing. The VA DTAP Briefing normally occurs as part of the VA Benefits Briefing and usually includes information about application procedures for vocational rehabilitation and employment assistance. This information is for servicemembers who have or think they have a service-connected disability. Members should always follow up once they return home by contacting the VA office closest to where they live.

- **VET VIP**
Call your VA regional office toll free at 1-800-827-1000.

Benefits Provided by the Department of Veteran Affairs

The Department of Veterans Affairs is responsible for ensuring that you receive the care, support, and recognition you have earned through your military service. You may be eligible for one or more of the following federal veterans' benefits.

Healthcare

In October 1996, Congress passed the Veterans' Health Care Eligibility Reform Act, paving the way for the Medical Benefits Package plan, available to all enrolled veterans. The Medical Benefits Package emphasizes preventive and primary care, offering a full range of outpatient and inpatient services.

Education and Training – GI Bill

Education benefits (up to 36 months) can be used for education, training, certification, apprenticeship, and on-the-job training programs. National Guard and Selected Reserve may also be eligible under previous active duty enlistment.

Home Loan Guaranty

Eligible veterans and servicemembers can purchase a home without making a down payment.

Veterans Group Life Insurance (VGLI)

The Veterans Group Life Insurance program allows servicemembers to convert their Servicemembers' Group Life Insurance (SGLI) coverage to renewable term insurance.

If you are unable to visit a VA counselor at your installation, call the nearest VA regional office at the toll-free numbers listed at the conclusion of this section. A veterans' service representative will be happy to provide information about specific benefits and how to file a claim.

To get complete information concerning all the VA benefits you and your family members may be entitled to, visit their website at www.va.gov.

You can also submit a specific question to the VA website by sending an inquiry through the VA Inquiry Routing and Information System (IRIS). This application provides VA clientele with secure communication of personal data, should they voluntarily choose to send it to VA.

Veteran Service Organizations (VSO)

Your state, county, or local Veteran Service Organizations have specially trained individuals who can offer transition assistance. A veteran service officer can provide counseling and help with everything from filling out VA claims and enrollment forms to assisting with claims appeals. You can call the VA toll-free number for assistance on finding the nearest VSO.

Veteran Centers

Veteran Centers provide readjustment counseling and outreach services to all veterans who served in any combat zone. Services are also available to family members for military-related issues. Veterans have earned these benefits through their service and are provided at no cost to the veteran or family members.

Readjustment counseling is part of the wide range of services provided to combat veterans in the effort to make a satisfying transition from military to civilian life. These services include the following benefits.

- Individual counseling
- Group counseling
- Marital and family counseling
- Bereavement counseling
- Medical referrals
- Assistance in applying for VA Benefits
- Employment counseling
- Guidance and referral
- Alcohol or drug assessments
- Information and referral to community resources
- Military sexual trauma counseling and referral
- Outreach and community education

Contact your nearest Veteran Center through the Veteran Center directory at www.va.gov/directory/guide/vetcenter.asp or review the listings in your local Blue Pages. The Veteran Center staff is available toll free during normal business hours at 1-800-905-4675 (Eastern) and 1-866-496-8838 (Pacific).

SOURCE: The Department of Vetwerans Affairs

VA VOCATIONAL REHABILITATION AND EMPLOYMENT TRACKS

Which Track Is Right for Me?

Plans for a successful transition will vary with individual needs and assessments. What's right for one person may be the worst decision for someone else. Only you can decide what approach is best for you and your circumstances.

Reemployment with Previous Employer

This track is designed for those individuals separating from active duty or in the National Guard or Reserves and who are returning to work for their previous employer.

What are some of the features of this track? A rehabilitation plan with the goal of reemployment may involve job accommodations, job modification, case management, coordination, and linkages of services with VA healthcare, reemployment rights advice, work adjustment services, and consultations with the employer.

Rapid Access to Employment

Rapid access to employment is targeted to those individuals who have expressed a desire to seek employment soon after separation or who already have the necessary skills to be competitive in the job market in an appropriate occupation.

What are some of the features of this track? A rehabilitation plan with the goal of immediate employment may provide for job readiness preparation, resume development, job search assistance, development of employment resources, job accommodations, and post-employment follow up.

Self-Employment

Self-employment is targeted to individuals who have limited access to traditional employment, need flexible work schedules, or who need a more accommodating work environment due to their disabling conditions or other life circumstances.

What are some of the features of this track? A rehabilitation plan with the goal of self-employment may provide for analysis of the viability of a business concept, development of a business plan, training in the operation of small businesses, marketing and financial assistance, and guidance in obtaining adequate resources to implement the business plan.

Employment Through Long-Term Services

Long-term services are targeted to individuals who need specialized training and/or education to obtain and maintain suitable employment.

What are some of the features of this track? A rehabilitation plan with the goal of training and/or education may provide for on-the-job training, apprenticeships, internships, job shadowing, work monitoring, work-study, public-private job partnering, or higher education sufficient to obtain suitable entry-level employment.

Independent-Living Services

Independent-living services are targeted to individuals who may not be able to work immediately and need rehabilitation services to live more independently.

What are some of the features of this track? A rehabilitation plan with the goal of independent-living may include assistive technology, independent living skills training, connection to community-based support services, etc.

What Other Benefits May Be Provided?

After a plan is developed, the counselor will assist the veteran in implementing plans to achieve gainful suitable employment or independent living. The counselor or case manager may provide medical and dental referrals, coordination of training allowance, tutorial assistance, adjustment counseling, or other services necessary to achieve rehabilitation.

Summary

A veteran who is found eligible for the VA Vocational Rehabilitation and Employment program and who has an employment handicap is entitled to vocational rehabilitation services. Following the vocational rehabilitation counselor's determination that a veteran has met the entitlement criteria, the counselor and veteran will jointly develop a plan for a rehabilitation program with a goal typically leading toward employment. In some cases, the plan may be related to an independent-living need. If so, it will provide all of the necessary services and assistance identified through the initial evaluation.

In cases where a veteran is found not to be entitled, the VA counselor will help him or her to use the information gathered in the initial evaluation to identify other options, goals, and programs that should contribute to sound vocational adjustment, for example, referral to the State Vocational Rehabilitation program, information about financial aid, and referral to the Department of Labor's Disabled Veterans' Outreach Program (DVOP).

Important VA Definitions

Employment Handicap

An impairment of a veteran's ability to prepare for, obtain, or retain employment consistent with his or her abilities, aptitudes, and interests. The impairment results in substantial part from a service-connected disability. For veterans rated at 20% or more, a finding of employment handicap results in a finding of "entitled."

Serious Employment Handicap (SEH)

A significant impairment of a veteran's ability to prepare for, obtain, or retain employment consistent with his or her abilities, aptitudes, and interests. The Serious Employment Handicap results in substantial part from a service-connected disability. For veterans rated at 10% and for veterans whose 12-year period of basic eligibility has passed, the finding of an SEH is necessary to establish "entitlement."

Suitable Employment

Work that is within a veteran's physical and emotional capabilities and consistent with his or her pattern of abilities, aptitudes, and interests.

Transferable Skills

Reasonably developed skills, knowledge, and abilities attained through both training and experience (civilian and military) that relate to current employment opportunities in the labor market.

SOURCE:
The Department of Veterans Affairs (www.vetsuccess.gov/fivetracks)

TAP
PRE-SEPARATION GUIDE

In recognition of the contributions made by so many patriotic men and women by volunteering to serve their country, the Department of Defense has developed a booklet to present information on the many transition services and resources available to veterans.

Once you know your options, you will be able to make informed decisions about the choices open to you and your family. If you haven't already visited your transition office, the DoD recommends that you do so 180 days prior to your separation date or earlier if possible. The *Pre-separation Guide*, available for download online (www.transitionassistanceprogram.com), serves as a ready reference to keep you focused on your transition process.

No two veterans are alike and no two experiences are exactly alike. The TAP *Pre-separation Guide* offers the following advice about making your transition to civilian service.

A carefully thought-out Individual Transition Plan is your game plan for a successful transition to civilian life. It is not an official form, but something you create by yourself, for yourself. Your transition assistance office will give you a head start with the *Pre-separation Counseling Checklist*, which can serve as an outline for your ITP. On this checklist, you indicate the benefits and services for which you want counseling. You are then referred to subject experts who will answer your questions. Your transition assistance office will furnish additional information and emphasize certain points for you to consider.

Create an Individual Transition Plan

The ITP identifies likely actions and activities associated with your transition. You can determine what these might be through consultation with your transition assistance office, your local Army Career and Alumni Program (ACAP) office, or command career counselor, as well as by using the *Pre-separation Counseling Checklist*.

Contact your transition or ACAP office or command career counselor and make an appointment to complete your pre-separation counseling and the checklist.

Your military service branch has samples of ITPs that can help you. Check with your transition or command career counselor to review them. You can start developing your ITP by answering seven important questions:

1. What are my goals after I leave the military?
2. Where do I plan to live?
3. Do I need to continue my education or training?
4. Will the job market, where I plan to relocate, provide me with the employment that I am seeking?
5. Do I have the right skills to compete for the job(s) I am seeking?
6. Will my spouse's and family's needs be met at our new location?
7. Am I financially prepared to transition at this time?

It's never too early to start planning for your transition into civilian life. Servicemembers of all branches have a wealth of recourse available to help with this process, as well as general assistance offered by the federal government— job fairs, websites, books, pamphlets, magazines and other printed resources, workshops, government programs, and experienced professionals. Investigate every resource available to you. There's lots of help out there, but remember that it's your transition and ultimately, it's up to you to make it work!

SOURCE: Transition Assistance Program *Preseparation Guide*

BASIC PRE-SEPARATION GUIDE TRANSITION STEPS

Step 1. Schedule Your Pre-Separation Counseling Appointment

You may schedule your pre-separation counseling appointment at your installation transition assistance office any time within a year before your planned separation date. However, since it takes time to prepare for an effective transition, be sure to contact your transition assistance office at least 180 days before your separation. By law, pre-separation counseling (completion of the *Pre-separation Counseling Checklist*) must occur no later than 90 days prior to separation; therefore, if you have not had an appointment 90 days before separation, call your transition assistance office or your Navy command career counselor and schedule a visit immediately. However, it is strongly recommended that you set up your pre-separation counseling appointment at least 180 days prior to separation.

Step 2. Review the Pre-Separation Counseling Checklist

Your transition counselor or command career counselor will walk you through the *Pre-separation Counseling Checklist*, which helps ensure that you will receive the necessary assistance and advice to benefit fully from the wide range of services and entitlements. The checklist is required by law to be filed in the official military personnel record of each servicemember receiving the counseling.

At this meeting, the transition assistance office or command career counselor will provide the following services:

- Assist you in developing an individual needs assessment.
- Identify helpful relocation resources.
- Offer immediate and long-range career guidance.
- Provide benefits counseling.
- Refer you to other service providers for any additional assistance you may require.

Step 3. Draft Your Individual Transition Plan

Information on drafting your Individual Transition Plan is available through the transition assistance office. You may choose to use your *Pre-separation Counseling Checklist* as a guide for developing your own unique ITP. Once you have created your ITP, show it to your transition counselor or command career counselor. They will provide further assistance or refer you to a subject-matter expert to assist you. Full participation in this process by you and your spouse is encouraged.

Phases of Individual Transition Planning

All military personnel transitioning out of the service go through the same fundamental phases, that can be divided into the following seven parts: Self-Assessment, Exploration, Skills Development, Intern Programs, Job Search, Job Selection, and Support.

Phase One: Self-Assessment

Ask yourself: *Who am I? What are my talents and experiences? Why would someone want to hire me?*

In this phase, document your portfolio of knowledge, experience, skills, talents, and abilities. For starters, create a list using your personal DD Form 2586, *Verification of Military Experience and Training*. Your VMET outlines the training and experience you received during your military career. It is designed to help you, but it is not a resume.

To get your verification document, go to the VMET website at www.dmdc. osd.mil/vmet. All separating military personnel can electronically download and print their VMET document and personal cover letter from the VMET website. Simply click the "Request Document" and "Request Cover Letter" tabs and print each of these documents after they have downloaded. (Note: This site can be accessed only from a government computer network)

You can get your verification document online as long as you have a current DoD Common Access Card (CAC) or a Defense Finance Accounting Service (DFAS) myPay Personal Identification Number (PIN). You should retrieve this information within 120 days prior to your separation. If you have problems getting your VMET and need assistance, check with your local transition counselor.

Add anything else you can think of to this list. In essence, you are now creating an "asset bank," from which you can draw when called upon to write a resume or attend a job interview. If you need help, use the professional guidance available through your local installation transition assistance office or education center. Or, refer to the self-help section of your local library or bookstore for useful career planning books.

In addition, you can get an official transcript of your education and training credits from your service branch. Each branch has their own system for recording your military (and civilian) education and experience.

Army/American Council on Education Registry Transcript System (AARTS)

The Army/American Council on Education Registry Transcript System automatically captures your military training, MOSs, and college-level examinations scores with the college credit recommended. The AARTS website address is http://aarts.army.mil.

Army Career and Alumni Program (ACAP)

Army veterans are eligible to use the services of the Army Career and Alumni Program (ACAP) for 180 days after their Enlisted Termination of Service (ETS). If you're still eligible for ACAP services, you can reconnect with ACAP online by going to www.acapexpress.army.mil or by contacting your local ACAP center. Even if you have been out of the Army for more than 180 days, you can still use the tools provided on the website.

ACAP Express

This resource gives speedy access to the Army's transition program. ACAP Express provides immediate online access to services for those considering transition or in the process of transition.

ACAP Express online offers the following services.

- Register for mandated pre-separation counseling.
- Schedule a Transition Assistance Program employment workshop.
- Schedule Veterans Administration briefings.
- Schedule other employment assistance training.
- Use ACAP tools to write resumes and cover letters.
- Connect with ACAP employment professionals for advice and support.
- Learn how to find a job.

Navy and Marines

The Navy and Marine Corps use the Sailor/Marine American Council on Education Registry Transcript (SMART) system. This system automatically captures your training, experience, and standardized test scores. Visit the SMART website at www.navycollege.navy.mil/transcript.html.

Air Force

The Community College of the Air Force (CCAF) automatically captures your training, experience, and standardized test scores. Transcript information may be viewed at the CCAF website at www.au.af.mil/au/ccaf.

Coast Guard

The Coast Guard Institute (CGI) requires each servicemember to submit documentation of all training (except correspondence course records), along with an enrollment form to receive a transcript.

Information can be found at the Coast Guard Institute homepage at http://www.uscg.mil/hq/cgi/Resources/Institute_Forms/CG_form_1564.html.

Phase Two: Exploration

Ask yourself: *What career options are attractive to me? Do the careers that interest me have long-term stability? Do these jobs coincide with my values and aptitudes? How do I find these jobs?*

You probably have some idea about what you want to do, and now is not the time to limit your opportunities. Maximize the list of job titles and career paths that appeal to you. If you can, broaden your geographic horizons to include several places where you might like to pursue your career. Many resources are available to help you explore your expanded career options.

The Transition Assistance Office is designed to help servicemembers focus on jobs that employers need to fill now and in the near future. Transition professionals can help you identify the geographic areas that have opportunities in your fields of interest.

The employment office in your state is another good resource during this second phase. They generally offer services for job-interviewing techniques; selection and referral to openings; job development; employment counseling; career evaluation; referral to training or other support services; and testing. Your state office can also lead you to information on related jobs nearby and acquaint you with the Department of Labor database, DoD Job Search, which has listings of thousands of jobs across the nation.

Public libraries are also an excellent resource. Most have a number of helpful periodicals and books related to employment and job searches.

Phase Three: Skills Development

Ask yourself: *How do I prepare myself to be an attractive candidate in the career fields that interest me? Do I need more education or training?*

As you continue through the exploration phase, you may find some appealing opportunities for which you feel only partially qualified. Your local transition assistance office and education center can help you determine the academic or vocational training you will need and how to get it.

Phase Four: Intern Programs

Ask yourself: *Do I have the aptitude and experience needed to pursue my occupational interests? Are there internships, volunteer jobs, temporary services, or part-time jobs where I might "try out" the kind of work that interests me?*

Some government-sponsored programs, such as the one designed to help educators obtain teaching credentials, can provide income and training in exchange for guaranteed employment. Check your local and base libraries and the education office for books containing intern program information.

Temporary agencies are also a great way to become familiar with a company or industry. Don't automatically turn down an interesting volunteer position. Volunteering increases your professional skills and can sometimes turn into a paid position.

Explore internship possibilities with private employers: Many companies have such programs but do not advertise them. To learn more about intern programs, inquire at your transition assistance office, your local civilian personnel office, or the state employment office.

Phase Five: Job Search

Ask yourself: *How do I do everything necessary to present myself well in the job marketplace? How do I write a resume, develop leads, conduct an interview, and complete a job application?*

Once you have honed in on your future career, you must begin the challenge of finding work. The job market is a competitive place, and can be a bit intimidating when you don't have a job. The best way to improve your odds of successful placement is to play your best hand: Seek the opportunities for which you are best prepared.

Work hard at finding a job. Until you find gainful employment, finding a job should be your job. By all means network! The vast majority of jobs are filled by referrals, not the classifieds.

Use your network of fellow servicemembers, friends, colleagues, and family, as well as the job listings provided by your installation's transition assistance office, the local human resources office, or even the nearest community college. Take advantage of job-hunting seminars, resume-writing workshops, and interviewing techniques classes. Attend job fairs and talk to as many company representatives as possible.

Phase Six: Job Selection

Ask yourself: *How do I select the right job?*

Although it may be tempting, you don't have to take the first job that comes along, especially if it is not really a good fit for you. When deciding whether the offer is right for you, consider the type of work, location, salary and benefits, climate, and advancement opportunities. Remember, even if you take the first job offered to you, you are not necessarily locked into it. You can choose to take a suitable position and then move on to a better one as quickly as possible.

Phase Seven: Support

Ask yourself: *How do I make a smooth transition to a civilian career?*

For your transition to be truly successful, you should manage the personal affairs related to your career change with the same professionalism and care as your job search. A successful transition means not just finding a job, but also taking care of the details related to things like out-processing, relocation, financial management, family matters, and coping with the inevitable stress of change.

Your local TAP office can offer support as you go through this process. Your individual transition plan is an opportunity for you to integrate these issues with the career-oriented activities that are the focus of your transition effort.

Note: Departing servicemembers are eligible for continued transition assistance for up to 180 days after separation.

Veterans

Under most circumstances, Veterans are eligible to use their former service branches transcript program. However, if you are not eligible for AARTS, SMART, CCAF, or CGI systems, you will need to fill out DD Form 295, *Application for the Evaluation of Learning Experiences During Military Service*, and provide DD Form 214, *Certificate of Release or Discharge from Active Duty*, to receive credit for your experience.

The investment you make now in conducting your assessment is crucial. It will bring the "professional you" into clearer focus, and it will have a major impact on your career decisions. The key to a smooth transition is to be prepared well before you separate from the military. Start early. Make connections and build networks that will help you transition into the civilian world.

Your transition success is an important mission. Like all important missions, your transition requires advance planning. The seven categories listed on the Individual Transition Plan represent the major education, training, and job assistance concerns you may face as you transition from the military. To help you develop and manage your transition plan, all branches of the military have developed resources to help with transition planning. These resources will help you identify the actions you should consider taking; they are valuable to setting goals and establishing a schedule for completing those goals.

SOURCE:
1. U.S. Department of Defense (www.turbotap.org)
2. Army Career and Alumni Program (www.acap.army.mil)

PRE-SEPARATION TIMELINE

The Department of Defense, Department of Labor and Department of Veterans Affairs play a role in helping service members and their spouses adjust to civilian life. DoD is required by law (PL101-510, 1990) to: (1) provide separatees with a skills verification document that translates their military experience and training into marketable job skills; (2) offer individual pre-separation counseling to separatees; (3) operate employment assistance centers for separatees and spouses; and (4) assist the DOL and VA in conducting seminars that separating personnel and their spouses can attend to help them find civilian jobs.

The following pre-separation timeline for retiring servicemembers and separatees follows the Department of Defense guidelines for separation from military service.

Two Years Prior to Separation (Retirees Only)

❑ Schedule your pre-separation counseling appointment.

❑ Review the *Pre-separation Counseling Checklist*. Identify individual service providers who will provide assistance.

18 Months Prior to Separation (Retirees Only)

❏ Attend a Transition Assistance Program workshop. If your service-connected disability makes you eligible or if you are planning to file for disability, attend the Disabled Transition Assistance Program workshop.

❏ Develop your Individual Transition Plan (at home, self-directed). Seek assistance from your ACAP center counselor, if needed.

❏ Make fundamental life decisions (continue working, change careers, volunteer, etc.) and determine future goals.

❏ Capitalize on current career stability to prepare for future career goals. Identify training, education, and/or certification requirements, and determine how to achieve goals (e.g., use tuition assistance). Start classes.

❏ Evaluate family requirements (college tuition, eldercare for parents, etc.).

❏ Determine post-retirement income requirements. Project retirement take-home pay. Identify if you need to supplement retirement take-home pay.

12-24 Months Prior to Separation (Retirees Only)

❏ Continue the training or education needed to qualify for your objective career.

❏ Investigate health and life insurance alternatives, including long-term healthcare coverage.

❏ Consider whether you will take terminal leave or cash in unused leave.

❏ Consider retirement locations.

❏ Identify medical/dental problems and arrange treatment for yourself and/or your family.

❏ Begin networking. Track potential network contacts you have lost or may lose contact with.

❏ Contact the installation Retirement Services Office (RSO) to receive pre-retirement and Survivor Benefit Plan (SBP) briefing.

❏ Consider spouse education and career desires.

❏ Update legal documents (will, powers of attorney, etc.).

12 Months Prior to Separation (Retirees and Separatees)

❑ Schedule your pre-separation counseling appointment (separatees only).

❑ Continue the training or education needed to qualify for your objective career.

❑ Review the *Pre-separation Counseling Checklist*. Identify individual service providers who will provide assistance.

❑ Develop your Individual Transition Plan (at home, self-directed). Seek assistance from your ACAP center counselor, if needed.

❑ Receive post-government (military) service employment restriction counseling.

❑ Attend a TAProgram workshop. If your service-connected disability makes you eligible or if you are planning to file for disability, attend the Disabled Transition Assistance Program workshop.

❑ Establish a financial plan to make ends meet during your transition to civilian life.

❑ Assess your job skills and interests. To determine how they relate to today's job market, take a vocational interest inventory. Contact your installation's education center and ACAP center.

❑ Begin researching the job market. Develop a career plan, including possible employers in your field.

❑ If you need additional educational or vocational training to compete in the job market, explore your options for adult education.

❑ Learn about the education benefits you are eligible for under the Montgomery GI Bill. If you enrolled in the Vietnam-era GI Bill, learn how you can convert to MGIB. Contact your local Department of Veterans Affairs representative for details.

❑ Visit the education center to take academic entrance exams, college admission tests, or challenge exams. Remember, this is free to service members on active duty.

❑ Discuss with your family possible options about your career and where to live next.

❑ If you need help with your finances, explore the options available to help departing servicemembers in your military branch.

❑ Review and make a copy of your personnel records.

❑ Start developing a resume.

❑ Join a professional association in your chosen career field and become involved in it.

180 Days Prior to Separation
(Retirees and Separatees)

❏ Continue the training or education needed to qualify for your objective career.

❏ Research specific job possibilities, job markets, and the economic conditions in the geographic areas where you want to live.

❏ Contact friends in the private sector who may help you find a job. Actively network.

❏ Seek assistance from your ACAP counselor after completing the first draft of your resume.

❏ Attend job fairs to connect with potential employers.

❏ Develop an alternate plan in case your first career plan falls through.

❏ Review and copy your medical and dental records. Get a certified true copy of each.

❏ Schedule medical/dental appointments as needed.

❏ Request your Verification of Military Experience and Training at www.dmdc.osd.mil/appj/vmet/index.jsp.

• •

150 Days Prior to Separation
(Retirees and Separatees)

❏ Continue the training or education needed to qualify for your objective career.

❏ Start actively applying for jobs. Make contact with employers for possible interviews.

❏ Start assembling a wardrobe for interviewing. Check with the ACAP center for Dress for Success® information.

❏ Seek help if the stress of your transition to civilian life becomes too much to handle.

❏ If you are separating prior to fulfilling eight years of active service, you must satisfy your obligations by becoming a member of the Reserves.

❏ Start posting resumes to career websites.

❏ Research websites for posting resumes and conducting online job searches (e.g., www.careers.org).

❏ Schedule your separation physical examination (separatees only).

120 Days Prior to Separation
(Retirees and Separatees)

❑ Complete the training or education needed to qualify for your objective career.

❑ If you are considering federal employment, visit www.USAJOBS.gov to determine the appropriate documents to submit. Explore special federal programs and hiring opportunities for veterans.

❑ Consider using Resumix, an automated tool that allows you to use an online application to create resumes for applying to federal jobs. You can print your resume, as well as save it to the system to retrieve and edit for future use. For some federal jobs, you may be able to submit your resume electronically. Obtain more information about Resumix from the USAJOBS website.

❑ Visit the relocation assistance program office, located at your service center, to learn about relocation options, entitlements, and assistance.

❑ If you live in government housing, arrange for a pre-inspection and obtain termination information.

❑ Contact appropriate offices at your installation to discuss extended medical care (if eligible) or conversion health insurance. Learn about your options for transitional healthcare. If you have specific questions about veterans medical care, contact the VA or access the VA website.

❑ Research Reserve programs to continue to receive part-time benefits, earn a future retirement, and continue to grow and train in your field. Even if you have fulfilled eight years of military service, you may want to explore the option of joining the Reserve or National Guard.

❑ Visit the Department of Veterans Affairs website at www.va.gov for valuable information for veterans.

❑ Start a subscription to a major newspaper in the area where you plan to move. Begin replying to want ads.

❑ Visit and evaluate the area where you plan to move. Attend job interviews there. Visit a private employment agency or executive recruiter in the area.

❑ Send out resumes and make follow up phone calls to check if they arrived. Submit your resume through the DoD job search website at http://dod.jobsearch.org.

❑ Schedule Part I of your separation physical. Part II will be scheduled upon completion of Part I (retirees only).

90 Days Prior to Separation (Retirees and Separatees)

❑ Continue to post resumes to websites. Conduct an automated job search for you and your spouse using ACAP online and other available employment data banks.

❑ Continue to expand your network.

❑ Visit websites that help you locate a home, realtor, or neighborhood, such as www.realtor.com.

❑ Once you have chosen where you will live next, arrange for transportation counseling. Learn about your options for shipment and storage of household goods.

❑ Schedule a final dental examination.

❑ Determine if you are eligible for separation pay.

❑ If you would like to update your will or if you have legal questions or problems, obtain free legal advice.

60 Days Prior to Separation (Retirees and Separatees)

❑ Begin planning additional visits to the area where you plan to move.

❑ Continue to send out your resume. In your cover letter, include the date you plan to move.

❑ Continue to network at all levels.

❑ Choose your transitional healthcare option: use military medical facilities or sign up for TRICARE, if eligible.

❑ For detailed information about disability compensation, benefits and programs, call the Department of Veterans Affairs at 1-800-827-1000.

30 Days Prior to Separation
(Retirees and Separatees)

❑ Continue to network.

❑ Review your *Certificate of Release or Discharge from Active Duty* (DD Form 214) [www.uscg.mil/hq/psc/DA/DD214.pdf] worksheet.

❑ Several government agencies offer special loans and programs for veterans. Check with your local VA office.

❑ If you are unemployed, you may qualify for unemployment compensation once you are a civilian. See your local state employment office for eligibility.

❑ Decide whether to sign up for the optional Continued Health Care Benefit Program medical coverage.

❑ Complete your *Veteran's Affairs Disability Application* (VA Form 21-526) and submit it to the appropriate office. Check with your local ACAP center or VA representative.

❑ Consider converting your Servicemen's Group Life Insurance to Veteran's Group Life Insurance (optional).

❑ Websites with worldwide relocation information on major military and associate installations for use by military personnel and their families who are relocating: www.militaryonesource.com and www.MilitaryHOMEFRONT.dod.mil/moving.

❑ Visit the website on the Military Health System at www.tricare.osd.mil.

SOURCE:
1. U.S. Department of Defense (www.turbotap.org)
2. Army Career and Alumni Program (www.acap.army.mil)

What Other Vets Are Saying...

It was the most important day of my life! At exactly 11:45 A.M., I received a call that I had graduated from the Community College of the Air Force, just a minute and a half earlier. That's right, I remember the exact time!

I cannot underestimate the importance of obtaining a CCAF degree prior to separating or retiring from the military.

When I joined the active duty Air Force, I already had an associate's degree. I separated from active duty and went back to school. Two years later, I joined the Air National Guard. I also obtained a Bachelor of Arts degree and started teaching. Throughout my entire military career, I always made sure that CCAF received a copy of my certificates from all the technical schools I attended.

For the last 12 of my 24 years in the military, I was a historian. After retiring from the military, I applied for a historian position. The first letter of consideration I received was from Randolph Air Force Base. I was told I was their number one choice.

A couple of days later, I received an e-mail stating that my consideration had been withdrawn. I was devastated! They informed me that even though I had a degree, it was not in history.

Fortunately, my credits for an Aerospace History degree were satisfied, and my AF Form 968 (*Community College of the Air Force Action Request*) had been submitted prior to retiring. Even with 12 years of experience as a historian, plus two degrees, it took my CCAF degree in my career field to make me eligible to apply.

No matter how many degrees you may have, you will never know when your career might require you to have a degree in your military career field.

So, check in with your education office and find out what you need to do to get your certification, credits, or degree before you separate or retire. You might not need it now, but you just might need it in the future!

Veronica S.
USAF Master Sergeant, Retired

CHAPTER TWO

THE MILITARY *IS* SCHOOL:
AN ACCELERATED COURSE!

Depending on your service, your time in the military has likely earned you college credit. Many schools and colleges will award academic credit toward a degree based on your training, coursework, and occupational specialty. If you qualify, you could potentially save both tuition dollars and classroom time!

Pursuing your college degree will be one of the best career moves you make, but it can also be very expensive and time consuming. That's why claiming credit for your military experience is vital. Even better, getting these college credits costs you nothing because you've already earned them!

It's possible for you to earn up to four semester hours of college credit simply because you completed your Initial Entry Training, otherwise known as basic training or boot camp.

The military offers a wide range of educational opportunities to servicemembers, and has created a comprehensive (although somewhat complicated) system that translates military courses, training, and occupations into potential college credit.

The Department of Defense's Voluntary Education Program website, www. voled.doded.mil, offers a variety of educational information of interest and use to separating servicemembers. The website has a mission to provide direct support to active and reserve components, servicemembers, and their families. This support includes information on all programs provided by the Defense

Activity for Non-Traditional Educational Support (DANTES), including the Distance Learning Program, Examination Program, Certification Program, Counselor Support Program, Troops to Teachers, and a wide variety of educational catalogs and directories.

American Council on Education (ACE)

The primary agency for aiding the transfer of military experience into measurable college credits is the American Council on Education. ACE was created in 1942 to recognize the educational value of military training and experience. Since then, ACE has continuously evaluated military schools, correspondence courses, and occupations to determine the amount and level of academic credit to be awarded. Through ACE, you may earn academic credit for much of the training you have received, including basic training. The ACE military evaluations program is funded by the Department of Defense and coordinated through DANTES.

After World War I, veterans were granted blanket credit for military training as a reward for length of service. This practice ceased after World War II. Educators concluded that trained educators should determine whether military experiences could be applied to civilian education courses. In December 1945, ACE established the Commission on Accreditation of Service Experiences (renamed the Commission on Educational Credit and Credentials in 1979) to evaluate military educational programs and assist institutions in granting credit for those experiences. One year later, the Commission produced the first edition of the *Guide to the Evaluation of Educational Experiences in the Armed Services*. Several subsequent editions of the *Guide* have been published.

Over the years, the recommendations contained in the *Guide* have assisted higher education institutions in granting credit to hundreds of thousands of servicemembers. Surveys indicate that most of the nation's colleges and universities use the formal course recommendations in awarding credit to veterans and active duty service personnel.

Courses listed in the *Guide* are service school courses conducted on a formal basis (i.e., approved by a central authority within each service and listed by the service in its catalog). These courses are conducted for a specified period of time with a prescribed course of instruction, in a structured learning situation, and with qualified instructors.

In 1975, the Commission implemented a program to evaluate learning acquired through proven proficiency in Army enlisted Military Occupational Specialties. The MOS evaluation procedures were developed, tested, and refined during a feasibility study conducted by ACE and sponsored by the Department of the Army. Evaluators made recommendations for educational credit and advanced standing in apprentice training programs. Subsequently, the occupational assessment program of the Commission was expanded to include Navy general rates, ratings, warrant officers, and limited duty officers; Army warrant officer MOSs; Navy warrant officer and limited duty officer specialties; Coast Guard enlisted ratings and warrant officers; and selected Marine Corps MOSs. A small number of Naval Enlisted Classifications (NEC) has also been evaluated.

Most courses are given on a full-time basis. After 1981, ACE began evaluating courses that are at least 45 academic hours in length. Prior to that time, evaluated courses were at least two weeks in duration; or, if less than two weeks in length, the course had to include a minimum of 60 contact hours of instruction.

The ACE Evaluation Process

Military courses are evaluated by teams of at least three subject-matter specialists (college and university professors, deans, etc.). Evaluators have two major tasks for each course: the formulation of a credit recommendation and the preparation of the course's description.

Evaluators are drawn from postsecondary institutions, professional and disciplinary societies, education associations, and regional accrediting associations. The Program Evaluations Content Review Committee selects evaluation teams.

Through discussion and applying evaluation procedures and guidelines, team members reach a consensus on the amount and category of credit to be recommended.

Evaluation materials include the course syllabus, training materials, tests, textbooks, technical manuals, and examinations. Additional information may be obtained from discussions with instructors and program administrators, classroom observations, and examination of instructional equipment and laboratory facilities.

But recent surveys conducted by ACE have found that 14% of colleges and universities do not award any military credit, and another 30% do not award credit for occupational experiences, only for coursework.

Finding a Military-Friendly College

When recruiting young men and women, all branches of the military emphasize the educational advantages associated with military service. Young people sign up expecting that military service will bring them a few steps closer to a college degree and a better career. But veterans' advocates and students alike claim that many of the thousands of veterans who attend college after tours of duty are denied credit for their military courses and specialized skills, despite an accreditation system set up to award it. These students must then take additional courses, further stretching their already lean GI Bill benefits.

Conversely, colleges assert they are fairly evaluating military courses and that a good deal of service training does not match with academic subjects. But, the denial of credits causes veterans to cast doubt on the academic qualifications of their military training, coursework, and specialties. Many are left feeling bitter and disillusioned. The issue is an increasing point of tension on college campuses as scores of veterans return home to take advantage of a range of public benefits, hoping to build on skills acquired during their military service.

Just as college students receive course credit through internships, veterans contend that military training and jobs that correlate to academic subjects deserve as much credit as college coursework. For example, veterans say working as an Army cook should earn credit in a culinary arts program; and a sergeant supervising 100 soldiers should receive credit in business management.

The evaluation process, which military officials describe as rigorous and fair, documents soldiers' skills and responsibilities and recommends how much college credit they should receive. Colleges widely recognize military transcripts, however, they are not bound to honor them. Those who work closely with veterans report that many colleges award the credits arbitrarily.

"Many people handling transfers aren't aware of it and don't know how to do it, so they just don't accept it," said one military education director at a four-year, liberal arts college. "It's a problem that comes up a lot."

These hindrances lead many veterans to attend colleges known to be military-friendly to maximize their credits. These colleges usually belong to Service Members Opportunity Colleges (SOC), a Washington, D.C. consortium of approximately 1,800 schools dedicated to helping servicemembers receive college degrees. For a complete listing of SOC institutions, consult the REF section at the end of this chapter.

Colleges that do not award credit for military training contend that most service-related experience is incompatible with academic programs.

ACE Military Programs

Since 1945, ACE has provided a link between the DoD and higher education institutions by reviewing the military training and experiences of Air Force servicemembers and the equivalent college credits to be awarded.

Your military schools and work experiences (MOS) or Air Force Specialty Code (AFSC) are evaluated for possible college credit using a reference from the ACE *Guide to the Evaluation of Educational Experiences in the Armed Services*. If the credits recommended by ACE match credits required in your SOC degree plan, they may take the place of courses you would otherwise have been required to complete.

In addition, you can get college credit by taking tests, for example, CLEP® (College Level Examination Program), DSST® (DANTES Subject Standardized Tests), ECE (Excelsior College Examination), and ASE (Automotive Service Excellence). The combination of credits earned for Army schools and occupational experiences and tests, along with the actual college courses taken, will eventually give you enough credits for a college degree.

The first step to claiming the credits you have earned is to request a transcript from your military service. Each service branch has their own system for recording your military education and experience credits. They will provide you with unofficial personal copies and send schools official copies at no charge.

Army

The Army uses AARTS, which automatically captures your academic credits from military training and standardized tests. The AARTS transcript is designed to help college officials award credit for learning experiences the soldier gained while in the military; provide the soldier or veteran with a supplement to his/her resume; and provide employers with a better understanding of the scope of responsibilities and skills acquired in the military.

The AARTS transcript contains the following information: current rank, military status (active or inactive), additional skill identifiers, (ASI) and skill qualification identifiers (SQI), formal military courses, MOSs held, standardized test scores, and descriptions and credit recommendations developed by ACE.

It is a valuable asset you should provide to your college or employer and is available for active Army, National Guard, and Reserve soldiers. You can view and print your own transcript at https://aartstranscript.army.mil.

The AARTS system is available to enlisted soldiers only. You are eligible for an AARTS transcript if you have enlisted in the Army, Army National Guard (ARNG), or U.S. Army Reserve (USAR). AARTS receives its data directly from the following sources:

- Regular Army Biographical Data and MOS history—Human Resources Command (HRC)

- Army National Guard Biographical Data and MOS history—National Guard Bureau

- Army Reserve Biographical Data and MOS history—Army Reserve: Human Resources Command (HRC)

- Formal Course Completions—Army Training Requirements and Resources System (ATRRS)

- Standardized Test Scores—Educational Testing Service (ETS), American College Testing (ACT), and Excelsior College Examination Program (ECEP), formerly Regents College Examination Program (RCEP).

- Course and MOS Descriptions and Credit Recommendations—American Council on Education (ACE)

Army officers must use Form DD 295, *Application for Evaluation of Learning*, to report their military training and experience.

For more information on AARTS, visit http://aarts.army.mil.

In addition to AARTS, several records may be used for Army MOS verification. The applicant may submit one or several of the following forms of documentation:

- DD Form 295, *Application for the Evaluation of Learning Experiences During Military Service*
- DD Form 214, *Armed Forces of the United States Report of Transfer or Discharge*
- DA Form 2166-5, *Enlisted Evaluation Report* (EER)
- DA Form 2166-5A, *Senior Enlisted Evaluation Report* (SEER)
- DA Form 2166-1, *NCO Evaluation Report* (NCOER)
- USAEREC Form 10A and EREC Form 10, *Enlisted Evaluation Data Report*
- DA Form 2-1, *Personnel Qualifications Record*
- DA Form 20, *Enlisted Qualification Record*
- *Individual Soldier's Report* (ISR)

For Army warrant officer MOS verification, several records may be used. The applicant may submit one or several of the following forms of documentation:

- DA Form 67-8, *Officer Evaluation Report* (OER)
- DA Form 67-8-1, *Officer Evaluation Support Form*
- DA Form 2-1, *Personnel Qualifications Record*
- DA Form 66, *Officer Qualification Record*
- DA Form 4037, *Officer Record Brief*

Navy and Marines

The Navy and Marine Corps use the SMART system, which automatically captures training, experience, and standardized test scores. The primary purpose of SMART is to assist servicemembers in obtaining college credit for their military experience. For more information, visit www.navycollege.navy.mil.

SMART is available to document ACE-recommended college credit for military training and occupational experience. It is an academically accepted record validated by ACE.

SMART has replaced the *Application for Evaluation of Learning Experiences during Military Service*, which is currently submitted to colleges by sailors and marines to verify their military experiences. The *Application for Evaluation* may still be necessary to document training and experience that is not contained in and cannot be added to current personnel and training databases.

Currently, within the Marine Corps MOS system, selected aircraft maintenance, avionics, and ground occupational fields have established a performance evaluation system that meets ACE's criteria for college credit. The evaluation programs known as the Individual Training Standards System (ITSS) and Maintenance and Training Management and Evaluation Program (MATMEP) provide for the evaluation of a marine's job performance in the aircraft maintenance and avionics fields. The MATMEP program is a standardized, documentable, level-progressive, technical skills management and evaluation program for enlisted aviation technical maintenance training.

The ITSS (MATMEP) is organized as a two-way grid. The row headings identify the specific duties and tasks that define a MOS. The column headings identify the skill levels at which each MOS duty and task are performed. When a marine can perform a particular task at a specified level of skill, the marine's supervisor evaluates the performance. When a marine's ITSS (MATMEP) summary sheet indicates that the marine has advanced to complete Level III, ACE credit recommendations may be applied. ACE grants credit recommendation for Levels III and IV in aircraft maintenance and avionics MOSs.

Several records may be used for Navy warrant officer and limited duty officer verification. Applicants may submit one or several of the following forms of documentation:

- NAVPERS 601-4, *Navy Occupation/Training and Awards History*
- DD Form 295, *Application for the Evaluation of Learning Experiences During Military Service*

- DD Form 214, *Armed Forces of the United States Report of Transfer or Discharge*

For Navy enlisted classification verification, applicants may submit one or several of the following forms of documentation:

- NAVPERS 1070/604, *Navy Occupation/Training Awards History*
- NAVPERS 1616/24, *Enlisted Performance Evaluation Report*
- NAVPERS 1070/613, *Administrative Remarks*
- DD Form 295, *Application for the Evaluation of Learning Experiences During Military Service*
- DD Form 214, *Armed Forces of the United States Report of Transfer or Discharge*
- Letter of designation from a commanding officer

Several records may be used for Marine Corps MOS verification:

- ITSS (MATMEP) summary sheet
- DD Form 295, *Application for the Evaluation of Learning Experiences During Military Service*
- DD Form 214, *Armed Forces of the United States Report of Transfer or Discharge*

Air Force

The Community College of the Air Force is a federal program offered by the United States Air Force, which grants two-year associate of applied science (AAS) degrees in association with Air University. CCAF offers and awards job-related associate in applied science degrees and other academic credentials that enhance mission readiness, contribute to recruiting, assist in retention, and support the career transitions of Air Force enlisted members. The college awards an associate's degree to students who have successfully completed a degree program designed for an Air Force specialty.

The college is one of several federally chartered degree-granting institutions; however, it is the only two-year institution exclusively serving enlisted personnel. The CCAF automatically captures your training, experience, and standardized test scores. More information may be obtained at the CCAF website at www.maxwell.af.mil/au/ccaf.

The CCAF is unique in that it provides instruction at numerous locations because of the geographic dispersion of the students pursuing their Air Force occupations. Civilian collegiate institutions provide the course work to satisfy the general education requirement of the degree programs. They also provide course work to satisfy technical education and Leadership, Management, and Military Studies (LMMS) requirements not completed at CCAF schools. Although this broad geographical separation is unusual, the college is organized into a single, highly effective educational system.

Over the years, CCAF has grown both in numbers and recognition. With more than 373,000 registered students, the college is the world's largest multi-campus community college. Its affiliated schools are located in 34 states, the District of Columbia, six foreign locations, and one territory. Nearly 6,500 CCAF faculty members provide quality instruction for the personal and professional development of enlisted personnel. More than one million transcripts have been issued in the last ten years; and in 2000-2001 CCAF students earned 1.41 million hours of college credit.

Since issuing its first degree in 1977, the college has awarded more than 215,000 associate in applied science degrees.

Coast Guard

The Coast Guard Institute (CGI) provides training and education services, information, and guidance for all CG members and the CG Education Services Officers (ESO) who assist members in pursuit of advancement, qualifications, and voluntary education. The Institute requires each servicemember to submit documentation of all training (except correspondence course records), along with an enrollment form, to receive a transcript. For more information, visit the CGI website at www.uscg.mil/hq/cgi.

Several records may be used for Coast Guard occupation verification. The applicant may submit one or several of the following forms of documentation:

- DD Form 295, *Application for the Evaluation of Learning Experiences During Military Service*
- DD Form 214, *Armed Forces of the United States Report of Transfer or Discharge*
- Achievement Sheet

For Coast Guard warrant officer verification, applicants may submit one or several of the following forms of documentation:

- Form CG-5311, *Officer Evaluation Report* (OER)
- DD Form 295, *Application for the Evaluation of Learning Experiences During Military Service*
- DD Form 214, *Armed Forces of the United States Report of Transfer or Discharge*

Veterans

Under most circumstances, veterans are eligible to use their former service branches' transcript program. However, if you are not eligible for AARTS, SMART, CCAF, or CGI systems, you will need to fill out DD Form 295 and provide your DD Form 214 discharge document to receive credit for your experience.

In most cases, ACE-recommended credits will be used to fulfill your free-elective requirements, but each college determines the number of credits it will accept, as well as how they will be applied toward your degree. Truthfully, some schools choose not to grant credit for military experience. For this reason, it is critical to search for and apply to military-friendly schools.

Before you start taking classes, have all of your official transcripts from previous colleges and service branches sent to your new school for evaluation. Many students waste valuable time and money duplicating

- **VET VIP**

CCAF-affiliated schools are located in 34 states, the District of Columbia, six foreign locations, and one territory. More than one million transcripts have been issued in the last ten years; and in 2000-2001, CCAF students earned 1.41 million hours of college credit.

course work because they enrolled before their military and prior college transcripts were evaluated.

Testing Available through Your Education Center

Testing can be an important first step in your civilian career development. Some colleges and universities may require you to provide test results as part of your application. Prior to your departure from military service, you can take advantage of the testing services offered by your education center, Navy college office, and Marine Corps Lifelong Learning Center. These services include the following benefits:

Vocational interest inventories: Most education centers, Navy college offices, and Marine Corps LifeLong Learning Centers offer free vocation interest inventories that can help you identify the careers most likely to interest you.

Academic entrance exams: Before applying for college or other academic programs, you may want to take a college admissions test such as the Scholastic Aptitude Test® (SAT®), American College Testing® (ACT®), or the Graduate Record Examination® (GRE®). Most colleges and universities require that you take one of these exams. Information on these tests is available from your education center, Navy college office, or Marine Corps Lifelong Learning Center. You must start early. These exams are offered only a few times each year.

Credit by examination: Your education center, Navy college office, and Marine Corps Lifelong Learning Center offers a variety of "challenge" exams that can lead to college credit. If you score high enough, you may be exempt from taking a certain class or course requirements—resulting in a savings of time and money as you earn your degree. The College Level Examination Program and the DANTES Subject Standardized Tests are free to service members on active duty.

Certification Programs

If your military training school doesn't offer college credit, don't lose hope. Your training may instead lead to certification in a specialized technical field. DANTES has approximately 80 agreements with nationally recognized certification and licensure associations. These agreements allow DANTES test sites to administer the majority of their certification and licensure exams, providing convenience and accessibility to servicemembers.

You may already have the experience and knowledge required to gain certification in your occupational specialty, and may have no problem passing the exam to earn certification or licensure in a profession. Certification and licensure documents a servicemember's level of competency and achievement in a particular area. Credentials provide the equivalent of a "professional badge."

Certification testing is available in the automotive, computing, electronics, management, broadcast engineering, emergency medical technician, medical technology, and food preparation fields, among many others. Passing a certification exam helps you begin your civilian career right away as a fully trained individual, without having to go through a long apprenticeship period at low pay.

Passing a certification exam helps you begin your civilian career right away as a fully trained individual, without having to go through a long apprenticeship period at low pay.

Other Perspectives...

"We don't have a process for evaluating [military service] for credit," said a senior-level college administrator at a major university. "I think that's fairly standard." However, her school does consider giving former servicemembers credit for academic classes taken while in the military but offered through accredited colleges.

Despite problems and inconsistencies, a Department of Defense official has offered that while some veterans are frustrated by colleges' denials, overall, they saved an estimated $140 million in annual tuition costs through credits earned during service.

He added, "Some academic advisers are fairly junior people who are not totally conversant with the system, especially if they aren't near a military base."

But one longtime VA administrator at a university has criticized the military for exaggerating the amount of academic credit veterans will receive. "Students have the expectation that they are going to walk into college and get all sorts of credit, and it just doesn't happen," he said. "I really think the problem is in what they are being told, rather than what the institutions are not doing."

More than a few college administrators claim that a good deal of military training is too technical to transfer to a college program.

Carson Bennett, a business major in college, left for basic training just prior to his senior year and joined the military. While in the Army, he took intensive classes in Army psychological operations. However, when he returned to college, his courses were not accepted for academic credit.

Carson chose to transfer to a college that accepted most of his military classes toward his degree. He earned his degree and returned to active duty.

Dan Kennedy is an Army reservist who worked in logistics during a tour in Iraq. His college of choice rejected his request for transfer credit, although ACE argues that his training should have counted toward a management or business administration degree.

"Veterans assume they are going to get taken care of when they get back to school, and so does the general public," Dan said, "but they're not."

DEPARTMENT OF DEFENSE VOLUNTEER EDUCATION PROGRAMS

The DoD's off-duty, voluntary education programs constitute one of the largest continuing education programs in the world. Each year, about 300,000 servicemembers enroll in postsecondary courses leading to associate's, bachelor's, master's, and doctoral degrees. Colleges and universities, through an extensive network, deliver classroom instruction to hundreds of military installations around the world.

Servicemembers are also afforded opportunities to earn college credits for learning that has taken place outside the traditional classroom. This is accomplished through programs such as college-level equivalency testing, assessment of prior learning, assessment of military training, independent study, and distance learning. Additionally, special opportunities exist for servicemembers to enhance their basic academic skills through the following programs: high school completion, functional/basic skills, and English as a second language. Many of these educational opportunities are provided to servicemembers at no cost or, as in the case of college courses, at significantly reduced fees by tuition assistance.

A servicemember's participation in DoD-supported continuing education programs begins with a visit to an installation education center. At these centers, education officers and counselors present members with an extensive menu of options, provide details about specific programs, help members design courses of study, and accomplish administrative tasks to ensure that servicemembers receive maximum exposure to and benefits from available programs. These centers are staffed, funded, and operated by the Services. The National Defense Appropriations Act annually provides each Service with funds designated for "off-duty and voluntary education."

Postsecondary Degree Programs

Programs that enable servicemembers to earn a college degree are the primary focus of DoD-sponsored continuing education programs. Congress has held that men and women serving in the Armed Forces should have at least the same opportunities to advance academically as do civilians who remain outside the military. Servicemembers can enroll in college, receive tuition assistance, and earn degrees. In many instances, they can join college classes being conducted on the military base where they are assigned. Those serving aboard ships or submarines can take courses while at sea. In some cases, servicemembers can even continue their studies while deployed.

Military Tuition Assistance Program

Since 1996, tuition assistance has been uniform across the Services. The National Defense Authorization Act for 2000 removed the long-standing restriction on the percentage of tuition assistance that the Services could pay and, for the first time, authorized assistance at 100%.

SOURCE:
U.S. Department of Defense (www.voled.doded.mil)

SERVICEMEMBERS OPPORTUNITIES COLLEGES

The Servicemembers Opportunity Colleges' consortium of colleges and universities is dedicated to helping servicemembers and their families get college degrees. Military students can take courses in their off-duty hours at or near military installations in the United States, overseas, and on Navy ships.

SOC was created in 1972 to provide educational opportunities to servicemembers who had trouble completing college degrees due to frequent transfers, deployments, etc. Today, SOC is a consortium of more than 1,800 colleges and universities that provide educational opportunities for servicemembers and their families.

SOC is co-sponsored by the American Association of State Colleges and Universities (AASCU) and the American Association of Community Colleges (AACC), in cooperation with thirteen other educational associations, the Military Services, the National Guard, and the Coast Guard.

Funded by the Department of Defense through a contract with AASCU, SOC coordinates associate's and bachelor's degrees in a variety of curriculum areas for the Army (SOCAD), Navy (SOCNAV), Marine Corps (SOCMAR), and Coast Guard (SOCCOAST). Colleges and universities that are on or accessible to Army, Navy, Marine Corps, and Coast Guard installations worldwide offer these degree programs. Due to the presence of CCAF, the Air Force does not offer an Air Force-specific SOC program; however, the Air Force is a member of SOC under its general program.

Within each curriculum or degree network, member colleges agree to accept each other's credits in transfers. Servicemembers and their family members in isolated locations can take courses through distance-learning methods as the Internet, correspondence, computer, or video.

Each year, hundreds of thousands of servicemembers and their family members enroll in programs offered by the SOC consortium of universities, colleges, community colleges, and technical institutes. Military students can enroll in associate, bachelor, and graduate-level degree programs on school campuses, military installations, and armories in the United States and overseas.

Military Evaluations Program

The ACE, under a DoD contract, develops credit recommendations based on its evaluation of Service school courses, military training, and most enlisted occupations. The recommendations are published in the *Guide to the Evaluation of Educational Experiences in the Armed Forces*. Most colleges and universities award some college credit based on these recommendations.

Independent Study and External Degree Programs

Many regionally accredited colleges and universities offer courses and degree programs that provide opportunities for academic advancement and incorporate flexible scheduling, little or no residency requirements, and other nontraditional approaches. Opportunities exist for distance learning using broadcast video, recorded video, interactive CD-ROM, teleconferencing, or the Internet. Servicemembers receive tuition assistance for these programs under the same terms offered to more traditional modes of instructional delivery. These programs are managed by DANTES.

Examinations Program

The DoD operates a testing program through which servicemembers can earn certificates, licenses, college credits, and a high school diploma; or satisfy entrance and employment requirements with successful completion of the GRE, SAT, ACT, and the National Teacher Exam (NTE). Tests are offered to members at no cost. The testing program is offered uniformly across the Services and is managed by DANTES through contracts with the College Board and the Educational Testing Service.

High School Diploma

For enlistees who enter the military without a high school diploma, all Services pay 100% of the cost of studies and the testing leading to its achievement. Servicemembers that pass a special examination designed for adults can earn a high-school equivalency credential, which is awarded by the Department of Education of the state or territory where the member has residency or a service assignment.

Academic Skills Programs

For members that may need to update or enhance basic academic competencies, all Services offer opportunities to improve skills in areas such as English, reading, writing, speaking, and mathematics. Basic and functional skills programs are provided at no cost to servicemembers. For those posted to overseas locations, these programs are also available to spouses without cost.

Military Installation Voluntary Education Review (MIVER)

The DoD contracts with ACE for a periodic third-party review of the voluntary education programs conducted at the installation level. Teams of highly qualified professors, deans, and other professionals from the higher education community are sent to the field to conduct the review.

Team members review the operation of the education center and the colleges providing services to that installation. They evaluate the self-studies prepared by the installation and the servicing institutions and they interview education officers, counselors, institutional representatives, instructors, and students. They meet with local command personnel. Their written report is issued to Service headquarters, local commands, and the institutions. Services generally require local commands to report on the actions taken in response to the recommendations within a year of the visit.

SOURCE:
Servicemembers Opportunity Colleges (www.soc.aascu.org)

THE NAVY
COLLEGE PROGRAM (NCP)

The Navy College Program provides opportunities for sailors to earn college degrees by providing academic credit for navy training, work experience, and off-duty education. NCP's mission is to enable sailors to obtain a college degree while on active duty. In support of its four Rs— Recruiting, Readiness, Retention, and Respect—the NCP is the portrait of the Navy's commitment to helping sailors apply themselves to new situations and challenges, better preparing them for advancement, building up their self-image, and producing higher quality servicemembers.

The Navy College Program integrates all components of DoD's voluntary education programs. While the NCP is primarily geared toward enlisted sailors, some NCP components are also available to officers.

Further, to assist you in your preparation for college courses, the Navy provides instruction in basic subjects. You may work on your English, mathematics, and reading skills ashore at the Navy College Learning Centers' (NCLCs) computer labs or in the Navy College Learning Program's (NCLP) instructor-taught classes. In either program, you will be given diagnostic tests and begin your instruction at a level appropriate to your needs. Instruction in academic skills is available at no cost to you or your command.

Combining the various components of the total program, the NCP serves the needs of mobile sailors. Servicemembers are provided uncomplicated access to information along the path to a degree, including transferability of college credit and access to education regardless of the sailors' location or duty station. Participation is voluntary. Sailors participate at their own pace when they are ready.

SOURCE:
U.S. Navy (www.navycollege.navy.mil)

THE SERVICEMEMBERS OPPORTUNITY COLLEGES STUDENT AGREEMENT

The student's home college (the college that offers a SOC Network System degree that the student wishes to pursue) issues the SOCAD, SOCNAV, SOCMAR, or SOCCOAST Student Agreement (SA). The agreement serves as the official evaluation by a home college of a student's prior education and experience as it applies to his or her degree program. The agreement gives the student a plan showing the courses and other requirements needed to complete the degree.

The SA is a "contract-for-degree" between the home college and the student. The SA also serves as the student's guarantee that he or she will be awarded the degree by the home college when all stated requirements have been met.

When degree-seeking students enroll in a program that is part of the SOC Network System, they are entitled to have a Student Agreement reflecting the college's official evaluation of the students' prior learning, plus remaining degree requirements after completing no more than approximately six semester hours, or two courses, at the home college.

SOC Consortium Military Student Bill of Rights

The following Military Student Bill of Rights spell out ten specific "Rights" that military students should have as they explore, enroll, and work toward degrees or certificates at SOC consortium colleges and universities. These "Rights" focus directly on fair and honest recruiting, marketing, and student services practices. The SOC advisory board approved the Military Student Bill of Rights in 2007.

All military student populations have basic rights to satisfactory college marketing, admissions, and student services practices, including the right to:

1. Accurate information about a school's programs, requirements, accreditation, and its potential impact on course transferability.

2. Access basic college/university information and fees without disclosure of student personal information.

3. Educational planning and career guidance without high-pressure registration and enrollment efforts from institutions.

4. A clear and complete explanation of course/program enrollment procedures and all resulting financial obligations.

5. Explore, without coercion, all financial aid options before signing up for student loans or other financial assistance.

6. Accurate scholarship information, free of misleading "scholarship" offers based on military tuition assistance.

7. Appropriate academic screening and course placement based on student readiness.

8. Appropriate, accessible academic and student support services.

9. Clearly defined institutional "drop/add" and withdrawal policies and procedures including information about the impact of military duties (e.g., mobilization, activation, and temporary duty assignments) on their academic standing and financial responsibilities.

10. Clearly defined grievance/appeals processes.

SOURCE:
Servicemembers Opportunity Colleges Consortium (www.soc.aascu.org)

SOC CONSORTIUM MEMBER INSTITUTIONS

The 1,800 colleges and universities that comprise the Servicemembers Opportunity Colleges consortium provide educational opportunities for servicemembers and their families. SOC is cosponsored by the American Association of State Colleges and Universities (AASCU) and the American Association of Community Colleges (AACC), in cooperation with thirteen other educational associations, the Military Services, the National Guard, and the Coast Guard.

Note: Consortium memberships are biannual and therefore subject to change. For more information on the SOC consortium and member institutions, visit www.soc.aascu.org.

Alabama
Alabama Agricultural and
    Mechanical University
Amridge University
Andrew Jackson University
Athens State University
Auburn University at Montgomery
Bevill State Community College
Bishop State Community College
Calhoun Community College
Central Alabama Community College
Chattahoochee Valley Community College
Columbia Southern University
Dothan Herzing College
Enterprise-Ozark Community College
Faulkner State Community College
Faulkner University
Gadsden State Community College

George C. Wallace State Community College
ITT Technical Institute – Birmingham
J.F. Drake State Technical College
Jacksonville State University
Jefferson Davis Community College
Jefferson State Community College
Judson College
Lawson State Community College
Lurleen B. Wallace Community College
Northeast Alabama Community College
Northwest-Shoals Community College
Oakwood College
Reid State Technical College
Remington College, Mobile Campus
Shelton State Community College
Snead State Community College
South University
Southern Union State Community College
Talladega College
Trenholm State Technical College,
    Trenholm Campus
Troy University
United States Sports Academy
University of Alabama at Birmingham
University of Alabama at Tuscaloosa
University of Alabama in Huntsville
University of Mobile
University of Montevallo
University of North Alabama
University of South Alabama
University of West Alabama
Virginia College at Birmingham
Wallace Community College – Selma
Wallace State Community College –
    Hanceville

Alaska
Alaska Pacific University
Charter College
University of Alaska Anchorage
University of Alaska Fairbanks
University of Alaska Southeast

Arizona
Argosy University/Phoenix
Arizona Western College
Art Institute of Phoenix
Axia College of University of Phoenix
Central Arizona College
Cochise College
DeVry University – Mesa Campus
DeVry University – Northeast Phoenix
DeVry University – Phoenix Campus

Estrella Mountain Community College
GateWay Community College
Glendale Community College
International Import-Export Institute
International Institute of the Americas
ITT Technical Institute – Tempe
ITT Technical Institute – Tucson
Mesa Community College
Mohave Community College
Northcentral University
Northern Arizona University
Paradise Valley Community College
Paralegal Institute Penn Foster College
Phoenix College
Pima County Community College
Prescott College – Adult Degree Programs
Rio Salado College
Scottsdale Community College
South Mountain Community College
University of Arizona – University of
    Arizona South
University of Phoenix Western
    International University

Arkansas
Arkansas Baptist College
Arkansas Northeastern College
Arkansas State University
Arkansas State University – Beebe
Arkansas State University – Newport
Arkansas Tech University
Central Baptist College
Cossatot Community College of the
    University of Arkansas
Henderson State University
Mid-South Community College
National Park Community College
Ouachita Technical College
Ozarka College
Pulaski Technical College
Southern Arkansas University
University of Arkansas – Fayetteville
University of Arkansas at Fort Smith
University of Arkansas at Little Rock
University of Arkansas at Monticello
University of Arkansas at Pine Bluff
University of Arkansas Community
    College at Hope
University of Central Arkansas

California
Allan Hancock College
Alliant International University
American Graduate University

American River College
Antelope Valley College
Argosy University/Orange County
Argosy University/San Francisco Bay
Art Institute of California – Los Angeles
Art Institute of California – Orange County
Art Institute of California – San Diego
Art Institute of California – San Francisco
Aviation & Electronic Schools of America
Azusa Pacific University
Bakersfield College
Barstow College
California Baptist University
California Coast University
California College - San Diego
California Design College
California Lutheran University
California Maritime Academy
California National University
California Polytechnic State University
   – San Luis Obispo
California State Polytechnic University
   – Pomona
California State University, Bakersfield
California State University, Channel Islands
California State University, Dominguez Hills
California State University, East Bay
California State University, Fresno
California State University, Fullerton
California State University, Long Beach
California State University, Los Angeles
California State University, Monterey Bay
California State University, Northridge
California State University, Sacramento
California State University, San Bernardino
California State University, San Marcos
California State University, Stanislaus
Cerritos College
Cerro Coso Community College
Chaffey College
Chapman University – University College
Citrus College
City College of San Francisco
Coastline Community College
Cogswell Polytechnical College
Coleman College
College of the Canyons
College of the Sequoias
Copper Mountain College
Cosumnes River College
Crafton Hills College
Cuyamaca College
De Anza College
DeVry University – Fremont
DeVry University – Fresno

DeVry University – Inland Empire/Colton
DeVry University – Irvine
DeVry University – Long Beach
DeVry University – Pomona
DeVry University – Sacramento
DeVry University – San Diego
DeVry University – San Francisco
DeVry University – San Jose
DeVry University – Sherman Oaks
District San Diego City College
Fashion Institute of Design
   and Merchandising
Feather River College
Fielding Graduate University
Foothill College for Advanced Studies
Fresno City College
Gavilan College
Gemological Institute of America
Golden Gate University
Golden West College
Grossmont College
Hartnell College
Heald College
Henley-Putnam University
Holy Names University
Hope International University
Humboldt State University
Irvine Valley College
ITT Technical Institute – Lathrop
ITT Technical Institute – San Bernardino
ITT Technical Institute – San Diego
John F. Kennedy University
LA College
Los Angeles Trade-Technical College
Maric College – North County
Merced College
MiraCosta College
Mission College
Monterey Institute of International Studies
Monterey Peninsula College
Moorpark College
Mount St. Mary's College
National Polytechnic College of Science
National University
Newschool of Architecture and Design
Orange Coast College
Oxnard College
Pacific Graduate School of Psychology
Palomar College
Patten University
Pierce College
Riverside Community College
San Diego Mesa College
San Diego Miramar College
San Diego State University

San Francisco State University
San Joaquin Delta College
Santa Monica College
Solano Community College
Sonoma State University
Southern California Institute of Technology
Southwestern College
Taft College
TUI University
University of La Verne
University of San Diego – Schools of
    Business Administration and Education
Victor Valley College
West Hills Community College District
    – Lemoore Campus
West Los Angeles College
Yuba Community College

Colorado

Adams State College
Aims Community College
American Sentinel University
Arapahoe Community College
Art Institute of Colorado
Aspen University
College for Financial Planning
Colorado Christian University
Colorado Northwestern Community College
Colorado School of Mines
Colorado State University
Colorado State University – Pueblo,
    Division of Continuing Education
Colorado Technical University
Community College of Aurora
Community College of Denver
DeVry University – Colorado Springs
DeVry University – Denver South
DeVry University – Westminster
Fort Lewis College
Front Range Community College
Jones International University
Lamar Community College
Mesa State College
Metropolitan State College of Denver
Morgan Community College
Northeastern Junior College
Otero Junior College
Pikes Peak Community College
Pueblo Community College
Red Rocks Community College
Redstone College
Regis University – College for
    Professional Studies
Remington College, Colorado Springs

Trinidad State Junior College
University of Colorado – Colorado Springs
University of Northern Colorado
Westwood College

Connecticut

Albertus Magnus College
Asnuntuck Community College
Briarwood College
Capital Community College
Charter Oak State College
Eastern Connecticut State University
    – School of Continuing Education
Manchester Community College
Middlesex Community College
Mitchell College
Naugatuck Valley Community College
Norwalk Community College
Post University
Quinebaug Valley Community College
Sacred Heart University
Southern Connecticut State University
Three Rivers Community College
Tunxis Community College
University of New Haven

Delaware

Delaware Technical and Community College
Goldey-Beacom College
Wesley College
Wilmington College

District of Columbia

American University
Catholic University of America
    – Metropolitan College
George Washington University
Georgetown University
    School of Continuing Studies
Howard University
Potomac College
Southeastern University
Strayer University
University of the District of Columbia

Florida

AI Miami International University
    of Art & Design
Argosy University – Sarasota
Argosy University – Tampa
Art Institute of Fort Lauderdale

Barry University – School of Adult and
  Continuing Education BARRYU
Bethune-Cookman College
Brevard Community College
Broward Community College
Central Florida Community College
College of Business and Technology
Daytona Beach Community College
DeVry University – Fort Lauderdale
DeVry University – Jacksonville
DeVry University – Miami Campus
DeVry University – Miramar Campus
DeVry University – Orlando Campus
DeVry University – Orlando North
DeVry University – Tampa Bay
Eckerd College – Program for
  Experienced Learners
Edison Community College
Edward Waters College
Embry-Riddle Aeronautical University
Everest University
Everglades University
Florida Agricultural and Mechanical
  University
Florida Atlantic University
Florida Community College – Jacksonville
Florida Gulf Coast University
Florida Institute of Technology
Florida International University
Florida Keys Community College
Florida National College
Gulf Coast Community College
Hillsborough Community College
IMPAC University
Indian River Community College
International College
ITT Technical Institute – Fort Lauderdale
ITT Technical Institute – Lake Mary
ITT Technical Institute – Miami
ITT Technical Institute – Tampa
Jacksonville University
Jones College – Distance Learning Program
Kaplan University Online
Keiser University
Key College
Lake City Community College
Lincoln College of Technology
Manatee Community College
Miami Dade College
North Florida Community College
Nova Southeastern University
Okaloosa-Walton College
Palm Beach Atlantic University
Palm Beach Community College
Pasco-Hernando Community College

Pensacola Junior College
Polk Community College
Polytechnic University of the Americas
Saint Leo University
Santa Fe Community College
Seminole Community College
South Florida Community College
Southeastern University
Southwest Florida College
St. Johns River Community College
St. Petersburg College
St. Thomas University
Tallahassee Community College
University of Central Florida
University of Florida
University of North Florida
University of South Florida
University of Tampa
University of West Florida
Valencia Community College
Webber International University

Georgia
Abraham Baldwin Agricultural College
Albany Technical College
Altamaha Technical College
American Inter Continental
  University – Dunwoody
Argosy University/Atlanta
Armstrong Atlantic State University
Art Institute of Atlanta
Ashworth University – Associate
  Degree Program
Athens Technical College
Atlanta Technical College
Augusta State University
Augusta Technical College
Beacon University
Brenau University – Evening
  and Weekend College
Brewton-Parker College
Central Georgia Technical College
Chattahoochee Technical College
Clayton State University
Coastal Georgia Community College
Columbus State University
Columbus Technical College
Covenant College
Darton College
DeVry University – Alpharetta
DeVry University – Atlanta/Buckhead
DeVry University – Atlanta/Cobb-Galleria
DeVry University – Atlanta/Perimeter
DeVry University – Decatur

DeVry University – Gwinnett
DeVry University – Henry County
East Central Technical College
East Georgia College
Emmanuel College
Georgia College and State University
Georgia Military College
Georgia Perimeter College
Georgia Southern University
Georgia Southwestern State University
Gwinnett Technical College
Heart of Georgia Technical College
Lanier Technical College
Luther Rice University
Mercer University
Middle Georgia College
Middle Georgia Technical College
North Georgia College and State University
North Georgia Technical College
North Metro Technical College
Northwestern Technical College
Paine College
Savannah State University
Savannah Technical College
Shorter College – School of
    Professional Programs
South Georgia College
South University
Southeastern Technical College
Southern Polytechnic State University
Southwest Georgia Technical College
Swainsboro Technical College
Thomas University
University of West Georgia
Valdosta State University
Waycross College
West Georgia Technical College

Guam

Guam Community College
University of Guam

Hawaii

Argosy University/Hawaii
Chaminade University of Honolulu
Hawaii Pacific University
Hawaii Theological Seminary
Honolulu Community College
Kapiolani Community College
Leeward Community College
Maui Community College
Windward Community College

Idaho

Boise State University
Brigham Young University – Idaho
College of Southern Idaho
Idaho State University
ITT Technical Institute – Boise
Lewis-Clark State College
North Idaho College
Northwest Nazarene University
University of Idaho

Illinois

Argosy University/Chicago
Argosy University/Schaumburg
Benedictine University
Black Hawk College
Carl Sandburg College
Chicago State University
City Colleges of Chicago –
    Richard J. Daley College
City Colleges of Chicago –
    Harold Washington College
College of DuPage
College of Lake County
Columbia College Chicago
DeVry University – Addison
DeVry University – Chicago
DeVry University – Chicago Loop
DeVry University – Chicago O'Hare
DeVry University – Elgin
DeVry University – Gurnee
DeVry University – Lincolnshire
DeVry University – Naperville
DeVry University – Oak Brook
DeVry University – Schaumburg
DeVry University – Tinley Park
Eastern Illinois University – Bachelor of
    EASTIL Arts Degree Program
Governors State University
Highland Community College
Illinois Central College
Illinois Eastern Community Colleges
    – Frontier, Lincoln Trail, Olney
    Central, Wabash Valley
Illinois Institute of Art – Schaumburg
    and Chicago Campuses
Illinois State University
Illinois Valley Community College
ITT Technical Institute – Orland Park
John A. Logan College
John Wood Community College
Joliet Junior College
Kaskaskia College

Keller Graduate School of Management
of DeVry University
Kendall College
Kishwaukee College
Lake Land College
Lewis and Clark Community College
Lewis University
Lincoln Land Community College
MacMurray College
McKendree University
Midstate College
Morrison Institute of Technology
National-Louis University
Northeastern Illinois University –
Bachelor of Arts Degree Program
Oakton Community College
Olivet Nazarene University
Parkland College
Quincy University
Rend Lake College
Robert Morris College
Rosalind Franklin University of Medicine
and Science – Chicago Medical School
Saint Xavier University
Sauk Valley Community College
Shawnee Community College
Southeastern Illinois College
Southern Illinois University, Carbondale
– College of Applied Sciences and Arts
Southern Illinois University, Carbondale
– College of Education and
Human Services
Southern Illinois University, Carbondale
– College of Engineering
Southern Illinois University, Edwardsville
Southwestern Illinois College
Spoon River College
Triton College
University of Saint Francis
Waubonsee Community College
Western Illinois University – School
of Extended Studies
William Rainey Harper College

Indiana
Ball State University
Bethel College
Calumet College of Saint Joseph
DeVry University – Indianapolis Campus
DeVry University – Merrillville Campus
Huntington University
Indiana Institute of Technology
Indiana State University

Indiana University – Purdue University,
Fort Wayne
Indiana University – Purdue University,
Indianapolis
Indiana University – School of
Continuing Studies
Indiana University, Kokomo
Indiana Wesleyan University
ITT Technical Institute – Fort Wayne
Ivy Tech Community College –
Central Indiana
Ivy Tech Community College – Columbus
Ivy Tech Community College –
East Central
Ivy Tech Community College –
Kokomo/Logansport
Ivy Tech Community College – Lafayette
Ivy Tech Community College –
Northcentral
Ivy Tech Community College – Northeast
Ivy Tech Community College – Northwest
Ivy Tech Community College – Richmond
Ivy Tech Community College – Southcentral
Ivy Tech Community College – Southeast
Ivy Tech Community College – Southwest
Ivy Tech Community College – Wabash Valley
Lincoln Technical Institute
Marian College
Martin University
Oakland City University
Saint Joseph's College
Saint Mary-of-the-Woods College
Tri-State University
University of Evansville –
Individualized Study Program
University of Indianapolis
University of Saint Francis
University of Southern Indiana
Vincennes University

Iowa
AIB College of Business
Ashford University
Briar Cliff University
Clarke College
Des Moines Area Community College
District Ellsworth Community College
Dordt College
Drake University
Eastern Iowa Community College
Graceland University
Grand View College
Hamilton College
Hawkeye Community College

Indian Hills Community College
Iowa Lakes Community College
Iowa State University
Iowa Wesleyan College
Iowa Western Community College
Kaplan University – Davenport
Loras College
North Iowa Area Community College
Northeast Iowa Community College
Northwest Iowa Community College
Northwestern College
Palmer College of Chiropractic –
    Technical & Bachelor of Science
    Degrees in General Science Programs
Scott Community College
Southeastern Community College
Southwestern Community College
St. Ambrose University
University of Dubuque
University of Iowa
University of Northern Iowa
Upper Iowa University
Western Iowa Tech Community College
William Penn University

Kansas

Allen County Community College
Baker University – School of Professional
    and Graduate Studies
Barton County Community College
Butler Community College
Cloud County Community College
Coffeyville Community College
Colby Community College
Cowley County Community College
Dodge City Community College
Donnelly College
Emporia State University
Fort Hays State University – Virtual College
Fort Scott Community College
Garden City Community College
Hutchinson Community College
    and Area Vocational School
Independence Community College
Johnson County Community College
    – Kansas City
Kansas Community College
Kansas State University
Kansas Wesleyan University
Neosho County Community College
Newman University
Ottawa University
Pittsburg State University
Pratt Community College

Seward County Community College
Southwestern College – Professional
    Studies
University of Saint Mary
Washburn University
Wichita State University

Kentucky

Ashland Community and Technical College
Beckfield College
Brescia University
Eastern Kentucky University
Elizabethtown Community and
    Technical College
Hazard Community and Technical College
Henderson Community College
Hopkinsville Community College
ITT Technical Institute – Louisville
Kentucky State University
Kentucky Wesleyan College
Lindsey Wilson College
Louisville Technical Institute
Madisonville Community College
Maysville Community and Technical College
Mid-Continent University
Midway College
Morehead State University
Murray State University
National College
Somerset Community College
Southeast Kentucky Community
    and Technical College
St. Catherine College
Sullivan University
Thomas More College
University of Kentucky
University of Louisville – College of
    Education and Human Development
West Kentucky Community and
    Technical College
Western Kentucky University

Louisiana

Grambling State University
ITT Technical Institute – St. Rose
Louisiana State University at Alexandria
Louisiana State University at Eunice
Louisiana Tech University
Louisiana Technical College – Northeast
Louisiana Technical College – Young
    Memorial Campus
Loyola University – New Orleans
McNeese State University

Nicholls State University
Northwestern State University
Our Lady of Holy Cross College
Remington College
Southeastern Louisiana University
Tulane University – School of
    Continuing Studies
University of Louisiana at Lafayette
University of Louisiana at Monroe
University of New Orleans – General
    Studies Program

Maine

Central Maine Community College
Eastern Maine Community College
Kennebec Valley Community College
Maine College of Art
Maine Maritime Academy
Northern Maine Community College
Saint Joseph's College of Maine – Division of
    Graduate and Professional Studies
Southern Maine Community College
Thomas College
University of Maine
University of Maine at Augusta
University of Maine at Fort Kent
University of Maine at Machias
    – Baccalaureate Programs
University of Maine at Presque Isle
University of Southern Maine
York County Community College

Maryland

Allegany College of Maryland
Anne Arundel Community College
Baltimore City Community College
Bowie State University
Capitol College
Cecil Community College
College of Southern Maryland
Columbia Union College
Community College of Baltimore
Community College of Baltimore County
    – Catonsville
Community College of Baltimore County
    – Dundalk
Coppin State University
DeVry University – Bethesda
Frederick Community College
Frostburg State University
Garrett College
Hagerstown Community College
Harford Community College

Howard Community College
Montgomery College
Morgan State University
Mount St. Mary's University
Prince George's Community College
Salisbury University
St. Mary's College of Maryland
Towson University – Undergraduate Programs
University College
University of Baltimore
University of Maryland
University of Maryland Eastern Shore
Villa Julie College

Massachusetts

American International College
Bay Path College
Becker College
Berkshire Community College
Boston University – Metropolitan College
Bridgewater State College
Bristol Community College
Bunker Hill Community College
Cambridge College
Cape Cod Community College
Eastern Nazarene College – Adult
    Studies Program
Elms College
Fisher College
Fitchburg State College
Massasoit Community College
Middlesex Community College
Mount Wachusett Community College
National Graduate School
Newbury College
Nichols College
North Shore Community College
Northeastern University – School of
    Professional and Continuing Studies
Northern Essex Community College
Quincy College
Quinsigamond Community College
Salem State College
University of Massachusetts, Amherst
Western New England College

Michigan

Albion College
Baker College
Bay Noc Community College
Central Michigan University –
    Off-Campus Programs
Charles Stewart Mott Community College

Cleary University
Concordia University – Ann Arbor
Davenport University
Delta College
District Western Michigan University
Eastern Michigan University
Ferris State University
Finlandia University
Glen Oaks Community College
Gogebic Community College
ITT Technical Institute – Canton
Jackson Community College
Kalamazoo Valley Community College
Kellogg Community College
Kirtland Community College
Lansing Community College
Lewis College of Business
Madonna University
Michigan Jewish Institute
Michigan Technological University
Mid Michigan Community College
Muskegon Community College
North Central Michigan College
Northern Michigan University
Northwestern Michigan College
Northwood University – University College
Rochester College – College of
    Extended Learning
Schoolcraft College
Siena Heights University
Southwestern Michigan College
Spring Arbor University
St. Clair County Community College
University of Michigan – Flint
Walsh College
Washtenaw Community College
Wayne County Community College

Minnesota

Alexandria Technical College
Anoka-Ramsey Community College
Argosy University/Twin Cities
Art Institutes International Minnesota
Augsburg College
Bemidji State University
Bethel University – College of Adult
    and Professional Studies
Capella University
Central Lakes College
Century College
College of St. Scholastica
Concordia University, St. Paul
Dakota County Technical College Online
DeVry University – Edina

DeVry University – St. Louis Park
Globe University
Hibbing Community College
Inver Hills Community College
Itasca Community College
Lake Superior College
Mesabi Range Community and
    Technical College
Metropolitan State University
Minnesota School of Business
Minnesota State Community and
    Technical College
Minnesota State University, Mankato
Minnesota West Community and
    Technical College – Worthington Campus
Normandale Community College
North Hennepin Community College
Northland Community and Technical College
Northwest Technical College
Northwestern College
Pine Technical College
Rainy River Community College
Rasmussen College – Multi-Campus System
Ridgewater College
Riverland Community College
Rochester Community and Technical College
Saint Paul College – Community and
    Technical College
Southwest Minnesota State University
St. Cloud State University
St. Cloud Technical College
Vermilion Community College
Walden University

Mississippi

Alcorn State University
Belhaven College
Coahoma Community College
Copiah-Lincoln Community College
Delta State University
East Central Community College
East Mississippi Community College
Hinds Community College
Holmes Community College
Itawamba Community College
Jackson State University
Jones County Junior College
Meridian Community College
Mississippi Gulf Coast Community College
Mississippi State University
Mississippi University for Women
Pearl River Community College
Rust College
Southwest Mississippi Community College

University of Mississippi
University of Southern Mississippi
William Carey University

Missouri

Calvary Bible College and Theological
    Seminary
Columbia College
Culver-Stockton College
DeVry University – Kansas City Campus
DeVry University – St. Louis West
Drury University, Mid-Missouri Region
    (Fort Leonard Wood) DRURY
East Central College
Fontbonne University
Global University
Grantham University
Hannibal-LaGrange College
Harris-Stowe State University
ITT Technical Institute – Arnold
ITT Technical Institute – Earth City
Lincoln University
Lindenwood University
Maryville University of Saint Louis
Mineral Area College
Missouri Southern University
Missouri State University – Springfield
Missouri State University – West Plains
Missouri Tech
Missouri University of Science
    and Technology
Missouri Western State University
Moberly Area Community College
North Central Missouri College
Northwest Missouri State University
Ozarks Technical Community College
Park University
Rockhurst University
Saint Louis University – Parks College of
    Engineering, Aviation and Technology
Saint Louis University – School
    for Professional Studies
Southeast Missouri State University
Southwest Baptist University
St. Charles Community College
State Fair Community College
Stephens College – School of Graduate
    and Continuing Studies
University of Central Missouri
University of Missouri – St. Louis
Webster University
Westminster College

William Jewell College
William Woods University – College
    of Graduate and Adult Studies

Montana

Blackfeet Community College
Carroll College
Dawson Community College
Fort Belknap College
Fort Peck Community College
Miles Community College
Montana State University – Billings
Montana State University – Bozeman
Montana State University – Great Falls
    College of Technology
Montana State University – Northern
Montana Tech College of Technology
Rocky Mountain College
Salish Kootenai College
Stone Child College
University of Great Falls
University of Montana
University of Montana – Helena College
    of Technology
University of Montana – Missoula
    College of Technology
University of Montana – Western

Nebraska

Bellevue University
Central Community College – Columbus
Central Community College – Grand
    Island
Central Community College – Hastings
Chadron State College
Hastings College
ITT Technical Institute – Omaha
Metropolitan Community College
Mid-Plains Community College
Midland Lutheran College
Nebraska Methodist College of
    Nursing and Allied Health
Northeast Community College
Peru State College
Southeast Community College
University of Nebraska – Lincoln
University of Nebraska at Kearney
University of Nebraska at Omaha
    – College of Continuing Studies
Wayne State College
Western Nebraska Community College

Nevada

Art Institute of Las Vegas
Community College of Southern Nevada
DeVry University – Henderson Campus
Great Basin College
ITT Technical Institute – Henderson Truckee
Meadows Community College
University of Nevada – Las Vegas
University of Nevada, Reno
Western Nevada Community College

New Hampshire

Chester College of New England
Colby-Sawyer College
Daniel Webster College
Granite State College
New England College
Southern New Hampshire University

New Jersey

Atlantic Cape Community College
Bergen Community College
Berkeley College
Bloomfield College
Brookdale Community College
Burlington County College
Caldwell College
Centenary College
County College of Morris
DeVry University – North Brunswick
Fairleigh Dickinson University
Georgian Court University
Gloucester County College
Hudson County Community College
Kean University
Mercer County Community College
Monmouth University
New Jersey Institute of Technology – College of Science and Liberal Arts
Ocean County College
Ramapo College of New Jersey
Raritan Valley Community College
Rider University
Saint Peter's College
Salem Community College
Sussex County Community College
Thomas Edison State College
Union County College

New Mexico

Clovis Community College
College of Santa Fe
College of the Southwest
Dona Ana Community College
Eastern New Mexico University – Main Campus
Eastern New Mexico University – Roswell
ITT Technical Institute – Albuquerque
Mesalands Community College
New Mexico Highlands University
New Mexico Junior College
New Mexico Military Institute
New Mexico State University
New Mexico State University at Alamogordo
Northern New Mexico College
San Juan College
Western New Mexico University

New York

Adelphi University
Adirondack Community College
American Academy McAllister Institute of Funeral Services
Art Institute of New York City
Broome Community College
Canisius College
Cayuga Community College
City University of New York Baccalaureate Program
City University of New York College of Staten Island
City University of New York – John Jay College of Criminal Justice
City University of New York – Medgar Evers College
Clinton Community College
College of Mount Saint Vincent
College of Saint Rose
Columbia-Greene Community College
Corning Community College
D'Youville College
DeVry University – Long Island City
DeVry University – Manhattan
Dominican College of Blauvelt
Dutchess Community College
Elmira College
Empire State College, State University of New York
Erie Community College
Excelsior College
Farmingdale State University of New York
Genesee Community College
Herkimer County Community College
Hilbert College
Hudson Valley Community College
ITT Technical Institute – Liverpool

Jamestown Community College
Jefferson Community College
Keuka College
Laboratory Institute of Merchandising
Long Island University – C.W. Post
Medaille College
Mercy College
Milano The New School for
    Management and Urban Policy
Mohawk Valley Community College
Monroe College
Monroe Community College
Mount Saint Mary College
Nassau Community College
Nazareth College of Rochester –
    Undergraduate Programs
New York Institute of Technology
Niagara County Community College
Niagara University
North Country Community College
Nyack College
Orange County Community College
Pace University – Adult Services Program
Plaza College
Purchase College, State University
    of New York
Roberts Wesleyan College
Rochester Institute of Technology
Schenectady County Community College
Skidmore College – University Without Walls
St. Bonaventure University
St. Francis College
St. John Fisher College
St. Joseph's College – Brooklyn Campus
St. Joseph's College – Long Island Campus
St. Thomas Aquinas College
State University of New York at Binghamton
State University of New York at Potsdam State
State University of New York College at
    Brockport
State University of New York College at
    Buffalo
State University of New York College at
    Fredonia
State University of New York College at
    Oswego
State University of New York College at
    Plattsburgh
State University of New York College of
    Agriculture and Technology at Cobleskill
State University of New York College of
    Agriculture and Technology at Morrisville
State University of New York College of
    Technology at Alfred

State University of New York College of
    Technology at Delhi
State University of New York Institute of
    Technology at Utica-Rome
State University of New York
    Maritime College
Suffolk County Community College
Sullivan County Community College
SUNY Canton College of Technology
SUNY Ulster County Community College
Syracuse University – University College,
    Professional Studies Program
Tompkins Cortland Community College
Touro College
University at Buffalo, State University
    of New York
University of New York at Stony Brook
    – School of Professional Development
Utica School of Commerce
Vaughn College of Aeronautics and
    Technology
Villa Maria College of Buffalo

North Carolina

Apex School of Theology
Art Institute of Charlotte
Beaufort County Community College
Bladen Community College
Brunswick Community College
Caldwell Community College and
    Technical Institute
Campbell University
Cape Fear Community College
Catawba Valley Community College
Central Carolina Community College
Central Piedmont Community College
Cleveland Community College
Coastal Carolina Community College
College of the Albemarle
Craven Community College
Davidson County Community College
DeVry University – Charlotte Campus
DeVry University – Raleigh-Durham
Durham Technical Community College
East Carolina University
Edgecombe Community College
Elizabeth City State University
Fayetteville State University
Fayetteville Technical Community College
Guilford Technical Community College
Halifax Community College
Haywood Community College
Heritage Bible College
High Point University

Isothermal Community College
John Wesley College
Johnson C. Smith University
Johnston Community College
Lenoir Community College
Mars Hill College
Martin Community College
Mayland Community College
Methodist University
Mitchell Community College
Montgomery Community College
Montreat College
Mount Olive College
Nash Community College
North Carolina Agricultural and Technical
    State University
North Carolina Central University
North Carolina State University
North Carolina Wesleyan College
Pfeiffer University
Piedmont Community College
Pitt Community College
Randolph Community College
Richmond Community College
Roanoke-Chowan Community College
Rockingham Community College
Rowan-Cabarrus Community College
Sandhills Community College
School of Communication Arts
Shaw University
South Piedmont Community College
Stanly Community College
Surry Community College
University of North Carolina at Charlotte
University of North Carolina at Pembroke
University of North Carolina Wilmington
Wake Technical Community College
Wayne Community College
Western Carolina University
Western Piedmont Community College
Wilkes Community College
Wingate University
Winston-Salem State University

North Dakota
Bismarck State College
Dickinson State University
Jamestown College
Lake Region State College
Mayville State University
Minot State University
North Dakota State College of Science
North Dakota State University
University of Mary

University of North Dakota – Main Campus
Valley City State University

Ohio
Ashland University
Capital University
Cincinnati State Technical and
    Community College
Clark State Community College
Cleveland Institute of Electronics
Cleveland State University
Columbus State Community College
Cuyahoga Community College
Davis College
DeVry University – Cincinnati
DeVry University – Cleveland Campus
DeVry University – Columbus Campus
DeVry University – Columbus North
DeVry University – Dayton
DeVry University – Rockside
Edison State Community College
Franklin University
Hocking College
Kent State University
Lakeland Community College
Lorain County Community College
Lourdes College
Malone College
Marion Technical College
Mercy College of Northwest Ohio
Miami-Jacobs Career College
National College
North Central State College
Northwest State Community College
Ohio Christian University
Ohio State University
Ohio University – Independent Study
    Program and Adult Learning Services
Ohio University – Zanesville
Otterbein College – Continuing Studies
Owens Community College
Shawnee State University
Sinclair Community College
Southern State Community College
Tiffin University
Union Institute & University
University of Akron
University of Findlay
University of Northwestern Ohio
University of Rio Grande
University of Toledo – Main Campus
Urbana University
Washington State Community College
Wilberforce University

Wright State University
Xavier University
Youngstown State University

Oklahoma

Cameron University
Carl Albert State College
Connors State College
DeVry University – Oklahoma City
East Central University
Eastern Oklahoma State College
Langston University
Mid-America Christian University –
    LEAD Degree Completion
    MIDAMERICA Program
Murray State College
Northeastern Oklahoma A & M College
Northeastern State University
Northern Oklahoma College
Northwestern Oklahoma State University
Oklahoma City Community College
Oklahoma City University – Prior Learning
    and University OKCITYU
    Studies Program
Oklahoma Panhandle State University
Oklahoma State University
Oklahoma State University – Oklahoma City
Oklahoma State University – Okmulgee
Oral Roberts University
Redlands Community College
Rogers State University
Rose State College
Southeastern Oklahoma State University
Southwestern Christian University
Southwestern Oklahoma State University
Spartan College of Aeronautics and
    Technology
Tulsa Community College
University of Central Oklahoma
University of Oklahoma
University of Oklahoma – College of
    Liberal Studies
University of Science and Arts of Oklahoma
Western Oklahoma State College

Oregon

Art Institute of Portland
Blue Mountain Community College
Clackamas Community College
Concordia University
Corban College
DeVry University – Portland Campus
Eastern Oregon University

Eugene Bible College
George Fox University
ITT Technical Institute – Portland
Lane Community College
Marylhurst University
Mt. Hood Community College
Northwest Christian College
Oregon Health and Science University
Oregon Institute of Technology
Oregon State University
Portland Community College
Rogue Community College
Southern Oregon University
Southwestern Oregon Community College
Treasure Valley Community College
Umpqua Community College
University of Oregon
Warner Pacific College
Western Oregon University

Pennsylvania

Arcadia University
Art Institute of Philadelphia
Art Institute of Pittsburgh
Butler County Community College
Cabrini College
California University of Pennsylvania
Cambria-Rowe Business College
Carlow College
Cedar Crest College – Continuing Education
    Programs
Clarion University of Pennsylvania
Community College of Allegheny
County Community College of Beaver County
Delaware County Community College
Delaware Valley College
DeSales University
DeVry University – Fort Washington Campus
DeVry University – Philadelphia
DeVry University – Pittsburgh Campus
DeVry University – Valley Forge
Drexel University
DuBois Business College
Duquesne University, School of Leadership
    and Professional Advancement
Eastern University
Edinboro University of Pennsylvania
Gannon University
Gwynedd-Mercy College
Harcum College
Harrisburg Area Community College
Holy Family University
Immaculata University
Indiana University of Pennsylvania

ITT Technical Institute – Bensalem
ITT Technical Institute – Mechanicsburg
ITT Technical Institute – Monroeville
ITT Technical Institute – Pittsburgh
    Johnson College
Kaplan Career Institute
Keystone College
King's College
La Roche College
Lackawanna College
Lancaster Bible College
LaSalle University
Lebanon Valley College
Lehigh Carbon Community College
Lehigh Valley College
Lincoln Technical Institute, Allentown
Lock Haven University of Pennsylvania
Luzerne County Community College
Mansfield University of Pennsylvania
McCann School of Business and Technology
Millersville University of Pe
    nnsylvania
Montgomery County Community College
Mount Aloysius College
Neumann College
Peirce College
Penn State University
Penn State University World Campus
Pennsylvania Highlands Community College
Pennsylvania Institute of Technology Point
    Park University
Robert Morris University
Saint Francis University
Seton Hill University
Shippensburg University of Pennsylvania
Slippery Rock University of Pennsylvania
St. Vincent College
Temple University
Thiel College
University of Pittsburgh at Bradford
Valley Forge Military College
Washington & Jefferson College – Office of
    Lifelong Learning
Waynesburg College
Westmoreland County Community College
Widener University
Wilson College
York College of Pennsylvania

Puerto Rico
American University of Puerto Rico
Inter American University of Puerto Rico

Inter American University of Puerto
    Rico – Arecibo Campus Universidad
    Metropolitana
University of Puerto Rico – Humacao
    University College

Rhode Island
Community College of Rhode Island
Johnson & Wales University
New England Institute of Technology
Providence College – School of Continuing
    Education
Rhode Island College
Roger Williams University – School of
    Continuing Studies
Salve Regina University
University of Rhode Island – Feinstein
    College of Continuing Education

South Carolina
Aiken Technical College
Benedict College
Central Carolina Technical College
Charleston Southern University
Coastal Carolina University
Coker College
Columbia Campus Southern Wesleyan
    University – Adult Programs
Denmark Technical College
Florence-Darlington Technical College
Francis Marion University
Greenville Technical College
Horry-Georgetown Technical College
ITT Technical Institute – Greenville
    Lander University
Limestone College
Midlands Technical College
Newberry College
North Greenville University
Northeastern Technical College
Orangeburg-Calhoun Technical College
Piedmont Technical College
South Carolina State University
South University
Spartanburg Community College
Spartanburg Methodist College
Technical College of the Lowcountry
Tri-County Technical College
Trident Technical College
University of South Carolina – Aiken
University of South Carolina – Beaufort
University of South Carolina – Columbia
University of South Carolina – Sumter

University of South Carolina – Upstate
Williamsburg Technical College
Wofford College

South Dakota
Augustana College
Black Hills State University
Dakota State University
Dakota Wesleyan University
Kilian Community College
Mitchell Technical Institute
Mount Marty College
National American University
Northern State University
South Dakota School of Mines and
    Technology
South Dakota State University
University of South Dakota
Western Dakota Technical Institute

Tennessee
Aquinas College
Argosy University/Nashville
Austin Peay State University
Bethel College
Bryan College – Adult Degree Completion
    Programs (ASPIRE) BRYAN
Carson-Newman College
Chattanooga State Technical
    Community College
Cleveland State Community College
Crichton College
DeVry University – Memphis
Draughons Junior College
Dyersburg State Community College
East Tennessee State University
Fountainhead College of Technology
Hiwassee College
ITT Technical Institute – Memphis
Jackson State Community College
King College
Lambuth University
LeMoyne-Owen College
Martin Methodist College
Middle Tennessee State University – Fort
    Campbell, Aerospace Degree Program
Milligan College
Motlow State Community College
Nashville Auto-Diesel College
Nashville State Community College
National College of Business and Technology
North Central Institute

Northeast State Technical Community
    College
Pellissippi State Technical Community
    College
Roane State Community College
Southern Adventist University
Southwest Tennessee Community College
Tennessee State University
Tennessee Technological University
Tennessee Temple University
Tennessee Wesleyan College
Tusculum College
Union University
University of Tennessee at Chattanooga
University of Tennessee at Martin
University of Tennessee, Knoxville
Walters State Community College

Texas
Abilene Christian University
Angelina College
Angelo State University
Argosy University/Dallas
Art Institute of Houston
Austin Community College
Central Texas College
Clarendon College
Coastal Bend College
College of the Mainland
Collin County Community College
Dallas Baptist University
Dallas County Community College District
Dallas TeleCollege
Del Mar College
DeVry University – Austin
DeVry University – Fort Worth
DeVry University – Houston Campus
DeVry University – Houston Galleria
DeVry University – Irving Campus
DeVry University – Plano Campus
DeVry University – San Antonio
District Frank Phillips College
District North Lake College
El Centro College
El Paso County Community College
Galveston College
Grayson County College
Hallmark Institute of Aeronautics
Hardin-Simmons University
Houston Community College
Huston-Tillotson University
ITT Technical Institute – Houston (West)
ITT Technical Institute – Richardson
    Jacksonville College

Jarvis Christian College
Kilgore College
Lamar State College – Port Arthur Lamar
    University
Laredo Community College
Lubbock Christian University
McMurry University
Midland College
Midwestern State University – Bachelor of
    Applied Arts and Science
Navarro College
North Central Texas College
North Harris Montgomery Community
    College
Northwest Vista College
Our Lady of the Lake University
Palo Alto College
Paris Junior College
Prairie View A & M University
Ranger College
Sam Houston State University
San Antonio College
Schreiner University
Southwest Texas Junior College
Southwestern Adventist University
St. Mary's University
St. Philip's College
Sul Ross State University
System Howard Payne University
Tarleton State University
Temple College
Texarkana College
Texas A & M University – Commerce
Texas A & M University – Corpus Christi
Texas A & M University – Kingsville
Texas Lutheran University
Texas State Technical College at Waco
Texas State Technical College West Texas
Texas State Technical College – Harlingen
Texas State Technical College – Marshall
Texas State University – San Marcos,
    Occupational Education Program
Texas Tech University – Undergraduate
    Programs
Texas Wesleyan University – School of
    Business Administration
Texas Woman's University
Trinity Valley Community College
University of Dallas – Constantine College
University of Houston
University of Houston – Clear Lake
University of Mary Hardin-Baylor
University of North Texas
University of St. Thomas
University of Texas – Pan American

University of Texas at Arlington
University of Texas at Austin
University of Texas at Brownsville
University of Texas at El Paso
University of Texas at San Antonio
University of the Incarnate Word
Vernon College
Wade College
Wayland Baptist University
Weatherford College
Western Technical College
Western Texas College
Wiley College

Utah

College of Eastern Utah
DeVry University – Sandy
Dixie State College of Utah
Independence University
Salt Lake Community College
Snow College
Southern Utah University
Utah State University
Utah Valley University
Weber State University
Western Governors University
Westminster College

Vermont

Community College of Vermont
Norwich University
University of Vermont
Vermont Technical College

Virgin Islands

University of the Virgin Islands

Virginia

Argosy University – Washington, D.C.
Art Institute of Washington
Averett University
Blue Ridge Community College
Bluefield College
Bryant & Stratton College – Virginia Beach
Central Virginia Community College
Dabney S. Lancaster Community College
DeVry University – Crystal City Campus
DeVry University – Tysons Corner
Eastern Shore Community College
ECPI College of Technology

George Mason University – Bachelor of
  Individualized Study
Germanna Community College
Hampton University – College of Continuing
  Education
ITT Technical Institute – Chantilly
ITT Technical Institute – Norfolk
ITT Technical Institute – Richmond
ITT Technical Institute – Springfield
J. Sargeant Reynolds Community College
James Madison University – Adult Degree
  Program
John Tyler Community College
Liberty University – Distance Learning
  Program
Lord Fairfax Community College
Marymount University
National College
New River Community College
Norfolk State University
Northern Virginia Community College
Old Dominion University
Patrick Henry Community College
Paul D. Camp Community College
Piedmont Virginia Community College
Regent University
Richard Bland College
Shenandoah University
Southside Virginia Community College
Southwest Virginia Community College
Stratford University
Thomas Nelson Community College
Tidewater Community College
University of Management and Technology
University of Virginia's College at Wise
Virginia Intermont College
Virginia State University – Bachelor of
  Individualized Studies
Virginia Western Community College
World College
Wytheville Community College

Washington

Argosy University – Seattle
Art Institute of Seattle
Bellevue Community College
Big Bend Community College
Central Washington University
Centralia College
City University of Seattle
Clark College
Clover Park Technical College
Columbia Basin College
Community Colleges of Spokane

DeVry University – Federal Way Campus
DeVry University – Seattle Bellevue Campus
Eastern Washington University
Edmonds Community College
Everett Community College
Grays Harbor College
Green River Community College
Heritage University
Highline Community College – A.A.S. in
  Paralegal Studies
ITT Technical Institute – Everett
ITT Technical Institute – Spokane
Lower Columbia College
Northwest University
Olympic College
Pacific Lutheran University
Peninsula College
Pierce College
Renton Technical College
Saint Martin's University
Shoreline Community College
Skagit Valley College – Whidbey
  Island Campus
South Puget Sound Community College
South Seattle Community College
Tacoma Community College
Trinity Lutheran College
University of Washington – Online Degree
  Programs
University of Washington, Tacoma
Walla Walla Community College
Washington State University
Wenatchee Valley College
Yakima Valley Community College

West Virginia

American Public University
Blue Ridge Community and Technical College
Concord University – Board of Regents
  Program
Davis & Elkins College
Eastern West Virginia Community and
  Technical College
Glenville State College
Marshall University
Mountain State College
Mountain State University
Ohio Valley University
Shepherd University
Southern West Virginia Community and
  Technical College
System Bethany College
University of Charleston
Valley College of Technology

West Liberty State College
West Virginia Junior College at Bridgeport
West Virginia Junior College at Charleston
West Virginia Junior College at Morgantown
West Virginia State Community and
    Technical College
West Virginia University
West Virginia University Institute of
    Technology
West Virginia Wesleyan College
Wheeling Jesuit University

Wisconsin
Blackhawk Technical College
Bryant & Stratton College
Cardinal Stritch University
Carroll College
Chippewa Valley Technical College
Concordia University – School of Adult
    Education
DeVry University – Milwaukee Campus
DeVry University – Waukesha Campus
Gateway Technical College
Herzing College – Madison
Lakeland College
Lakeshore Technical College
Madison Area Technical College
Marian College
Marquette University
Mid-State Technical College
Milwaukee Area Technical College
Milwaukee School of Engineering
Moraine Park Technical College
Mount Mary College
Nicolet Area Technical College
Northcentral Technical College
Northeast Wisconsin Technical College
Northland College
Silver Lake College
Southwest Wisconsin Technical College
St. Norbert College
University of Wisconsin – Eau Claire
University of Wisconsin – Green Bay
University of Wisconsin – La Crosse
University of Wisconsin – Madison
University of Wisconsin – Manitowoc
University of Wisconsin – Milwaukee
University of Wisconsin – Oshkosh
University of Wisconsin – Parkside
University of Wisconsin – Platteville
University of Wisconsin – River Falls
University of Wisconsin – Stevens Point
University of Wisconsin – Stout
University of Wisconsin – Superior

University of Wisconsin – Whitewater,
    Undergraduate Program
University of Wisconsin Colleges
Viterbo University
Western Technical College
Wisconsin Indianhead Technical College

Wyoming
Casper College
Central Wyoming College
Eastern Wyoming College
Laramie County Community College
Northern Wyoming Community College
District Sheridan College
Gillette Campus
Northwest College
University of Wyoming
Western Wyoming Community College

What Other Vets Are Saying...

I've found that there are times when some military jargon can be used, for example, if you're applying for a job in the defense or military-contracting industries. But if you're seeking career opportunities outside of those industries, such as financial, materials, education, real estate, manufacturing, or automotive, the rules are different.

Don't take a chance. The hiring managers in these industries may be unfamiliar with military-speak or the industries may have their own nonmilitary terminology.

I found this out during my first post-Navy job hunt about 20 years ago. Having no experience with this, I filled my resume with military jargon, thinking that companies would understand my electronics training and experience. I got very few interviews, and when I did, the most common question was, "What is a MK 23 Gyrocompass Technician (NEC 4723)?"

Ultimately, I found employment through networking. Fortunately, the company that hired me was filled with ex-military personnel who understood my resume. When I left that company and had to rewrite my resume, however, I used the terms of the industry I was now working in. Not surprisingly, potential employers understood my resume and I received several interviews within just a few weeks of sending it out.

Charles Freeman
Former First Class Petty Officer
U.S. Navy

CHAPTER THREE

BUILDING YOUR
POST-MILITARY RESUME

In an ideal world, the best candidate always gets the job. Unfortunately, that's not how it works in the real world. You may be the best-qualified applicant for a job, but unless you can communicate your qualifications in a way that makes an employer want to interview you, you'll never get a chance to prove yourself. That's why creating a resume that brings your qualifications to life and shows that you're a perfect fit for the job is such a challenge. How do you use a couple of pages to tell a prospective employer who you are and what you have done during your military service?

All resumes are not created equal. Some resumes are quickly dismissed, while others yield calls from employers in a matter of weeks. What's the difference? Resumes can either open doors or eliminate you from the running. An effective resume will demonstrate how you and your skills, experience, training, and education best match the employer's needs. Your resume or application very well may be an employer's first impression of you, so it's important that you put your best effort into ensuring your resume is an attention-getter.

Job-hunting may have changed quite a bit since you entered military service. No doubt your military career includes a number of noteworthy accomplishments, but even the most decorated veteran needs to figure out how to successfully transition to a civilian position. In today's market, you have to figure out how to position yourself to effectively compete against candidates who may have substantial corporate experience.

Formatting Your Resume

The type of resume you choose will depend partly on the type of work you've performed and whether you're going to continue doing the same kind of work.

Generally, there are three types of resumes—chronological, functional, or combined. Your career interests may determine the format you use. There is a resume style that's best for you, but only you can decide that style. While a career counselor can help you to select the format that will best display your abilities, only you can make the final decision about the format that is most comfortable for you. Which one you choose will depend partly on the type of work you've performed and whether you're going to continue doing the same kind of work.

Chronological

In this style, the emphasis is on a chronological listing of employment and employment-related experiences. The chronological resume is a good format for those with a consistent employment history, no gaps in employment, and whose past employment experiences are related to their current employment goals. A chronological resume showcases a steady work record with increasing upward responsibilities. This format may not work best for recent graduates, individuals with employment gaps, or persons changing careers.

Functional

The functional resume highlights skills, experiences, and accomplishments without identifying specific dates, names, and places. This format is organized by functions or skills that advertise the specific qualifications needed for an occupation and works well for people changing careers. It's also effective for those re-entering the workforce, first-time job seekers, and applicants wanting to highlight experiences that occurred in the distant past. Since there is no chronological listing of employment, some employers don't like this format because they suspect that the person may be trying to hide something.

Combination

The combination resume combines the best of both the chronological and functional styles. It features a functional section that highlights skills, accomplishments, and experiences. Then, it gives a chronological listing of employment, education, and employment experiences. This format is very effective for a broad spectrum of job seekers. The best chronological resume is enhanced with a section that highlights skills, accomplishments, and experiences. The best functional resume is strengthened with a chronological listing of employment experiences.

Resume writing is about writing to the future, to the job that you want or the career path you wish to pursue.

Look Ahead, Not Behind

Resume writing is *not* about rehashing your past history, listing what you've done and where you've done it. Rather, resume writing is about writing to the future, to the job that you want or the career path you wish to pursue. This is critical to keep in mind throughout every phase of developing your resume and conducting your job search. Write a resume that reflects your future rather than your past.

As you look ahead, clearly define your objectives, identify the skills and qualifications that support your current goals, and then focus on these elements throughout your job search. Don't position yourself as someone who *wants to be* a professional accountant; rather, position yourself as someone who *is* a well-qualified accounting professional with excellent skills in delivering fiduciary responsibilities, actuarials, spreadsheets, budgeting, and more.

Highlight where you want to go, not simply where you've been. For example, if you served as a foreign language linguist in the Army and now want to establish a career in marketing communications with a global company, you would write a resume that positions you as a well-qualified marketing communications professional rather than positioning yourself simply as a well-qualified foreign language linguist who wants to be a marketing communications professional. Truthfully, many of the skills required for foreign language translation are also required for a marketing communications position (e.g., writing, editing, data interpretation, and analysis).

Most military resumes consist of little more than education or training and military job task experience as the foundation. In that way, your flags are only highlighting the basics. Today, employers increasingly look beyond the basics or foundation layers of a resume. Employers may look for flags such as industry experience, people skills, work ethic, job experience, education, product experience, and so forth.

When employers search for candidates, they are not looking at your career record; rather, they are looking for flags that are tagged with the specific skills they need. Unless specific military skills are needed, military-focused resumes do not work because they do not have the flags employers can readily see. By flagging your resume with key information a prospective employer can see, you can turn your resume into one that works.

Avoid a traditional resume format and style. In most cases, military experience is featured in a modified, functional resume because it highlights work experience in professional categories rather than chronological achievements by job title or rank. A functional resume has an up-front career objective that explains your skills and experience, as well as other outstanding areas of expertise.

When composing your resume, statements following your career objective should categorize your experience in particular commercial areas, such as Management Experience, Operations Experience, or Human Resources Experience. This simplified format allows you to neatly connect all of the components of your military experience into a continuous, comprehensive picture that communicates clearly and quickly. This format also helps you to weave seemingly fragmented assignments to read as parts of one position, showing progressively more duties and responsibilities along the way.

Define Your Career Objective

You can't effectively market yourself if you don't have a clearly defined goal. An eye-catching resume starts with a career objective that gives a distinct focus to your job hunt. If you have more than one major skill, you may need more than one resume so that you can appropriately target your job skills to a prospective employer. Your career objective is the skeleton that connects the resume body. Once you have a solid objective, you can begin to determine what employers are looking for, their needs, and how your skills can fit.

Before you begin writing your resume, do some soul-searching to determine what you really want to do and how your skills can relate.

Many service people have diverse backgrounds and often make the mistake of creating a resume that is too general to be effective. Before you begin writing your resume, do some soul-searching to determine what you really want to do and how your skills can relate. Then, research occupations and pinpoint a specific career path. If you are having trouble with this step, tap into your local transition office or enlist the help of a career coach. If you are torn between two or more potential goals, create different resumes for each.

One size never fits all, and this is true for resumes as well. Don't assume that you can use one resume to apply for many different jobs. Otherwise, your success will be much more difficult to achieve. Start with a basic resume that matches well with your objective occupation. Then, as you respond to job opportunities, tailor your basic resume to match the employer's requirements.

Smart job seekers know that in today's world of electronic job searching, you must have three distinct versions of your resume—a doc (word processing file) or pdf (Portable Document Format) version, an ASCII (American Standard Code for Information Interchange) text version, and a hard-copy version. Use the doc/pdf version when submitting your resume as an attachment

BASIC RESUME COMPONENTS

Name
- First, Middle Initial, Last

Contact Information
- Include address, telephone (land and mobile), fax, and e-mail.

Career Goal/Objective
- A brief statement of the field of endeavor you desire upon entering the workplace.

Professional Profile
- Provide a brief description of your professional background and relevant education. Include a summary of the skills you possess in this portion of your resume.
- Describe these skills in one or two words. It is not necessary to list all of your skills. Emphasize those skills most relevant to your employment interest.

Professional Accomplishments
- List relevant achievements according to related fields.

Employment History
- Job title
- Company name/location
- City and state
- Dates of employment

- Pay series/grade/classification (if federal civilian position): list highest grade held and period of time spent at that grade level. If experience describes federal civilian positions at different grade levels, include month and year promoted.

- All major tasks: include any systems on which you have worked, software programs or special tools and equipment you have used, as well as special programs you have managed.

- Other relevant information: licenses/certificates (including date(s) certified and location), performance awards, language proficiencies, professional associations, etc.

Education
- Give your highest level of education. If you completed your degree, list your major field of study, name of college or university, the year in which you received the degree awarded, and grade point average (GPA).

- If your highest level of education was high school, list either the highest grade you completed, the year you graduated, or the date you were awarded your General Equivalency Diploma (GED).

Limit resume information to no more than three pages, preferably two, printed on a single side of 8.5" x 11" white bond paper.

- List specialized training pertinent to your career goals
- Degree(s) earned and certification(s)
- Granting institutions
- Dates of graduation

References
- Note that references are available upon request.

to an e-mail message. A pdf file may be the safer version as companies may use various word processing applications or fonts that are not compatible with the version you use. If you use a word processing application, save the document in rich text format (RTF), which will make the document universally accessible.

The ASCII text version will be needed when completing online applications or when you know the company will not open a doc attachment. Finally, the hard-copy version is needed incase employers request one, which they will scan into a resume database.

What Can You Do for Me?

How you present your skills and experience in your resume helps determine whether or not you are invited to interview for a job. Ultimately, your resume has to speak to a potential employer. Does your resume answer an employer's question, "What can this person do for me?" A good way to consider employers' needs is to research your ideal job. What types of skills and experiences are employers in the field seeking? What aspects of your military background are most relevant?

In addition to tailoring your resume to the employer's requirements, it's important to portray yourself as a "doer" whose skills match the requirements of the position and who demonstrates the ability to do the job. This is easy to do when you include results, achievements, and accomplishments you've produced that relate to the desired position.

Usually, employers will receive dozens of resumes for any given position. Since they don't always have a great deal of time to review resumes fully, it's important that you make it easy to quickly peruse your qualifications and see what you can do for them. A summary of your qualifications written as bullet statements, a brief paragraph, or keywords can be an effective way to introduce your resume and a quick way for the employer to view your ability and areas of expertise.

Any information that does not relate to your goal should be eliminated or de-emphasized, including unrelated military awards, training, and distinctions. For example, a medal you received for rifle marksmanship is irrelevant on a civilian resume. This "pruning" is often the hardest step for ex-military personnel.

But this is also the reason why so many ex-military resumes are five pages or longer—in other words, too long. As you determine relevant information to include, ask yourself, "Will a potential employer care about this?" Use that question as a barometer for relevancy. Only include information that will capture an employer's attention and help you land an interview.

De-Militarize Your Terminology

When you entered military service, you were unfamiliar with much of the language you heard and the terms that were used to identify people, equipment, and locations, but you soon learned to understand and speak military jargon. Now that you are entering the civilian workforce, you will need to translate this jargon for the employers who will read your resume.

Employers who do not know anything about the military don't understand the terminology and acronyms. So you need to translate these into civilian terms. De-militarize your job titles, duties, accomplishments, training, and awards to appeal to civilian hiring managers. To be sure that you target all terms, show your resume to nonmilitary friends, and ask them to point out terms they don't understand. You can also use job postings as a guide to help you substitute civilian keywords for military terms.

An article in the *Los Angeles Times* reported that an estimated 76% of military servicemembers do not know how to translate their military skills into civilian positions. ("Vets Face Grim Job Prospects," *Los Angeles Times*, March 28, 2008.) Fortunately, veterans have assistance available to them to help bridge the gap between military service and a civilian career.

Some retirees simply copy and paste a military job description into a resume that has been gleaned from a military career manual or the write-up from an annual performance evaluation. If you choose to copy and paste, you will have a great resume for applying to the armed forces. But when a civilian hiring manager reviews your resume, your skills and qualifications will be as incomprehensible as instructions for networking a computer system to a computer novice.

While military terminology is easier and quicker for you to use, understand that it inhibits potential employers from digesting the information quickly and easily. Make your resume easy to read so that employers can quickly grasp your qualifications and make sense of your experience.

It is important that you use nonmilitary terminology to prepare your resume and cover letter and strategize how you will market yourself throughout the process. Develop a resume that steers a recruiter or potential employer away from your military rank or title. Instead, focus on matching your resume and professional capabilities to the company's needs.

There are three very good reasons why you should avoid military terminology in your resume. First, while it may make your resume specific and detailed, it makes reading too difficult—whether the reader has a military background or not. Read the following narrative and determine how difficult it would be for a person with no military background to assess skills and abilities:

> Analyzes manpower programming and budgeting data in the Army Materiel Command portion of the Army Program Objective Memorandum (POM), the Army Budget Estimate Submission (BES), and the Command Plan for AMC MSC/SRA, to ensure that MTOE/TDA developed under TAADS reflect the approved military and civilian manpower program by appropriation and authorization, and that authorization data tracks to that reflected in the DA Standard Army Manpower Authorization System (SAMAS).

While the preceding paragraph is well written, specific, and detailed, it would require the reader to spend a considerable amount of time digesting the information and then determining if the applicant's experience matches the requirements for the open position.

Sometimes the jargon may be necessary to fully describe your skills or work experience. If this is the case, you can prepare resume readers for the terminology by opening with direct, clear language anyone can understand, and then use the jargon to repeat what you stated earlier. This will help your resume communicate effectively, whether the reader understands military lingo or not.

Second, military jargon can be indirect at times, lacking the specific terms or terminology of classic jargon, and using phrases that clump job tasks into vague terms. The use of non-specific language will muddy the connection between your qualifications and the employer's needs. For example, "Developed and implemented a training program for the technical enhancement of the junior enlisted soldiers." This statement does not provide a clear understanding of the candidate's experience. The training mentioned probably included a number of skills that were clumped under the ambiguous term "technical enhancement." Only persons who had experience in the training would know exactly what was involved.

Third, being detailed and exact is usually a plus, but such precision creates a whole new problem—wordiness—that only makes resumes longer and harder to read. For example:

- "Performed all duties required for the Personnel Management and Human Resources requirements, including the interviewing and hiring of new employees.

- "Spearheaded the implementation of our company's drug-free workplace policy."

While the candidate gives a detailed account of responsibilities and duties, terms such as "spearheaded the implementation" only add to the word count and make the material more difficult for the reader to digest quickly. In this instance, the word implemented would accurately convey the applicant's responsibilities.

There are resources available to assist in skills translation. One resource, HireVetsFirst.gov, is funded through the U.S. Department of Labor and the president's National Hire Veterans Committee. The website offers a Veteran's Zone that includes access to O*Net®, the Occupational Information Network, a comprehensive database of occupational skills, knowledge, and abilities that can help you align your military experience, education, and training curricula with current civilian workplace needs. Use a list of your skills to find matching O*NET-SOC occupations.

Showcase Your Track Record of Accomplishments

Your military career has provided excellent opportunities for training, practical experience, and advancement. Emphasize your accomplishments so civilian employers understand the significance of your achievements and the measurable outcomes. A de-militarized accomplishment statement would look something like this: "Increased employee retention rate by 16% by focusing on training, team building, and recognition. Regarded as one of the most progressive and innovative IT organizations in the Navy's communications and IT community."

If you received a significant award that would be important to an employer, you may want to phrase it along the following lines, "Awarded Air Force Achievement Medal for developing a patient database using MS Access, which tracked patient demographics, records, medication, appointments, and status and resulted in improved reporting functions."

Show Off Your Skills

You might have heard you need to downplay your military experience, but in reality, your military experience is an asset and should be marketed as such. Many employers realize the value of hiring veterans. When hired, former military personnel often bring dedication, leadership, teamwork, positive work ethic, and cross-functional skills to the position. Make sure your resume clearly communicates the value your military skills bring to the table.

Careful! Don't Give Too Much Information

Defending our country and its interests is one of the most admirable accomplishments a person can pursue. Nevertheless, the realities of actual combat can leave many employers squeamish. The fact that you worked in a short-range air defense engagement zone may have no relevance to your future career goal, so de-emphasize battlefield references.

Put It to the Test

Developing a resume that works in the civilian world may be an ongoing process. After you have polished your resume, start its distribution and keep track of the response rates. Seek out feedback and listen carefully and objectively to suggestions for improvement. Then, continue making modifications until your resume successfully generates job interviews.

Military and veteran candidates are often diamonds in the rough. They possess leadership skills in diverse, fast-paced, stressful environments and have proven themselves capable of adapting to an accelerated learning curve in various environments. They have the abilities, and the resources are available to help. In tandem, there are companies waiting to hire competent, disciplined former military personnel. By developing the right resume, you can correctly position yourself to get the job you want.

Proofread, Proofread Again, and Then Ask a Friend to Help

Submitting a resume with errors is a quick way to eliminate yourself from employment consideration. A prospective employer is first introduced to you via a paper or electronic file that should effectively and succinctly demonstrate the quality of work you can produce. If you want your resume to pave the way for an interview and then a job, be sure that it is accurate and reflective of the quality of work you will perform for that company.

In addition to checking for common spelling and grammatical errors, take a good look at the overall appearance. Is your resume appealing and easy to read? Is the text clumped together without white space? Are the margins appropriate? Do the headings stand out? Have bold and italic styles been used effectively? Did you use a word processing program to create the document? Was it printed from a quality printer using bond paper?

As you review it, keep in mind that your resume gives employers their first impression of you. Make sure it makes the best impression possible, just as you did when you went before a promotion board.

Tapping Technology

Technological advances have caused a number of changes in the job-search market. The federal government has at least four automated systems for submitting electronic applications. Resumix, a HotJobs software program used by defense agencies, relies on advanced optical character recognition (OCR) software to scan your resume and assign your skills. Other federal automated application systems include QuickHire®, used by the Environmental Protection Agency (EPA), United State government, and many other non-defense agencies;

Avue Digital Services used by the Library of Congress; and USASTAFFING, used as a staffing service by the Office of Personnel Management (OPM) for federal agencies.

Developing a Cover Letter

Once you have finely honed your resume so that it accurately presents your experiences and abilities, there is another important component that may determine whether or not you are granted an interview: A well-written cover letter is your chance to explain to employers why they should consider you for the job. The best cover letters are specific and give examples that directly relate to the job. Your cover letter is a targeted sales tool that should be tailored to the specific position you are seeking.

The cover letter is also a good opportunity to show potential employers your writing skills, if that is important to the position you seek. Regardless of your writing and language skills, however, make sure that your letter has no mistakes. Proofread the letter several times, and then ask a friend to read it for spelling, grammar, and comprehension.

A general cover letter should include three basic parts:

The first paragraph should state who you are, how you heard about the position or company, and why you are writing. Use this paragraph to convince the employer that you are the only candidate to interview.

In the second paragraph, share why you are interested in the position and/or company, and how your qualifications fit the specific skills needed for the job. Also, include specific examples of how your experience has prepared you to do the job for which you are applying, along with any other relevant skills, qualities, achievements, and experiences that make you the best candidate. This second paragraph is your chance to shine. Here, you can discuss the qualifications that match the requirements for the position.

In the third paragraph, repeat your desire to be considered for the job. Give specific information about your plans to follow up, and thank the employer for his or her consideration. Closing the letter with "Sincerely," "Respectfully," or "Sincerely Yours," along with your typed name and signature is appropriate.

Sample Cover Letter

2842 Southfork Drive
Cleveland, OH 44103
May 18, 2009

Stephanie K. Peterson
Director of Human Resources
National City Bank
500 National City Plaza
Cleveland, OH 44115

Dear Ms. Peterson:

The accompanying resume is in response to your listing in the *Plain Dealer* for a senior security officer.

I am particularly interested in this position because my experience as a senior security professional in the Navy has prepared me for a disciplined, secure work environment and the challenges associated with unexpected events. I'm looking forward to using this experience for enhancing the security of a growing and community-conscious bank.

I would appreciate an opportunity to meet with you to discuss how my experience will best meet your needs. My ideas on how to enhance your bank's security posture may be of particular interest to you. Therefore, I will call your office on the morning of May 23 to inquire if a meeting can be scheduled at a convenient time.

I look forward to meeting you. Thank you for taking the time to review my letter and credentials

Respectfully,

James Richardson

James Richardson

Sample Query Letter

821 West Paces Ferry
Atlanta, GA 30253
November 4, 2009

Reginald Paxton
Personnel Director
Honeywell Corporation
6311 W. Peachtree Street
Atlanta, GA 30203

Dear Mr. Paxton:

Felix Morgan suggested that I contact you about my interest in personnel management. She recommended you as a very knowledgeable person to talk to regarding careers in human resources.

I am leaving the U.S. Army after twenty years of experience in personnel administration. Because of my positive Army experience, I would like to continue working in a large organization. Before I venture further into the civilian job market, however, I would like to benefit from the experience and knowledge of other professionals in the field. I am seeking advice on opportunities for someone with my qualifications.

If you are available, perhaps we can meet briefly sometime within the next two weeks to discuss my career plans. I have several questions that I believe you could help clarify. I will call your office on April 22 to arrange a meeting time.

I look forward to discussing my plans with you.

Sincerely,

Karla Jernigan

Karla Jernigan

Cover Letter Dos and Don'ts

Your cover letter is a prospective employer's first glimpse of you, so you don't want to blow it. Following are some steps you should take that will positively impact your cover letter:

Do

- Use the first paragraph to name the title of the job for which you are applying and tell exactly how you heard about the position or company.

- If you can, use the name and title of the person who will be hiring you instead of writing a generic "Dear Sir" or "Dear Madam."

- Target your letter to precisely what the employer is seeking.

- Give an example from your experience for every qualification listed in the ad, if possible.

- State in the letter that you are enclosing a resume.

- Type the letter and use a quality paper and readable font that is the same as or looks similar to your resume. Avoid fancy script or italic fonts.

- Keep the letter brief—less than one full page.

- Use short paragraphs (two to four sentences each).

- Include your phone number and/or e-mail address in the last paragraph. Proofread the letter carefully and check for spelling, grammar, missing words, and punctuation. It's a good idea to have someone else proofread the letter as well.

- Make sure the envelope is clearly and properly addressed.

Don't

- Send a resume without a cover letter.

- Discuss salary unless the ad or job listing requires it.

- Tell what the job will do for you.

- Offer unnecessary personal information.

- Repeat information contained in the resume, except brief, introductory references.

- Generalize about personal qualities or past job titles. Instead, give specifics about your skills and experience.

- Include information that you will not be able to explain in an interview.

- Send photocopies.

- Offer to follow up without having a specific plan to do so.

- Staple or paper clip items.

- Send a stained, wrinkled, or otherwise messy resume.

- Use hard-to-read fonts or colored paper (ivory is acceptable).

- Forget to sign your name.

Where to Get Help

Creating an attention-getting resume can be a daunting task, but there are resources available to help you. Check the REF section at the end of this chapter and the Internet resources section, listed in Chapter Eight: Online Resources for Veterans.

RESOURCES FOR BUILDING YOUR RESUME

Many announcements for federal government positions require online applications, resume builders, or Resumix formats, which are scanned into computer databases. These electronic formats can be restricting, and can prove difficult for those who are not computer-savvy. If done incorrectly, your application will be rejected.

Online resumes and applications are searched electronically for the keywords required for the position. If you do not include the right keywords, your resume will not be selected for further review by the hiring authority. Once your resume is selected electronically, it is manually reviewed by the hiring authority and compared to the others selected. Therefore, it is important that your resume includes all relevant keywords. The restrictive nature of many online formats (limited length for describing jobs and experience) makes this difficult.

The Applicant Notification System Web-Enabled Response (ANSWER) tool is designed to allow users to check the status of their resumes, track application history, view self-nomination history, and access their current resumes and supplemental data listed in the central Resumix database. Users can toggle between the Resumix and ANSWER.

What are Online Application Formats?

Some of the agencies that require many (if not most) applicants to use online formats include the following:

Army—The Army Resumix format is a highly restrictive three-page format and is used for most Army job postings, but not for some higher-level positions. Resumes can be posted online using the Army resume builder. In this format, you must also include answers to all the KSA (Knowledge, Skills, and Abilities) questions in the Resumix (they are not separate answers).

Navy—The Navy Resumix format is less restrictive than the Army format, which allows five pages. In this format, you must also include answers to all the KSA questions in the Resumix (they are not separate answers). The Navy Resumix format is used for most, but not all Navy postings.

Air Force—The Air Force Resumix format is five pages and must include answers to all the KSA questions in the Resumix (they are not separate answers). This format is used for certain positions, generally those serviced by Randolph Air Force Base. Most positions handled through Warner Robins Air Force Base and higher-level Air Force positions still use a regular federal resume format.

Coast Guard—The Coast Guard uses Avue Digital Services to produce online resumes. This format is not as limiting as the Army, Navy, or Air Force formats. KSAs are answered separately, allowing up to 3,000 characters each. You will also need to post a doc file version of your federal resume and KSAs.

U.S. Department of Commerce—The U.S. Department of Commerce uses Commerce Opportunities Online for some of their job openings. This system allows up to eight jobs to be entered, and will sometimes ask a series of questions. You can cut and paste from the federal resume format to prepare these pages.

Other agencies have different online formats, including the Federal Aviation Administration (FAA), Federal Bureau of Investigation (FBI), and Defense

Intelligence Agency (DIA). The U.S. Post Office has its own format as well. Stay current on formats, and know how to research new requirements (they are constantly changing).

Resume-Building Sites

A helpful online tool for resume building can be found at www. careeronestop.org, a website sponsored by the U.S. Department of Labor that offers career resources and workforce information to job seekers, students, businesses, and workforce professionals to foster talent development in a global economy. The site features an online tutorial for developing resumes, and can be downloaded as a pdf electronic file. This comprehensive resource offers step-by-step instructions on Getting Started (resume preparation, thought, and revision); Types of Resumes (basic resume formats); Resume Design and Presentation (instructions on how to add interest with an effective layout); Essential Features (required versus optional parts of a resume); Methods of Delivery (distribution options); Cover Letters (telling the employer why you're the one for the job); Follow Up (thank you letters, follow up communications); and Interview Techniques.

Another online tool to help you write, edit, and post resumes is the TurboTAP™ website, www.TurboTAP.org. Its section on "Resume Writing for the New Millennium," contains tips for resume writing, as well as a link to TurboTAP's resume builder. To access the resume builder, you'll need to register at TurboTAP, which will take only a couple of minutes. No personal or contact information will be shared and once you're registered, the site offers a wealth of essential information on benefits and transition assistance customized to fit your needs. TurboTAP is the official Transition Assistance Program website, operated under contract on behalf of the U.S. Department of Defense, U.S. Department of Labor, and U.S. Department of Veterans Affairs.

KNOWLEDGE, SKILLS, AND ABILITIES (KSA) AND RESUMES

As you may have noticed, if you intend to do a federal job search, agencies have varying and unique application procedures to meet their hiring needs. One application format may be acceptable for one agency and not another. In the past, this proved to be frustrating for job seekers applying to multiple positions.

In an effort to drive the federal hiring process toward a universal application format, the Office of Personnel Management convened several government agencies to create one resume format that would include all crucial data required for a federal application.

The end product was the USAJOBS resume builder (www.usajobs.gov), which allows you to create a uniform resume that provides all of the information required by hiring government agencies. Instead of creating multiple resumes in different formats, you can build your resume once and be ready for all job opportunities.

When you apply for a position with the federal government, you will most likely need to prepare an accompanying KSA statement. Knowledge is the practical information you have gained to perform the job. Knowledge statements refer to an organized body of information, usually of a factual or procedural nature, which, if applied, makes adequate performance on the job possible.

Skills are your ability to work competently with materials and data, verbally, manually, and mentally. Skill statements refer to the proficient manual, verbal, or mental manipulation of data or things. Skills can be readily measured by a performance test where quantity and quality of performance are tested, usually within an established time limit. Examples of proficient manipulation of things are skill in typing or skill in vehicle operation. An example of proficient manipulation of data is skill in computation using decimals or skill in editing for transposed numbers.

Ability is your capacity to perform an activity. Ability statements refer to the power to perform an observable activity at the present time. This means that abilities have been evidenced through activities or behaviors that are similar to those required on the job; for example, the ability to plan and organize work. Abilities are different from aptitudes, which relate to the potential for performing the activity.

You will need to present your KSAs to perform the job you want on the statement you submit to the OPM.

Don't Ignore KSAs

Some job applicants, especially those looking for their first federal position, are not sure whether the KSA requirements apply to them, or whether they should include them in places where a response is optional. There's an easy way to decide when to pay attention to KSAs—always.

Federal agencies may emphasize the most important aspects of a job by assigning relative weights to each KSA. Others will designate particular KSAs as being mandatory (M) or desirable (D). As a job applicant, you will want to focus on responding to the more heavily weighted KSAs or the mandatory ones, but it is important to remember that you need to address every KSA on the list. If a vacancy announcement makes no distinction among the position's KSAs, you should assume that all KSAs are equally important.

KSAs Must Be Job-Related

An agency cannot ask for anything in a KSA that is not in the job's position description. Stop and think about keywords you need to add. You may be the most qualified person for the position, but your information could be lost in a sea of applicants without the right keywords. Do not assume that reviewers will pull the information out of your application package and pick up the salient points.

Clearly state your KSAs and jobs so the reader can understand your responsibilities. Number and title each KSA in bold and type responses in single space. Include your name, social security number, and the job vacancy number at the top of each page submitted. Be very detailed and specific, answering what, who, why, when, where, and how. Avoid repeating your resume or referring the OPM to another part of your application. Write in first person and make sure the reader knows what position and experience you are discussing. Instead of using puffed-up language, use simple but specific examples and descriptions that allow readers to draw their own conclusions. Include as much as possible to show your qualifications.

The federal OPM offers several guidelines and directives for blending your resume with KSAs.

A Single Keyword Communicates Multiple Skills and Qualifications

When a recruiter reads the keyword *analyst*, he or she might assume you have experience in collecting data, evaluating effectiveness, and researching and developing new processes. Just one keyword can have tremendous power and deliver a huge message.

Study Job Announcements

Make sure you understand what the KSAs are and what they mean. This step is critical. If you do not understand each KSA, you will not be able to write effective responses. A KSA by itself tends to be general in nature. The vacancy announcement usually contains a brief summary description of the duties of the position. Read this summary description very carefully.

Reviewing a number of interesting job announcements and their questions is the best way to determine important KSA keywords. The jobs don't have to be in your geographic target area. The idea is to find skills, experience, education, and other credentials important in your field. You will probably find keywords frequently mentioned by different agencies. Focus on the "requirements," "skills," or "qualifications" sections of job ads, and look for buzzwords and desirable credentials for your ideal job.

Do some brainstorming and review your experiences. Find things that relate to the KSAs. For example, if the KSA that you are writing about is the ability to communicate orally, you need to think about the times when you used oral communication skills.

Example: If you were a file clerk in the military, you instructed other clerks on new filing procedures. Or, as a management analyst you had to present recommendations on workflow procedures to top staff members.

Example: A training program in effective briefing techniques that you completed or an award you received that relates to your ability to communicate orally. Do not forget experiences you have had in non-work related areas, for example, volunteer activities or in school-related activities.

Example: While you were a Cub Scout leader, you acted as chairperson for a fundraising activity; or while in school, you were a student council representative. These experiences are just as valid as work-related examples, as long as they are relevant to the position's KSA.

Try reviewing your employment history from the earliest to the most recent so that you don't miss a job or experience relevant to the KSA. Review your total experience, both paid and volunteer, and training, and look for situations that apply to the particular KSA. Experiences that you have in one job or one area may apply to more than one KSA.

Do not worry about being repetitious in writing KSA responses. Each KSA is rated separately by the subject matter expert (SME)/promotion panel, and as long as the information you give is relevant, it does not matter if you've used it in another KSA.

Telling your story does not mean drafting an autobiography. Recruiters are inundated with applications and faced with weeding out the qualified from the unqualified. Their first step is to quickly skim through submissions and eliminate candidates who clearly are not qualified. Your resume needs to pass the skim test. Look at your resume and/or KSAs and ask yourself the following questions.

- Can a hiring manager see my main credentials within 10 to 15 seconds?
- Does critical information jump off the page?
- Do I effectively sell myself on the top quarter of the first page?

Analyze the Experiences You Identified

Scrutinize the experiences you identified and focus on the ones that really matter—it is here that you identify how to use the knowledge, skill, or ability in your job or experiences. This kind of information is at the core of the KSA process (sometimes called *task analysis*). Ask yourself specific questions about the experience you have identified. The answers that you come up with will be used to complete the actual writing of the KSA.

Take a look at the kinds of questions you need to ask about your experiences.

What kind of knowledge or skills do I use in my job?
- What are the steps, procedures, practices, rules, policies, theories, principles, or concepts that I use in my job?
  - How do I apply the knowledge, principles, or concepts that I use in my job?
  - How do I apply the knowledge that I have to accomplish my work?

What kind of supervision do I receive?
- How is my work assigned?
- What is my responsibility to accomplish work?
- How independent are my actions?
- How is my work reviewed?

What guidelines do I use to accomplish my work?

- Are the instructions that I use to perform my work in written or oral form, or both?
- Do I use procedural manuals?
- What other written procedures do I use?
- What kind of oral instructions do I use to perform my work?
- How much judgment do I have to use to apply the guidelines for my job?
- Are the guidelines I use very easily applied or do they require interpretation?
- How difficult are they to interpret?

How complex is my job?

- What is the nature of the work I do?

Example: Tasks are clear-cut and directly related to each other; or the work involves different and unrelated processes and methods; or the work consists of broad functions and processes of an administrative or professional nature.

- How difficult is it to identify what needs to be done?

Example: Little or no choice in deciding what needs to be done; or decisions depend on an analysis of the situation, as there are many alternatives; or extensive analysis is required to even define the nature of the problem.

- How difficult or original is the work I do?

How does my work affect other processes or individuals?

- Who do I have contact with on a daily basis?
- Why do I have contact with these individuals?
- What is my role in these discussions or meetings?

Example: Provide information; receive information; influence or advise someone; convince someone of something.

Now that you have a better understanding of the KSAs and the facts about your experiences, you are ready to move to the next step—selling yourself.

The Sales Pitch

Because applications are quickly skimmed during the first pass, it is crucial that your resume and KSAs go straight to selling your credentials. Your key selling points need to be prominently displayed at the top of the first page of the resume and directly address each question asked in the KSA section. For example, if an advanced degree is an important qualification, it shouldn't be buried at the end of a four-page resume. If a KSA question asks about your writing ability, immediately detail your experience.

Show that the facts you have gathered about your experience relate to the individual KSAs. Talk about your experiences in a way that clearly shows how they are related to knowledge, skill, or ability. In other words, you need to show a link between your own experience and the KSA. Do not assume that the link is obvious to someone else, even though it may be obvious to you.

The SME/promotion panel member(s) who rates your application can only credit what you tell them in your KSA response. They will not be able to give you proper credit for your experiences unless you give them specific examples showing how and why your experience is related to a particular KSA.

In communicating this information to the SME/promotion panel, remember a few important facts:

- It is the content of your responses that is rated, not the writing style you use. It is acceptable to use brief sentences or phrases as long as the SME/promotion panel knows what you mean.

- Do not use abbreviations, acronyms, or jargon. Chances are the SME/promotion panel will not know what you are talking about if you write this way. They will not be able to give proper credit for your experience if they do not understand what you have done.

- Very long responses do not guarantee a high rating. Give the SME/promotion panel direct and to-the-point responses.

Use an Editor's Eye

Many workers are proud of their career and believe their resumes should reflect everything they've accomplished. However, a resume shouldn't contain every detail, and KSAs should only address the questions at hand. So, be prudent. If your college days are long behind you, does it really matter that you delivered pizza after class? The editing step will be difficult if you are holding on to your past for emotional reasons. It may be beneficial to ask a friend to help you weed out irrelevant details.

If you were a recruiter looking at a resume or an answer to a KSA, which of the following entries would impress you more?

- Wrote news releases;

  or

- Wrote 25 news releases in a three-week period under daily deadlines.

Clearly, the second statement carries more weight because it uses numbers to quantify the writer's accomplishment and gives context to help the interviewer understand the degree of difficulty involved in the task. Numbers are powerful resume tools that help your accomplishments draw the attention they deserve from prospective employers. With just a little thought, you can find effective ways to quantify your successes on your resume.

Think Money

For-profit, nonprofit, and government organizations are always concerned about money. As you contemplate your accomplishments and prepare to present them on your resume or in your KSAs, think about ways you've saved money, earned money, or managed money in your assignments, internships, part-time jobs, and extracurricular activities so far. Your statements, as shown in the following examples, should be very specific, giving employers an idea of your experience and clearly stating your ability to impact the bottom line.

- Achieved *50% reduction* (from 12 to six months) in the amount of time required for building minimum competence in new employees.

- Implemented programs on customer orientation that contributed to the *improvement in product quality by 25%*.

- Managed a manufacturing supply chain operation through subordinate supervisors that resulted in a *20% reduction in costs* to the supplier.

- Ten years of experience in quality-analysis/quality-control practices and preservation of materials.

- Fifteen years of experience in carrying out cost engineer functions and responsibilities on large-scale industrial construction projects.

- Knowledge of treasury and credit control with some training in risk management and financial analysis.

- Initiated new supply chain concepts and implemented potential cost reduction and quality improvements across the supply chain.

- Revamped agency purchasing process that resulted in *$50,000 annual cost reduction*.

- A proven track record in cost reduction and control that created a *15% savings quarterly*.

- Implemented a product delivery system resulting in a 15% reduction in the normal development time with a *30% reduction in cost*.

- Improved proficiency and effectiveness of the estimating department, which included providing an accurate cost savings analysis for budgeting and scheduling, as well as all procedures. Resulted in a *cost savings of over $250,000 per year*.

Think Time

You've heard the old saying, "time is money." It's true. Companies and organizations are constantly looking for ways to save time and do things more efficiently. They're also concerned about meeting deadlines, both internal and external. Demonstrating on your resume or in your KSAs that you can save, maximize, or manage time will grab your reader's immediate attention. Here are some time-oriented entries that might appear on a typical college student's resume:

- Assisted with *twice-monthly* payroll activities, ensuring employees were paid as expected and on time.

- Attended high school basketball games, interviewed players and coaches, and composed 750-word articles by an *11:00 P.M. deadline*.

- Suggested procedures that decreased average order-processing time from *ten minutes to five minutes*.

Hypothetical KSA #1

Secretary, GS-5

KSA Title: Ability to write non-technical correspondence

KSA Response #1

I type letters every day. Sometimes I have to type them from a draft that the manager gives me. I also use form-letters or the manager tells me what he wants me to write. I write memos requesting supplies or advising employees of training classes. I have been a secretary in my unit for three years and always finish my work quickly and correctly.

KSA Response #2

I am the secretary in my unit. I write responses for most non-technical correspondence and for all administrative matters within the unit. I respond using various form-letters. Sometimes, I have to draft a letter from start to finish, depending on the nature of the inquiry. For example, I may have to write a statement regarding leave balances for an employee or a memo to a warehouse regarding supply shortages. When managers write memos, they are given to me as drafts and I rewrite them to ensure proper grammar and correct format.

Which Response is Better?

The writer of the first response seems to be confusing typing with writing. It is not until the third sentence that we get some specific information regarding a writing activity. And then, in the last sentence, the writer gives us some new information (how long the writer has been a secretary and how well the writer does the work of the position) that has nothing to do with the KSA as defined for the job. Remember that the SME/promotion panel rates your responses as they relate to the crediting plan. If what you have written is not relevant to the KSA, it will not relate to the crediting plan and you will not receive any credit.

The second response gives more relevant and useful information. The writer has provided specific information related to the KSA and has given examples to show the kind of writing being done. This response has given the SME/promotion panel enough information to properly credit the writer's experience.

Hypothetical KSA #2

Management Analyst, GS-12

KSA Title: Ability to communicate in writing

KSA Response #1

One of the most important things I do in my position is prepare reports and studies of the various components in our organization. They always have to be written in a clear and concise manner, and often involve very complex issues like organizational structures, work methods and procedures, manpower utilization, delegations of authority, and other issues. I usually have to pull together a lot of different information and from different sources. I usually have to work within very short time frames to produce a needed study or report.

Here are some examples of the materials I have written. Staffing/workload reports: In particular I am involved in the WMS/FTE weekly reports—this includes components in fiscal control and also DTB PLUS studies. These studies are done on an "as needed" basis and involve many operational and technical issues. They are only required when management sees a need for them and specifically requests an analysis. We set up a team and review the targeted work. These reports require a lot of data-gathering activity.

Director's reports: These also involve a lot of data analysis from the HAL reports and are sent to the director's staff advisor.

KSA Response #2

I write technical and administrative memos and study reports, which identify actual and potential problem areas in interrelated work processes, the underlying source of operating difficulties, trends, significant management accomplishments, merit/deficiency situations, and areas of imbalance. These reports always include recommendations for improvement in the studied areas.

Some examples of the kinds of studies or reports I produce are as follows: I write memos that represent the regional office (RO) position on proposed procedures or work processes. This involves evaluating the effect of alternative actions on the work processes under consideration and how best to use manpower and resources, as well as the identification of other alternatives worthy of consideration. This almost always involves the consolidation of information and comments from multiple components into one memo representing the regional office position on a given issue. An example of this type of product is the formulation of office comments on the design of the new national fishery control system. A committee reviewed the release to evaluate if all pertinent work processes were included and to identify more efficient design alternatives. In most cases, I consolidated the comments of the committee and formulated the final office comment memo.

I have been involved in periodic reports on national TS/incubation workloads since 1978. These reports were researched and written by a team of analysts. The final product was usually consolidated from other area reports and issued to the secretary.

I also wrote position papers detailing the regional office position on administrative, workload processing, or work measurement issues. An example of this type of product is a memo prepared for the central office in July 1989 stating the RO's position on the issue of productivity measurement in field stations. This memo presented our views on the secretary's productivity analysis project and pointed out flaws in their basic assumptions. It then listed the major problems with areas that should be addressed in order to provide valid productivity measures for all the field stations. The RO's concerns and ideas concerning the elements necessary for an acceptable productivity measure were presented.

In addition, I have also completed six semester hours of writing courses in college. I am presently the corresponding secretary for Tri Sigma National Sorority, Incorporated.

Which Response is Better?

The writer of the first response has borrowed some of the language from the duties described in the vacancy announcement in order to tell the SME/promotion panel what he or she does in the job. Unfortunately, this does not give the panel any more specific information about his or her experience than they would get by reading the announcement. The examples given by the writer sound like they could be relevant to the KSA, but the writer does not provide any specific information to explain how these activities relate to the KSA. The writer also uses a lot of acronyms. These are sure to confuse a SME/promotion panel and should not be used without explanation. Finally, the writer does not tell us what his or her specific role is in any of these activities. For example, what is the meaning of "I am involved in" and what is the writer's role when he or she says, "We set up a team"?

The second response gives more relevant and specific information. The writer provides a general introductory statement, which acts as a background to the examples that follow. The first and last examples are very specific and give enough information so that the SME/promotion panel will understand what the writer does and how it relates to the crediting plan. The second example, however, falls short. The writer uses some jargon ("TS incubation workloads"), which may mean little or nothing to the SME/promotion panel. It is also not clear what the writer's involvement is in the described "periodic reports." Should the SME/promotion panel assume that this means involvement as a writer or just as a team member? Regardless of this problem, the second response is the better of the two.

In each of the hypothetical responses you have just read, the second response, although the better of the two, is not the best possible response. With practice you could write an even better KSA response.

Tips for Developing Your KSA Responses

- Read the vacancy announcement carefully.
- Gather the information needed to begin writing.
- Get to the point.
- Do not use acronyms.
- Be specific.
- State specifically what you have done.
- Be precise.
- Present yourself in clear and simple language.
- Use lots of examples.
- Do not ramble.
- Do not borrow language from the position description.

SOURCE:
Outreach and Marketing Branch, Human Resources Management Office of the Centers for Disease Control, U.S. Department of Health and Human Services

PURSUING A JOB WITH THE FEDERAL GOVERNMENT

Applying for a civilian position with the federal government is usually a bit different from seeking a corporate position. According to the Army Career and Alumni Program, the following compliance information must appear on your federal resume. Leaving out any of these components will render you ineligible for the position.

Vacancy Information—Include the announcement number, the job title, and the grade(s) for the position.

Heading—Include your full name, address with zip code, home and work phone numbers with area codes, e-mail address, and social security number. Also, incorporate a section with personal information that includes country of citizenship, veterans' preference, civil service status, and whether your present supervisor can be contacted. You can list your education after that, or it can come later in the resume, depending on the type of emphasis you want. List your most recent degrees first with years of graduation or attendance and the university or school and its location. You may want to list specific courses that are relevant to the job. Next, include your professional training or job-related training courses with dates.

Work Experience—This section should cover your jobs for the last ten years. Start with your most recent, but if a prior experience is more relevant or was a civil service job, it may be to your advantage to begin with that position first. Include your job title, company name and address, dates of employment, salary (if required), hours worked per week, and supervisor's name and contact information. For each position, detail your duties and accomplishments as they relate to those listed in the vacancies that interest you. Indicate how you will be able to do the job better than anyone else. You can also summarize your qualifications and position the summary before your work experience. Be sure to include the keywords from the job announcement in your summary and in the details of your work experience.

Job-Related Awards, Honors, Memberships, and Volunteer Experience— In this last section, you can include your job-related awards, honors, memberships, and volunteer experiences that are directly job-related or enhance your KSAs, which are discussed in a supplemental statement. The KSAs can be grouped into the following four areas:

1. occupational and subject-matter knowledge and skills
2. ability to plan and organize
3. person-to-person relationships
4. communication skills

These can be written on plain paper or agency forms, if required, with one KSA to a page and your name and date at the bottom of each page. This is an additional opportunity to write about the skills, knowledge, and abilities regarding your work experiences (paid and volunteer), education, and life experiences that will show you to be the best person for the position.

Applying for a federal job requires entering your resume using an OCR program (Resumix, QuickHire, AVUE, and USASTAFFING). First, write your resume and delete all formatting. You can use capital letters for emphasis and titles. Then, carefully following the instructions, copy and paste your resume into the required fields. You can use an online resume builder to write your resume. A supplemental data sheet giving a profile of your jobs will be required.

First, write your resume and delete all formatting. You can use capital letters for emphasis and titles. Then, carefully following the instructions, copy and paste your resume into the required fields. You can use an online resume builder to write your resume. A supplemental data sheet, giving a profile of your jobs will be required.

Of course, finish your federal employment package with a knockout cover letter. If you are sending your packet electronically, the letter can be sent as an attachment or pasted directly into your e-mail message.

SOURCE:
Army Career and Alumni Program
(www.acap.army.mil/veterans/job_assistance/federal_job.cfm)

SAMPLE MILITARY RESUME

Mark L. West
555 Carmine Drive
Westbury, NY 12121
212-555-6789 /Home
212-555-4637/Mobile
212-555-0090/Fax
E-mail: mlwest2000@aol.com

PROFILE

Top performer with exceptional interpersonal, communication, and public-relations skills that allow the development of strong rapport with individuals on all levels. Outstanding record of achievement coupled with the ability to build and direct a business to profitability through leadership, creativity, effective management, and the motivation and development of staff to maximum potential. Adept at analyzing and resolving problems and developing and instituting the needed procedures and responses. A consistent high-level of performance dealing with people and services requiring solid management, organizational, time-management, and negotiating abilities. Results oriented, highly motivated to succeed.

Energetic and assertive, adept at the coordination and implementation of multifaceted operational procedures in established operations. A sound professional attitude with pride in personal performance. Seeking a position that will challenge and use management and sales experience, education, and acquired skills to positively impact company performance and profitability, while providing personal and professional growth.

MANAGEMENT/ADMINISTRATION EXPERTISE

- Train and evaluate staff, providing appropriate feedback regarding performance and training requirements.

- Identify corporate objectives, organize needed resources, and direct operational efforts to achieve desired results.

- Attend and participate in meetings, seminars, and conferences.

- Enforce, track, and ensure compliance with all organization policies and procedures.

- Gather and disseminate information for status reports for presentation to management staff.

OPERATIONS/FINANCE EXPERTISE

- Demonstrated effectiveness in problem evaluation coupled with the ability to generate and implement effective solutions.

- Troubleshoot operational functions to ensure productivity and optimize quality.

- Solid experience in the development and administration of annual budgets, cost containment, purchasing, and inventory control.

PUBLIC RELATIONS EXPERTISE

- Conceive, develop, and execute innovative, targeted media messages, story placement, radio promotion, and coordination of special events.

- Generate and enact public relations, advertising promotional and special event programs, as well as campaigns to increase public awareness.

- Develop and execute prepared and unprepared speeches for various community organizations.

- Prepare presentations and represent the organization during speaking engagements at local schools and colleges to promote strong community relations and represent organization efforts.

- Institute strong networking capabilities to recruit and retain personnel.

- Coordinate daily with personnel to ensure timely application processing.

CAREER HISTORY / ACHIEVEMENTS

UNITED STATES AIR FORCE, Westbury, NY (1981–Present)

Air Force Recruiter, Operations Department (10/93–Present)

Air Force Recruiter, Officer Recruiting (2/93–10/93)

Air Force Recruiter, Advertising & Public Relations (2/92–2/93)

Air Force Recruiter, Operations Department (7/89–2/92)

Non-Prior Service Recruiter (3/85–7/89)

Medical Service Specialist, NCIOC Recovery Room (10/81–3/85)

Air Force Recruiter, Operations Department

- Track every aspect of the production of non-prior service, officer, nurse, and physician recruiting. Maintain an up-to-date account of all jobs, assignments, reassignments, and dismissals. Run waiver program, verify candidates, and recommend those qualifying for approval. Evaluate applicants for job placement. Administer the following programs to stimulate production: Competition Program, Awards Program, Leads Program and the ROTC Scholarship Program. Coordinate all recruiting activities at the medical processing station. Perform detailed analyses of lead generation, trending, and short- and long-term programs to inform recruiters of more effective means of job performance. Design and execute marketing research to establish job positioning, target markets, and competition. Analyze competition and market trends, and institute required changes. Generate and enact creative public relations, advertising, promotional, special events, and presentations to increase public awareness and recruitment.

- Top Operations NCO for entire Northeast

- Top Support NCO for Squadron, four times

- Top Squadron NCO

- Commander's Annual Extra Effort Award, three times

- Took over the entire squadron Officer Training School Recruitment Program servicing five states, during a non-productive period and successfully submitted 35 Officer's Training School applications, which allowed the squadron to meet its goals. This is normally done over a 12-month period by several recruiters.

- Designed squadron regulation for competition to increase production.

- Squadron named "Top in Northeast, Fiscal Year 1991."

Air Force Recruiter, Advertising and Public Relations

- Increased community awareness of Air Force opportunities through effective advertising, promotional events, and public relations. Developed and implemented marketing programs to increase production. Raised educator confidence in the Air Force as a viable opportunity for all students. Prepared presentations and represented the Air Force during speaking engagements at local schools and colleges to promote strong community relations. Made speeches and presentations for various community organizations. Doubled squadron advertising and promotions program in every aspect through advertisements, community events, and radio interviews.

- Designed and administered the advertising and promotion plan.

Non-Prior Service Recruiter

- Responsible for local advertising, school programs, career days and lectures, daily telephone prospecting, and cold calling. Conducted interviews in offices, residences, and high schools. Qualified candidates for the Air Force.

- Met or exceeded goals four years consecutively. Received numerous monthly and quarterly awards.

- Named one of top five recruiters in the Northeast.

Medical Service Specialist, NCIOC Recovery Room

- Directed the daily activities of the recovery room of the Wilfred Hall Medical Center, a 1,000-bed hospital. Supervised, scheduled, trained, evaluated, and counseled 16 active duty medical technicians and two civilian LPNs. Performed all administrative functions including supply order, inventory control, and updating and maintaining regulation manuals.

- Most junior NCO put in charge of the recovery room of the third largest medical facility in the world.

- Received excellent rating on Inspector General Inspection.

EDUCATION

University of Texas, Westley, TX
General Studies/Marketing

Craigsville Junior College, Marquette, GA
General Studies/Marketing
(Total of 88 Credits)

NCO Academy
Management Theory; Total Quality Management
Management by Objective; Motivation, Counseling & Communication

SEMINARS/COURSES/WORKSHOPS

Advertising & Promotion; Recruiting School; NCO Leadership School
Supervisor Prep Course; Corpsman School (Basic Nursing, Emergency)

COMPUTER EXPERIENCE

SOFTWARE: Enable; Alice; Windows; e-mail; Microsoft Office
HARDWARE: Z-248; Laserjet; ALPS Printers; Plotter

CERTIFICATIONS

EMT Certified; CPR Certified

What Other Vets Are Saying...

I thought that the hard part was over, but it wasn't. I'd put my life on the line for my country—twice. After doing two tours of duty in Iraq, you would think I could handle anything, but there was something else I had to deal with.

It was great when I came home to Birmingham. People were cheering us at the airport when we got off the plane. My family and friends threw me a big welcome home party. For a few weeks after that, I just chilled. I needed a break. No more dawn patrols. No screams from soldiers hit by a roadside bomb. No more worrying about who would be next. But then my funds started running low. I needed a job.

I spent 18 months in Iraq taking orders and being told what to do at every step. The next thing I knew, I was out on job interviews and people I'd never seen before were asking me questions and opinions on this and that. I knew I had the skills and could do the job they were hiring for. But for some reason, when they asked the questions, I just couldn't get the answers out right. After a few times, I started to get paranoid.

I was gone a long time fighting a war, not looking for a job. That was my job. The military is very structured. They don't ask you questions or your opinion. They just tell you what to do and you do it.

A lot of my buddies have found it really, really hard to get back to civilian life. They didn't know what was out there for them. They had been away from civilian life since they'd gotten out of school. Me too. We all needed some help learning how to field questions in an interview and not look like a total idiot.

Chris Pearson
Former Army Medic

CHAPTER FOUR

MASTERING THE INTERVIEW PROCESS

You've finally achieved what you wanted. Your hard work has paid off—writing resumes, checking job banks, making endless telephone calls, and sending e-mails—and now, you've landed the all-important job interview. Like most job seekers in your position, you are excited, yet anxious; confident, and yet unsure.

You get to the interview, and as you sit there waiting to be called into an office and asked who knows what, you look down and your hands are trembling ever so slightly. You try to calm them by flipping the pages of a magazine. You haven't read a word, but at least it's keeping you busy. Soon you're called into the interviewer's office. As you walk in, you notice that your palms are sweaty, but it's too late to do anything about it, so you shake with a sweaty hand. As the interviewer is grilling you, you both notice that your voice is shaky. He's throwing a barrage of questions at you and you answer them to the best of your ability. But, his facial expressions give you a clue that he's not exactly impressed.

It's a great job and a rare opportunity. Competition is fierce. As he takes notes, you wonder what he's really thinking and how you're doing compared to the other applicants.

Then, your worst nightmare begins. He asks you a question that you have no idea how to answer. You circle around a response like an airplane in a holding pattern. You stumble over your words and give a totally lame response. It's clear from his reaction that your answer wasn't what he wanted to hear. And now that you've embarrassed yourself, it's too late to try and clean it up.

The interview concludes and you drive home beating yourself up. You pound the dashboard, wondering, "Why did I say something so incredibly stupid?" But the damage is done. A few days later, you get a letter thanking you for interviewing with the company, but the job was awarded to someone else. The job goes to someone whose resume wasn't as impressive as yours, but unfortunately for you, the successful candidate had polished job-interview skills.

A critical factor in getting the job has to do with how you present yourself in the interview.

If you had known the right words to say, how to answer the questions appropriately, and how to compose yourself after being sidelined by an unexpected question, the job could have been yours.

Yes, it's possible to be the most qualified candidate for the job, and yet the offer is extended to someone else. A critical factor in getting the job has to do with how you present yourself in the interview.

For most of your military career, you got a new position because you were assigned to it. You didn't have to interview or compete for it as it happens in a nonmilitary environment, or did you? Did you ever sit before a promotion board? Were you screened for other special programs and positions? If so, you were interviewed and you seized the opportunity to sell yourself, your skills, and experience by talking about your achievements and how they would help you perform in the new position. Well, a job interview is no different.

A job interview is a two-way process for sharing information. It's an in-depth conversation with a prospective employer about your skills, experience, and training as they relate to a job opportunity. An interview is also a time for you to display your enthusiasm, interest, and understanding of the job and the hiring company.

During a job interview, information is exchanged through both words and actions during four basic stages: (1) introduction and warm-up through preliminary conversation and pleasantries; (2) employer questions; (3) applicant questions; and (4) closing. Because employers are interested in finding the most qualified applicant who best matches the company, you could be interviewed several times for a position. Hiring and training a new employee is timely and costly. Consequently, companies often interview several times to ensure that the first interview was not simply a fluke or a lucky shot.

Screening Interviews

Screening interviews offer the applicant's first contact with a company representative and can take place in person or over the telephone. This also guards against glaring problems with a candidate. With increasing frequency, companies are screening candidates by conducting telephone interviews, especially for out-of-towners.

The purpose of a screening interview is to determine whether you meet the basic requirements for the position—related experience, education, licenses, etc. A human resources representative may conduct the screening interview.

A phone interview saves time for the employer and you. If you can't get the answers to basic questions correct on the phone, there's no point in employers watching you fumble through a face-to-face interview. Also, the screening interviewer is looking for you to make a mistake

The purpose of a screening interview is to determine whether you meet the basic requirements for the position— related experience, education, licenses, etc.

to rule you out—for example, taking the call with your kids screaming in the background.

A phone or screening interview is more than just a step toward a live meeting with an employer. Since it can actually eliminate you from a face-to-face interview, learn the rules and prepare for the screening interview. Today's hiring managers have many tools at their disposal to determine whether you are qualified for a job. They can obtain your personal history with a few clicks on the Internet. They may even find information regarding the content and quality of your work. A phone screening can give an employer a sense of your communication skills.

Technical Interviews

If you represent yourself well during the screening interview, you may be called again for a technical interview. Employees, who are very familiar with both the position and the job requirements, generally conduct technical interviews. These individuals may be supervisors or workers with a long history in the industry or with the company.

The face-to-face meeting helps determine whether or not you connect with an employer. That's why it's important to make a good impression when you meet. This is what the face-to-face interview is all about. So, make a great first impression and focus on making sure the interviewer likes you.

Have you ever watched the president of the United States hold a press conference? On the surface, it may seem like the reporters spontaneously ask a series of questions related to the purpose of the media event. In reality, when the president walks into a press conference, he doesn't really worry about what the journalists are going to ask. They already have all the answers he is going to provide, no matter what the questions are. These answers are called *talking points*.

Politicians such as presidents, governors, and mayors generally hold press conferences in order to frame an issue. They listen to a question and then determine which talking point they will use to answer the question. Each question presents an opportunity to get their point across.

Talking points can be a useful tool during job interviews as well. By using talking points, you control the topics you want to discuss. Prior to the interview, pick five or six pivotal points about yourself that you want to get across in an interview; each point should come with some sort of story or example. Listen to each question and then determine the point that best fits the question.

Unlike the president, you can't ignore questions that don't fit into one of your points; however, you may be surprised how often you can answer an interview question with one of your prepared points.

Above all, a job interview is a sales call, and any good salesperson knows that there is no deal until it's closed. In the same way, no matter how good the interview, there's no job until the deal is closed. If your interview has gone well, do not be afraid to ask if the employer has reservations or concerns about hiring you. Most will give you an honest answer. Admittedly, this is a hard question to ask because you'll be faced with your weaknesses in the midst of the interview. But the good news is that it gives you an opportunity to address those weaknesses and the ways you can overcome them.

Behavior-Based Interviews

Employers interview differently than they did five or ten years ago. Many hiring personnel today conduct what is known as behavior-based interviews. They are filled with behavior-based questions designed to bring out patterns of accomplishment that are relevant to the employer's situation. These are specific questions designed to challenge candidates to provide concrete examples of their achievements in various situations.

Behavior-based interviews are rooted in the simple belief that how a job candidate responds to certain types of situations in the past is a good predictor of how that person will behave in a similar situation in the future. Behavior-based questions are likely to begin with some variation of the following inquiries.

- Tell me about a time when you. . .
- Give me an example of a way you have. . .
- Please tell me about how you. . .

Behavior-based interviewing focuses on experiences, behaviors, knowledge, skills, and abilities that are job-related. In giving a response, you may use a variety of examples—work experience, volunteer work, school projects, social organizations, activities, hobbies, community projects, and family life—as evidence of your past behavior. There is a strong, growing trend towards this type of interviewing and you may very well be confronted with it in your job interviews.

The good news is that a behavior-based interview is an opportunity for you to sell your positives with only an example or two. When a question is posed, briefly describe the situation, enthusiastically explain what you did, and indicate the outcome.

You can prepare for behavior-based questions by outlining some of your major positive experiences prior to the interview. Obviously, you want to select examples that promote your skills and have a positive outcome. As you prepare for your interview, consider situations where you accomplished any of the following tasks:

- Increased company profits or productivity
- Helped to support a team effort
- Demonstrated leadership, especially in a crisis situation
- Implemented positive change
- Solved a problem
- Made a good decision
- Made a poor decision that yielded some type of positive result
- Handled criticism
- Improved relations with a coworker
- Helped build employee morale
- Met a deadline/missed a deadline
- Achieved goals

No matter how much preparation you do, you can't anticipate every kind of question that will be asked. Even if the interviewer asks about a time when something negative happened, you can still select an example where you were able to turn the situation around and yield a positive outcome. For example, if asked by an interviewer, "Tell me about a time you went out on a limb to implement a project that turned out to be a bad idea," try to identify an example where: (1) even though it wasn't the best decision, you were able to get something positive out of the situation; or (2) you learned from it and used that experience as groundwork to make a good decision or will do so when a similar situation arises; or (3) the negative impact was minimal in overall damage. Be honest in your assessment of the experience, but try to conclude with a positive outcome that occurred or a lesson you learned.

Decision-Making Interviews

Reaching the decision-making interview means you have all the requirements for the job. Why, then, another interview? Only company officials with hiring authority can offer you a position. Before they do, they want to be sure you fit the company culture. The decision-making interview is your final interview.

During this series of interviews, you may meet with one interviewer or a panel of interviewers. Their style may be casual or abrupt or they may ask set interview questions. Depending on the interview style, you may experience little or a great deal of stress. The best way to cope with interview stress is to prepare for the interview in advance. You can do this by researching the company, its products and purpose, key individuals and facts, and its culture and language.

Anticipate the kinds of questions you might be asked, and prepare answers that use examples of your achievements related to the job. Make sure you dress for success at the interview. Research requirements and select clothing and accessories that are appropriate for the position.

While hiring officials make the final determination to offer you the job, they often do so after consulting a number of other employees at the company. Anyone who observes you may be asked—a receptionist, a human resources clerk, and so forth. Therefore, each interview begins as soon as you arrive at the interview location. Be keenly aware of how you interact with everyone you meet and what you do while waiting for the interviewer. Always be poised and professional. Never divulge anything you would not want the hiring manager to know.

Finding a job is tough. And until you find a job, looking for jobs and interviewing becomes your job. At some point, you simply get tired of going on interview after interview, trying to present your best self and putting your

The best way to cope with interview stress is to prepare for the interview in advance.

best foot forward. It's important to develop and execute an interview strategy that includes preparation, enthusiasm, and a positive attitude.

We have established that an interview is a selling opportunity to present yourself as the product and the employer as the buyer. So, it stands to reason that you should apply the basic steps of a successful sale to the job interview process. Before you interview, learn about the company and position from a variety of places, including the following sources.

- Company website
- Internet search
- Job description
- Trade periodicals
- Chambers of Commerce
- Employer brochures
- Professional organizations
- Better Business Bureau
- Annual business reports
- Manufacturers' guides
- School placement offices
- Union representatives
- Local and state employment service offices
- Current employees

Answering Interview Questions

Typically, there are three types of questions asked in interviews: behavioral, leading, and theoretical.

Behavioral questions seek demonstrated examples of behavior from your past experience and concentrate on job-related functions. First, they may include questions that require more than a simple yes or no response, known as open-ended questions. For example: *Describe a time you had to be flexible in meeting a tight deadline with a project that could only yield a narrow profit.* Second, close-ended questions require a simple, definite answer. For example: *Where did you do your undergraduate studies?* Finally, there are questions that ask why. These are used to reveal your rationale for certain decisions you have made or to determine your motivation. For example: *Why did you choose to enter sales even though your major was political science?*

Leading questions hint at the answer the interviewer is seeking by the way they are phrased. For example: *I see that you have quite a bit of experience doing freelance writing? That requires you to pay close attention to deadlines, doesn't it?*

Theoretical questions place you in a hypothetical situation. These questions look to possibilities rather than probabilities. They challenge your ability to answer questions rather than seeking answers about whether or not you can do a good job. For example: *How would you organize your neighbors to have a yard sale at your local community center?*

These questions can be answered very effectively by individuals who know the correct answer, but do not necessarily practice it. Some interviewers believe they can see a pattern in your answers to such questions. They may ask questions like, *"If you could spend an evening with anyone in history, who would it be? What color best describes you? If you could be an animal, what would you be?"* There has been no research offered that correlates the answers to these questions with success on the job; nevertheless, you should be prepared for such questions.

Informational Interviews

There are times when you may have an opportunity to talk with a professional to help define your career options or research a company where you want to work. It is not a job interview and is not designed for a job offer.

In an informational interview, the roles are reversed. You are the interviewer, and as such, should prepare plenty of questions to keep the conversation moving. You don't want the person being interviewed to feel like he or she is wasting time. Include questions about working in the field or the company business, but ask about other things, too. How did they get into the field? Do they enjoy their work? What are the current job prospects in the field? How has the field changed in the last ten years? What does a typical day look like day? You can insure that the conversation remains fluid by avoiding questions that require only a yes or no response.

If you don't know someone already in the field, ask the people in your circle for potential contacts in the industry, company, or job that strikes your interest.

Once you obtain a contact name and number or e-mail, make arrangements for a meeting. A possible script (adjust for telephone, e-mail, or letter) might read along the following lines, "Mrs. Martin, your name was suggested to me by Ricardo Henderson. My name is Edward Porter and I am interested in a career in the field of video game design and development. I could use advice from someone who is in this growing and innovative field. I realize that you have a very demanding job and are very busy, but do you have any time this week when I can meet with you? There are so few people who have expertise in this field, so if you are able to spare about 15 or 20 minutes to answer a few questions, it would really be of great benefit to me."

If the person agrees to meet with you, dress and act just as you would during an employment interview. In other words, dress and act professionally, be upbeat, and demonstrate your enthusiasm for working in their field. Even though this interview is not designed to get you a job, the person may provide additional leads or referrals that could lead to a job.

Keep it short. Limit your initial interview to 15 to 30 minutes based on how the conversation is going. Pay attention to the interviewee's reactions. If the person seems ready to get the interview over with or rushed, do not overtax the person's time. You may want to interview someone who has no hiring power, as they often know more about day-to-day activities related to the job and can provide more specific information for you.

Take notes as you ask questions, and close the interview with an action plan. Ask the interviewee if you can contact him or her again with additional questions. Send a thank-you note after your meeting.

> *If you don't know someone already in the field, ask the people in your circle for potential contacts in the industry, company, or job that strikes your interest.*

Types of Job Interviews

The purpose of a job interview is for you and an employer to learn about one another. Employers want to evaluate your qualifications, and you also want to evaluate the employer.

There are several different types of interviews:

TYPE	WHAT TO EXPECT	TIPS
Telephone Screening Interview	A call from an employer to screen you and other candidates for essential criteria.	Have your job search records organized and handy. Refer to your resume as needed.
In-Person Screening Interview	An in-person screening for initial impressions of your attitude, interest, and professional style.	You may not be meeting with the final decisionmaker, but don't slack off. Sell yourself as you would in a regular interview.
Selection Interview	In-depth questions on your qualifications used to evaluate your ability to fit in.	Establish rapport with everyone you meet (before and after the actual interview). Sell yourself as a natural addition to the team.
Work Sample Interview	An opportunity to demonstrate your specific skills. It may be a display of your portfolio or a demonstration of your skills.	Run through different ways to describe the projects in your portfolio. Practice your presentation until it is smooth.

TYPE	WHAT TO EXPECT	TIPS
Peer Group Interview	A meeting with your prospective coworkers, who will evaluate how well you fit in.	Don't forget to smile. It shows confidence.
Group or Panel Interview	Three or more people who will ask you questions on your qualifications and evaluate how you fit in.	Direct your answer to the person who asked the question, but try to maintain eye contact with all group members.
Luncheon Interview	Interview conducted in a restaurant to assess how well you handle yourself in social situations.	Pick easy things to eat so you can answer questions and pay attention to the conversation.
Stress Interview	Questions intended to make you uncomfortable. This is usually a test of how you will handle stress on the job.	Keep your cool and take your time in responding to the questions. Don't take anything personally.
Video Conference Interview	A person-to-person interview by video.	Practice before a video camera or mirror if facing a camera during an interview makes you nervous.

SOURCE: *Creative Job Search Guide,* Minnesota Department of Employment and Economic Development. Copyright © 1994 - 2008. Used by permission.

Finding Your Corporate Match

Gathering facts about a company helps you answer potential interview questions. It also gives you important information on how to match your skills to the company or position.

To complete a successful match, try the following exercise. Divide a piece of paper in half by drawing a line down the middle. On one side, list specific skills, experiences, and abilities needed by the employer. On the other side, write down your qualifications that meet each requirement. Then, draw lines from each employer-need to your matching qualification. Identify your weaknesses by highlighting any areas where you did not have a matching qualification. At the bottom of the page, write down how you can address the skills you lack or list other skills that make up for this weakness. This exercise will help you successfully communicate your qualifications to an employer. Targeting your skills to an employer's needs will show how serious you are about the position or company.

Dress for Civilian Success

Your resume is perfectly fine-tuned and you successfully maneuvered the screening interview. They called you back for a face-to-face interview. Now, it's show time! Your first impression must be a strong one, and that begins with the right attire.

You already know about the importance of appearance. It was drilled into you from day one at boot camp and basic training. You know that your uniform, and how you care for it, says much about your discipline and commitment to the service. And when it comes to uniforms, you've got a whole footlocker full of them. If you're an enlisted Marine, for example, you have your dress blues, evening dress, blue-whites, reds, service uniforms, and utilities. You don't have to guess which uniform is appropriate to wear for a particular occasion. It was all figured out for you and was a distinct part of your military education.

Use your good judgment in dressing for an interview. For example, if you were scheduled to visit the White House, you would not wear desert camies. The same rule applies with a professional job interview. Wear your best. The safest interview uniform is a dark suit (blue, black, grey) and a white shirt,

Dress codes in the workplace are changing and relaxing, but that does not extend to the interview. Once you get the job, you can ask about the appropriate code of dress, written or understood.

with a conservative tie for men. Red is a good color for interview ties. Don't wear the pink panther tie that your kids gave you for Father's Day, even if it is your lucky tie! If you need help, look at what corporate executives profiled in television and magazines wear. Look at what Donald Trump or Condoleeza Rice wears to a business meeting.

For women, a dark suit and a tailored blouse, or a simple dress works well. Pantsuits are perfectly acceptable for today's corporate environment. If you wear a dress or skirt, the hemline should not fall above the knee and the blouse or neckline should not be revealing. Avoid wearing very high heels. In the interview, you want to assure the employer that you know how to exercise good judgment, including how to dress appropriately.

Observe how local politicians dress for an official event. Even if you live in a warm state like California or Florida, where dress tends to be more casual, it's advisable to dress conservatively, regardless of the type of job you seek. Overall, make sure your interview clothes are appropriate for the job. Don't wear a suit to an interview at a construction site or jeans (even black ones) and a blazer to an office setting. Pay attention to the differences in the way people dress, depending on the industry and region of the country. To help you decide what to wear to an interview, visit the company, if possible, and notice what people similarly employed are wearing.

Dress codes in the workplace are changing and relaxing, but that does not extend to the interview. Once you get the job, you can ask about the appropriate code of dress, written or understood.

A company's hiring process may include two or three interviews, especially for professional positions. This doesn't mean you have to buy three different suits if you only have one that's appropriate for interviewing. Still, it's a good idea to invest in three different ties so you can rotate them for different interviews. It's also wise to have more than one dress shirt or blouse, in case one is dirty or at the cleaners and you get a call at 4:45 P.M. to be at an interview at 8:00 A.M. the next morning.

Until you find a job, you want be interview-ready at a moment's notice. Keep your interview suit, ties, and shirts ready to wear. Keep your blouses clean and pressed and make sure you have panty hose with no runs. Keep your shoes clean and polished.

Don't forget what the military taught you about your personal appearance. Like the military, corporate employers generally frown on long or messy facial hair, extreme hairdos, body piercings, and obvious tattoos. Avoid wearing flashy jewelry or strong cologne because they can be irritating and distracting. Likewise, for women, heavy makeup, broken nails, wild nail colors or chipped polish, and poorly fitted clothing reveal a lot to an employer—mainly that you are probably not a good fit for their corporation. Your transition to civilian life will be much smoother if you stick to the standards of neatness and formal dress that you were taught in the military.

Regardless of the position you seek, whether entry-level or executive, office or factory, dress as well as your budget will allow. Your appearance is the first indicator of whether you fit in with the company and the kind of judgment you will use if you are given the job. Dress as if you already have the job— whether executive or factory worker at a company. The bottom line is to invest in one good outfit for your interviews. Always show up to the interview as well groomed as possible. Keep your hair and nails clean and neatly trimmed. It will be worth the expense in the long run.

If you are interviewing for a job that requires special attire and will be expected to demonstrate your skills, wear an appropriate outfit or uniform and be sure it is clean and well pressed. Your appearance will demonstrate your enthusiasm for the work and that you take pride in your skills. For example, if you are applying for a mechanic's position, you may be asked to demonstrate your skills during the interview. Have your work clothes and tools available at the interview, just in case.

Your attire is not just about receiving respect, but conveying it. Your appearance at an interview is a mirror that reflects your personal presence in the work culture. It says a great deal about your work and your judgment. Remember that the very first contact you have with people is visual. Make the first impression a good one. Dress appropriately, dress well.

CHECK YOURSELF...

Create an interview checklist, if you think it might help, so you can guard against costly appearance mistakes during the interview. Don't take a chance that the following behaviors or traits won't negatively affect that first impression:

- Chewing gum

- Smoking (most companies have banned smoking in the workplace; it's a good idea not to come to the interview smelling strongly of tobacco)

- Distracting physical habits such as tapping fingers or clicking pens, bouncing legs or shuffling feet

- Messy or unclean hair

- Extreme hairdo (i.e. lettering cut into it, odd colors, mohawk, spiked)

- Body odor or strong odor of cologne or perfume

- Mini-skirt or revealing cleavage

- Visible tattoos

- Jewelry worn in body piercings

- Dirty, worn or tattered clothing, missing buttons

- Too much jewelry or jewelry attached to odd places visible on the body (such as a nose piercing)

- Extremely worn or unpolished shoes; athletic shoes

- Careless grooming

- Dirty fingernails, chipped polish, or extreme polish colors, like neon or black

Unless you are interviewing for a position in a highly creative field, like a tattoo artist or night club performer, where unusual dress may be an asset, play it safe. Unlike the military, no one dictates what you must wear, but your capacity to exercise good judgment is revealed in the choices you make regarding your attire.

Handling Social Situations during the Interview Process

At times, employers conduct dinner or lunch interviews, which can give insight into your judgment and people skills. Or, they may invite you to attend the company picnic to gauge your interpersonal skills. They may want to know if you can represent the company well at functions. How are your table manners? Are you curt or demeaning to wait-staff? How do you handle yourself if someone jumps in front of you in line or steps on your toe accidentally? Can you dress well for semi-formal or formal company functions? Are you courteous to others? Can you engage appropriately in social conversations? Do you maintain control of your alcohol consumption? Do you treat your spouse with respect around others?

Even if you're having a great time, never forget that you are still being interviewed. You may pass all other aspects of the interview process with flying colors, but lose out on the job because you did not engage well in a social setting.

Selling Yourself

There are few experiences worse than being with an interviewer with whom you don't connect. So, the first step is to build rapport with the interviewer. Some applicants find this easy to do while others consider it a challenge. Building rapport requires finding common ground. Offer a firm handshake and a smile when introducing yourself. Then, break the ice by complimenting the interviewer's company based on your pre-interview research. Say something like, "I understand from my research that your company is the industry leader. That says a lot about your management team and your workforce." Most employees appreciate positive comments about their employer and probably will reinforce the compliment. By starting the conversation on a positive note, you have opened the door to a successful interview because you have established rapport.

Once the initial barrier has been crossed, you can uncover what the interviewer personally seeks that may or may not have been mentioned in the job announcement. You can ask, "Who is your best project manager (or the job title you are seeking), and what makes that person stand out from his or her peers?" In most cases, the interviewer will tell you the most important attributes, so take care to remember the qualities mentioned. For example, the interviewer responds that Gavin Phillips is the top manager because he always meets or exceeds deadlines and maintains cost effectiveness.

As the actual interview progresses, interviewers commonly ask something akin to "Tell me something about yourself." Or, "Tell me about your work experiences." It is at this point that many candidates make a crucial mistake by starting with their schooling or last job experience. In so doing, they miss an outstanding opportunity. This open-ended question is the ideal time to deliver a brief but impactful personal career presentation.

Your personal career presentation is a short, power-packed description of you and your career....Think of the exercise as a minute-long commercial advertising you and why you are the best-qualified candidate.

Your personal career presentation is a short, power-packed description of you and your career. This one-minute presentation is so powerful that you can set the tone for the entire interview because it enables you to favorably impress your interviewers.

Here are guidelines for creating your short talk when preparing for a job interview. Keep it short, giving a quick verbal summary of your career background, skills, and interests. It is a powerful, enthusiastic presentation about you, made by you. It's best to keep this quick oral summary to one minute or less. Otherwise, you will risk losing the interviewer's attention.

Your background research should have given you a good idea of what the employer is looking for. Equipped with this knowledge, you can tailor your presentation to their specific interests and needs. Focus on the highlights of your career, and only those relevant to the current available position. Think of the exercise as a minute-long commercial advertising you and why you are the best-qualified candidate.

Start the process with a statement of who you are—your profession or specialty. Be sure to mention some of the organizations you have worked for or your clients. Highlight a specific accomplishment in your career and talk about the skills and abilities of which you are especially proud.

In professions that require extensive academic preparation (e.g., the legal or medical profession), mention your educational background, qualifications, and professional memberships.

Give the interviewer an assessment of your career progression and how this position will fit well with your experiences. Wrap up your minute with a question that can lead to further discussion on your skills and qualifications. Remember, this is not a repetition of what is written on your resume.

Throughout the remainder of the interview, seize as many opportunities as you can to inform the interviewer of your ability to perform in the ways that have already been identified as important—above and beyond the job description. Show that you have a reputation for timely project delivery. Cite projects you managed that came in at or under budget. The more you mention these attributes, the more you will sound like the kind of top-quality person the company is seeking.

Another important component in selling yourself involves summarizing your background, expertise, and assets, while emphasizing your important attributes whenever possible. During many interviews, the conversation strays from the core competencies you want to emphasize. So, at the conclusion of your interview, say "Thank you for taking the time to interview me and giving me the opportunity to share with you how my people-management skills and track record of exceeding expectations can have a positive impact on your operations."

A Word about Body Language

Have you ever talked with someone who was in the midst of an exciting venture, yet you could tell he or she wasn't the least bit enthused about it? Could you tell that a person was irritated, even though she had a smile on her face? It was probably their body language that gave them away.

Few people are savvy enough to keep their body language on guard at all times. Your body movements communicate just as loudly as the words you speak. Body language often tells others how you feel about yourself, but it also reveals how you feel about the situation in which you're currently engaged.

In a job interview, if your body language is not good, you're going to distract or annoy the people with whom you're talking. We've all seen it. Maybe you've been talking with a person who looks at his watch every two minutes, while trying to appear interested in the conversation. Or, a person walks into a meeting with strangers and keeps her shoulders tight and arms folded, giving a signal that she's not comfortable or confident in the situation. It may not be noticeable to them, but it is extremely noticeable to you.

The first step in gaining control of your body language during the interview is to be conscious of your behavior. Don't make it a big deal; simply do a mental check as the interview progresses. Assess your body language and eye contact. If they are not good, fix it. Stop shaking your leg. Stop the nervous sniffling. Lean back in your seat and sit straight. Relax. Only you will know the particular change in your actions, but the atmosphere in the room will improve because you will be more relaxed. But if you continue an irritating habit of tapping your fingers on the table, the interviewer will remember.

When you speak, lean forward a bit and speak to the person, but sit back while listening. Let your body language be engaging and avoid appearing indifferent to the interviewer. Conversely, don't appear to be nervous and desperate by leaning in too closely.

Regular eye contact is a good thing, but total and complete eye contact is definitely not the way to go in an interview. Frankly, too much eye contact can be downright creepy. Whether speaking or listening, look into your interviewer's eyes frequently, but not constantly.

Pay attention to your body language when you meet a friend or are engaged in conversation with family members. Carry yourself in a similarly comfortable manner when speaking with a potential employer.

Post-Interview

Spend some time thinking about the interview and consider what you have learned from the experience. Evaluate the success and failures and the points at which you excelled and fell short. The more you learn from the interview, the easier the next one will become. You will become more confident because you've had good practice.

Finally, no matter how the interview went overall, write a thank you letter or send an e-mail to each person who took part in the interview. Thank the interviewer(s) for their time, restate your interest in the job, and remind them of your intent to follow up. Mail the letter or send the e-mail the day of or after the interview.

A Winning Attitude Wins the Job

Good companies don't like to hire people who appear desperate, so attitude is critical. Interview with a confident style that shows you *want* the job, but don't give the impression that you desperately *need* the job. The key to an interview that leads to getting the job is a positive attitude. The job interview is no time to be reticent or shy about who you are and what you can do. Modesty can be a fine thing, but it won't impress the employer regarding your capabilities. The interview is about you and no one knows more about you than you. The interview is your turn to show all that is great about you. Remember, resumes don't get hired; people do.

Be prepared for difficult questions and unexpected events, such as delays. Never let these affect your positive attitude. Even if the interviewer looks like he just got through sucking on a sack of lemons, turn those lemons into lemonade. Some interviewers may be difficult intentionally because they want to trip or intimidate you to find out what you're made of. But you have the upper hand when you determine that you will not allow anything to steal your winning attitude. If an interviewer asks you a question that's totally off base (or even illegal), you can salvage the situation by keeping a positive attitude. For example, if an interviewer asks "How will you be able to

The interview is about you and no one knows more about you than you. The interview is your turn to show all you have to offer.

165

work overtime as a single parent with three children?" Instead of getting bent out of shape, you can keep a positive attitude and explain that you are fully aware of the job's demands and are prepared to meet the challenges.

Suppose that you are in the middle of an interview for a great job with a company you really want to work with. Then, you commit a most unfortunate faux pas and you put your foot in your mouth. No matter what it is that makes you think you blew the interview, it is possible to salvage the situation. If you commit a faux pas during the interview, don't assume your chances for the job are blown. Minor transgressions can be overlooked by the interviewer if you follow up in a professional manner and simply apologize for being tardy, a ringing cell phone, using profanity, or whatever it is that happened in the interview.

Another strategy is to remedy the situation with follow up communication. Today, it is common for interviewees to follow a first interview with an acknowledgment of thanks. If you really want the job, try to correct your error with a well-written thank you note. The interview process can be stressful and you may not even realize something went wrong until after you are gone. Thank you notes are a good way to clarify any misunderstandings from the interview. If you made a major mistake, don't over-apologize; simply add a polite sidebar to the standard thank you note that you would have written anyway.

Are you willing to relocate? Talk about your flexibility. Don't make it seem like you are willing to do the employer a favor by moving and don't discuss that you really don't want to move.

What is your greatest weaknesses as an employee? Only give an answer that can be turned around to your benefit. Don't mention that you are quick-tempered. Instead, mention that you sometimes grow impatient

The interview process can be stressful and you may not even realize something went wrong until after you are gone.

with people who do not live up to their potential on the job. Always present the positive side to any weakness you may have.

Why do you want to change jobs? If you are asked about a current or former employer, never talk negatively about him or her. Speaking poorly about former employers only reflects negatively on you. No matter how terrible a current or former employer may be, focus on the positive aspects of the company and what you gained from employment there.

There have been times when less qualified candidates have been given the job because of their positive attitude. That's one reason why employers can't rely on resumes and applications alone. Confidence in a job interview is a good thing. Show your potential employer that no matter who the other candidates are, or how qualified, you know you're the best person for the job.

Consider the following tips to help you communicate your winning attitude to an employer:

- Be on time.
- Leave your cell phone in the car or turn it off until the interview is over.
- Smile and demonstrate that you are happy to be granted an interview.
- Maintain frequent eye contact during the interview.
- Don't watch the clock.
- Dress a step above what you would wear on the job and wear an outfit that makes you feel as though you can conquer the world.
- Get a good night's sleep before the interview so you'll be well rested and alert.
- Eat a good breakfast so your stomach won't be growling during the interview.
- Don't discuss illegal, sensitive, or discriminatory subjects such as politics, race, gender, age, religion, or national origin.
- Don't discuss salary (unless pressed).
- Don't tell the employer how much you need a job.
- Maintain a professional attitude and don't get too comfortable with the interviewer.
- Stay aware of your non-verbal cues and body language.

Thank You Letter

It is standard procedure and good corporate etiquette to send the interviewer a thank you letter a day or so following the interview.

3073 W. 135th Terrace
St. Petersburg, FL 33404
May 28, 2009

Theresa F. Spencer
Vice President of Marketing
Seacoast Products Incorporated
8300 Lakeside Drive
Clearwater, FL 33714

Dear Mrs. Spencer:

Thank you again for the opportunity to interview for the marketing position. I especially appreciated your hospitality and enjoyed meeting you and members of your staff.

The interview convinced me of how compatible my background, interest, and skills are with the goals of Seacoast Products, Inc. As I mentioned during our conversation, my 11 years of international experience as an Army international information officer and multilingual abilities have prepared me well for the global markets position with your company. I am confident my work for you will result in market expansion within the first two years.

For more information on my impact while in the service, feel free to contact Colonel Dexter Love at 202-726-0132. I spoke with Dexter this morning and mentioned your interest in this program.

I look forward to seeing you again.

Sincerely,

Lawrence Valentine

Lawrence Valentine

Acknowledgment Letter

If you find out almost immediately that you didn't get the job, it's still a good idea to send an acknowledgment by letter. Companies hire all the time and a good follow up letter may help you to stand out in an employer's memory when the next position vacancy opens.

51614 Post Road
#224
Dallas, TX 75231

April 29, 2009

Mr. Cedric Armstrong
Myers Research Corporation
1296 Sweetwater Crossings
Plano, TX 75072

Dear Mr. Armstrong:

I greatly appreciated your consideration for the research associate position. While I am disappointed in not being selected for employment, the interview process provided me with an opportunity to learn a great deal about your corporation. It was a pleasure to meet you and your team of highly competent researchers.

When another position becomes available with your company, please keep me in mind. I have a strong interest in working in this field, especially with the Myers Research Corporation. I believe that my skills and training would fit well with the company. I will be closely following the progress of your company over the coming months. Perhaps we will be in touch at some later date.

Best wishes,

Rasheed Martin

Rasheed Martin

Job Acceptance Letter

Congratulations! You got the job. Now, all you have to do is let your employer know that you accept the position. Even though you cinched the job, you still need to make a good impression. Continue on the path that got you the job by writing a short but professional acceptance letter.

8585 St. James Court
Minneapolis, MN 55439

June 7, 2009

Samuel Greenlee
Vice President
New Horizon Aircraft Corporation
5000 New Horizon Road
St. Paul, MN 55102

Dear Mr. Greenlee:

I am pleased to accept your offer of employment, and I look forward to joining you and your staff next month.

The systems engineer position is ideally suited to my background and interests. I am excited to give New Horizon the best of my many years of training and experience in the field.

I understand from my communication with the human resources division that I am scheduled to begin work on July 1, 2009. In the interim, if there are any pre-employment tasks that need to be completed, please contact me at 612-555-4321.

It was a pleasure meeting with you and the other departmental staff. I appreciate the proficient manner in which the hiring was conducted and am excited to be affiliated with such an innovative, professional organization.

Sincerely,

Alicia Gilmore

Alicia Gilmore

EFFECTIVE ANSWERS TO LIKELY INTERVIEW QUESTIONS

Few interview questions are as simple as they seem. Behind one interview question lies a concern or another question. Your goal is to project what the interviewer is looking for in an answer. In other words, why is the interviewer really asking you this question?

A Likely Question: Why do you want to work for the Trisys Tech Corporation?

The interviewer's concern is whether you are genuinely interested in working for their company or you are using a machine-gun approach to finding a job.

A Good Response: I have carefully considered my career options, along with the companies where I have applied. When I saw the announcement for this position, I knew I had found a good match. I can bring to this job seven years of knowledge and leadership experience, plus my ability to communicate effectively while building customer relationships. That, along with my flexibility and organizational skills, makes me a perfect fit with this company's mission. From what I have observed, there are some challenges here, but I am excited to be taking them on. I hope you believe, as I do, that I have the skills and qualifications you need to get the job done.

A Likely Question: How long have you been looking for a job?

The interviewer is trying to determine whether some major issue has kept you from gainful employment or whether you're not particularly interested in regular employment. Is there something wrong with the way you conduct yourself that other employers have picked up on?

A Good Response: After being discharged from the service, I decided to take some time off to assess my career interests and set some goals. I gained many new skills while serving in the U.S. Marines, and I wanted to make sure that I chose a career path that would support my life goals. I have been actively job searching for about four weeks. Since I have a definite goal, I've been judicious in selecting the positions I consider. Your company and this position are of great interest to me because I believe I possess the kind of skills needed.

A Likely Question: What steps did you take to prepare for this interview?

The interviewer is trying to determine the extent of your interest in the position, and perhaps in the company as well. Do you want the position badly enough to do something extra to find out about the job?

A Good Response: When I became aware of the position, I immediately visited the company's website and read the mission statement. I was instantly interested in the position. I was impressed with the information given about the company's history, its founders, and current executive staff. Once the interview was established, I inquired among friends and acquaintances to find out more about the company's reputation. Everything I read and everyone I spoke to confirmed that this is a good company to work for and that it has a strong standing in the community.

A Likely Question: How do you stay current and informed regarding the industry?

The employer wants to know whether you are only trying to get a job or whether you are self-motivated and will keep your skills current with industry standards.

A Good Response: I enjoy staying informed about current events, especially regarding topics of interest to this industry. My time in the military only served to broaden my interest in the field. I do a lot of reading—including the business section of newspapers and magazines. I recently joined a professional organization so that I can network with colleagues on a national level. I have taken classes and seminars whenever they are made available. I also stay current with several newsgroups and blogs that specialize in the field.

A Likely Question: Have you had any experience with planning and coordinating a project from start to finish?

The interviewer is looking for specific information regarding your success in past endeavors as an indicator of your future performance.

A Good Response: I had the opportunity to establish a service technicians' training module and develop the project from creation to implementation. After developing a draft for the project, I conducted a series of ideation sessions to engage in creative brainstorming with industry professionals. With their input, I completed the module proposal, incorporating the best ideas from those sessions. Then, I created a production schedule to ensure that we remained on target with implementation. We had a deadline to meet, so I did periodic checks with the teams. Within three months, the impact of the training module exceeded all projections. The training module led to a 20% increase in work productivity among the technicians and a 30% cost savings. It was a great team effort and a big success. I received a commendation for my leadership, but what I was most proud of was the team spirit and cooperation that made it a true success.

A Likely Question: What kinds of people do you find it most difficult to work with?

This question is designed to determine whether you are able to work in a diverse environment and if you are flexible enough to be a good team member.

A Good Response: In the military, you work closely with a group of people, sometimes in true life-and-death situations. You become a family very quickly for the sake of survival. I'm grateful for that experience because it taught me a lifetime lesson about teamwork and cooperation. Naturally, I bonded with some personalities more quickly than with others. Nevertheless, because we were thrust into a situation in which we had to cooperate, I managed to work with everyone. My primary challenge was working with a fellow soldier who was dishonest about work issues. He often attempted to take credit for work that the entire team had accomplished. So that we could continue working together, however, I decided to talk with him and emphasize how his actions were affecting the entire team. From that conversation, I learned something about his own trust issues and all of us discovered ways that we could help each other and make our team stronger. That experience taught me that sometimes what we perceive about others is not always the reality.

A Likely Question: Our managers often have to work longer than eight hours in a day. Would that pose a problem for you?

By asking this question, the interviewer is determining whether you are a workaholic or a person who requires strict balance. Are you willing to do what is necessary to get the job done?

A Good Response: When I was deployed to Afghanistan, I would often work 12- to 16-hour days. So I have no problem working long hours. I don't consider myself a workaholic; I strive to work smarter, not necessarily longer. My goal is to get the job done well, and in the most efficient manner.

A Likely Question: How do you adapt to new situations?

In other words, will you be difficult to work with or do you have a "that's not my job" kind of mentality?

A Good Response: Being in the military has prepared me for this part of any job. Being on-call 24 hours a day, as I was in the Marines, I quickly learned to move first, think second. Being flexible and adapting quickly is essential to military service. Lives depend on it. I bring that same orientation and skill to my post-military service. I will do whatever it takes to get the job done as scheduled.

A Likely Question: What is your minimum salary requirement for this job?

The interviewer is trying to determine whether the company can afford to hire you or whether you can be hired for less than the amount budgeted.

A Good Response: Before we discuss salary, I need more information about the job and the responsibilities involved. Can you give me an idea of the salary range budgeted for this position?

A Likely Question: If we make you an offer today, are you prepared to accept it?

The employer is genuinely interested in you and doesn't want to risk losing you to another offer elsewhere.

A Good Response: Based on my preliminary research and the information I have gathered during the interview process, I am in a position to consider a reasonable offer. I do, however, require 24 hours to firmly consider such a major life decision. If I am given an offer today, I can give you a firm decision by this time tomorrow.

THE INTERVIEW: DRESSING THE PART

The first few minutes of your interview are the most critical because you only get one chance for a good first impression. Before you speak your first word, your appearance has already revealed volumes about you. Your attire cannot communicate your job skills, but you'll be judged to some degree according to what you wear. The clothes you choose for an interview should not only make you feel good about yourself but should project a professional image that fits the requirements of the position and the company. A simple key to projecting a professional image is to dress tastefully and conservatively. This holds true for both men and women.

Dressing for Success: Women

Suit/Dress

Choose a conservative, matching business suit or dress (preferably made from a natural or woven-blend fabric) in a color that complements your skin and hair color, such as blue, navy, gray, beige, tan, or brown. If you wear a skirt or dress, the length should fall no higher than the bottom of your knee.

Blouse/Top

Choose a simple cut or shell, either white or a soft, solid color. Avoid very frilly styles and low-cut necklines.

Shoes

Wear sensible, comfortable well-polished shoes—business pumps or medium heels in a color that matches your outfit. Stay away from stiletto heels for the interview.

Hosiery

By all means wear them to a professional interview. Choose a color that matches your skin tone. Avoid patterned or lacy hosiery.

Purse

If you carry a portfolio, choose one that can accommodate your keys, identification, and perhaps a few dollars. Leave your cell phone in your car or turn it off during the interview. If you do carry a purse, choose a small or medium-sized bag that complements yours shoes and outfit. Avoid sporting designer purses that attract attention.

Accessories

Choose simple jewelry and other accessories; don't use too many. If you are wearing a scarf, you don't need a necklace too. Stay away from bangles or other jewelry that make a lot of noise. Wear one set of earrings only and no more than one ring on each hand. Take out all body piercing jewelry.

Nail Polish

Make sure your nails are manicured and clean, with either clear or a conservative color of polish; no chipped polish or broken nails.

Makeup

Use a minimal level of makeup and avoid loud colors of eye shadow or lipstick. Stay away from dramatic looks. You want to emphasize your skills, not your face or any part of your body.

Dressing for Success: Men

Suits

Dark blue, gray, brown, or very tiny pinstripes made from the best quality fabric that you can afford. Your suit should be properly tailored and freshly dry-cleaned.

Shirts

A quality white, classic collar preferred. Most importantly, make sure the shirt is pressed.

Ties

Complement your suit with a good silk or good quality-blend tie that is either solid or has a subtle pattern, like stripes or dots. The tip of your tie should end near the center of your belt buckle. If you need to invest a little more in a longer tie because you are taller or heavier, by all means do so. It's worth the investment.

Shoes

Wear highly polished loafers or laced dress shoes in a dark color like black or brown, complemented by dark, thin socks.

Facial Hair

Employers tend to prefer no beards; and mustaches are sometimes negative. If you do have facial hair, always make sure it is neatly trimmed.

Jewelry

Keep chains or necklaces tucked inside you shirt collar. Do not wear rings other than a wedding ring or college ring. If you wear an earring or any other body piercing, take it out for the interview.

Attire Tips for Both Men and Women

- Maintain a well-groomed hairstyle.
- Always have clean, manicured fingernails.

- Use a minimal perfume or cologne. If used, apply it at least two hours before the interview.

- Empty your pockets/purse of noisemakers and bulging objects—tinkling coins, mobile phone, gum, cigarettes, etc.

- No body piercing jewelry (nose rings, eyebrow rings, etc.).

- Ask a friend to critique your attire.

Employers notice the little things. Therefore, you must pay attention to even smallest details. Interviewers often consider the condition of your shoes as a way to tell whether you pay attention to detail. To that end, avoid shoes that are dusty or have run-down heels.

If at any time you are unsure, just remember to use common sense. If you come to your interview dressed in business attire and your potential employer is not, don't worry. You are the one looking for a job. It is far better to be dressed professionally than to be dressed too casually. Employers want people who are flexible and broad-based in their abilities to learn, grow, and contribute. Being dressed in a suit won't hurt your ability to be seen as someone employable, but being inappropriately dressed could.

Appearance can be a powerful and useful tool in influencing the kind of message you send to others. With a little common sense and attention to details, you can easily make sure that the first impression is your best.

MANAGING
BEHAVIOR-BASED
QUESTIONS

The following is a list of typical behavior-based questions from *The Ultimate Job Search Kit* by Damir Joseph Stimac (Seaton Corp, 1997). The competencies sought by the interviewer are listed in parentheses.

- Describe a situation in which you had to use reference materials to write a research paper. What was the topic? What journals did you read? (Research/Written communication)

- Give me a specific example of a time when a coworker or classmate criticized your work in front of others. How did you respond? How has that event shaped the way you communicate with others? (Oral communication)

- Give me a specific example of a time when you sold your supervisor or professor on an idea or concept. How did you proceed? What was the result? (Assertiveness)

- Describe the system you use for keeping track of multiple projects. How do you track your progress so that you can meet deadlines? How do you stay focused? (Commitment to task)

- Tell me about a time when you came up with an innovative solution to a challenge your company or class was facing. What was the challenge? What role did others play? (Creativity and Imagination)

- Describe a specific problem you solved for your employer or professor. How did you approach the problem? What role did others play? What was the outcome? (Decision making)

- Describe a time when you got coworkers or classmates who disliked each other to work together. How did you accomplish this? What was the outcome? (Teamwork)

- Tell me about a time when you failed to meet a deadline. What things did you fail to do? What were the repercussions? What did you learn? (Time management)

- Describe a time when you put your needs aside to help a coworker or classmate understand a task. How did you assist them? What was the result? (Flexibility)

- Describe two specific goals you set for yourself and how successful you were in meeting them. What factors led to your success in meeting your goals? (Goal setting)

Finally, the toughest interview question of all: What salary are you looking for? Most people aren't comfortable talking about salary requirements. Somehow it seems rude or impolite. But in a job interview, it can be a make-or-break question. If you are asked the question, know how to cut the best deal you can without sounding too greedy or pricing yourself out of the market.

If you can, try to get the interviewer to give you an idea of the salary range before you commit yourself. If you find the salary range unattractive, make the case for a higher one. If the company can't agree to your salary requirement, then decide whether to consider their offer.

Tell Me about Yourself

During the job interview, you want to impress the interviewer by providing brief, to-the-point answers that relate your skills and experience to their needs. Where possible, your answers should blend your knowledge of the firm based on your research and networking activities. This is also the time to impress the interviewer with your knowledge of the organization by asking insightful questions that demonstrate your knowledge and interest in their company. In so doing, you will help the interviewer see you as the right person for the job. Your goal at this stage in the process is to motivate the interviewer to ask you back for a second interview. You should practice for the interview by mentally addressing several questions most interviewers ask. Most of these questions will relate to your educational background, work experience, career goals, personality, and related concerns. Some of the most frequently asked questions include the following areas.

Education

Describe your educational background. How have you improved your education while in the military? What plans do you have to continue your education? What military training courses did you take? How did you do in these courses? How are they relevant to this job? Did you take any correspondence courses? What were they? Why did you attend university (college or school)? Why did you major in this particular field? What was your grade point average? What subjects did you enjoy the most? The least? Why? What leadership positions did you hold? How did you finance your education? If you started all over, what would you change about your education? Why were your grades so low? So high? Did you do the best you could in school? If not, why not? What skills do you hope to acquire through education during the next five years?

Work Experience

How many different jobs have you held? What were your major achievements in each of your past jobs? What did you do in the military? Tell me about your different jobs. How does your military experience relate to this job? What did you enjoy the most about your military career? The least? What is your typical workday like? What functions do you enjoy doing the most? What did you like about your boss? Dislike? Which job did you enjoy the most? The least? Why? Have you ever been fired? Why?

Career Goals

Why did you decide to leave the military? Why do you want to join our organization? Why do you think you are qualified for this position? Why are you looking for another job? Why do you want to make a career change? What ideally would you like to do? Why should we hire you? How would you improve our operations? What do you want to be doing five years from now? How much do you want to be making five years from now? What are your short-range and long-range career goals? If you could choose a job and organization, which would you choose? What other jobs and companies are you considering? When will you be ready to begin work? How do you feel about relocation? Traveling? Working overtime? What attracted you to our organization?

Personality and Other Concerns

Tell me about yourself. What are your major weaknesses? Your major strengths? What causes you to lose your temper? What do you do in your spare time? Any hobbies? What types of books do you read? What role does your family play in your career? How well do you work under pressure? In meeting deadlines? Tell me about your management philosophy. How much initiative do you take? What types of people do you prefer working with? How creative, analytical, tactful, etc., are you? If you could change your life, what would you do differently?

What Other Vets Are Saying...

I spent 25 years in the Air Force and would not trade a minute of it. My family and I made some of the best friends anyone can make and the jobs I had were literally the best.

Like the Air Force, the outside world or civilian community is no different in many regards. Networking is critical. Having a good resume is important because it will tell potential employers what you bring to the table; but networking is what will get you in the door for an interview.

If you're making a career out of the military, it's best to plan and prepare for your transition five years before retirement. One of the best ways to network is to take that HQ job, get on new program initiatives, or take on responsibilities that will expose you to the industry or the civilian world. As you are exposed to them, make contacts and keep the names of contacts and their numbers where you can readily locate them. Be sure you call them a few times a year to keep in touch so they don't forget you.

Today, I have a very rewarding job in the military aviation industry that I would not trade for anything. I was qualified for the job and had all of the credentials, but it was the networking and the actual contacts I'd made that got me where I am today.

You can't get ahead without someone helping you and having faith in you and giving you a chance—just like in the military.

It's really critical today to be prepared educationally and to have the experience. But if no one knows who you are and what you can do, it won't matter. Networking makes the difference!

Bernard G.
Retired Air Force

CHAPTER FIVE

NETWORKING—USING YOUR MILITARY CONNECTIONS

Job search and career networking are two of the most successful ways to find a new job; but to a novice, both strategies can seem intimidating. It doesn't have to be. While traveling back to his base, one Air Force officer ended up in a conversation on an airplane with someone who was looking for an aeronautical engineering job. The man sitting next to him just happened to be an ex-military who was in the same field. In the end, he assisted the fellow passenger in getting the kind of job he was looking for to make his career transition by making a couple of telephone calls to veterans in the field who were in hiring positions. It turned out that the man was well respected in the field. The telephone calls from him helped the Air Force officer to make a smooth transition into civilian employment.

Jobs can sometimes come unexpectedly, simply because a friend or acquaintance knows your background and skills. You've developed a great network in the military. Your service-related connections can be an extremely powerful tool, but for most people, it is very informal. You will need to use every advantage available to you, so network!

More than ever, organizations are looking for well-rounded individuals, and your military experience and network can be a strong foundation for the next step in your civilian career path. The military has a very strong culture and great internal networks. Many people have discovered career opportunities through their military relationships. Potential employers with military experience understand the value of your training and understand the diligence, character, and skills developed within the military.

Finding a job, especially when making a significant career change like a military transition, is hard work. The best shot you have at finding a job or getting on a career path in the least amount of time is using your network. Use your network of friends, colleagues, and family, job listings provided by your installation's transition office, the local personnel office, or even the nearest community college.

It's not just about who you know, it's also about who they know. When you tell your friends, family members, acquaintances, and fellow servicemembers that you're looking to venture into a certain field, you can ask them to spread the word. You may be amazed at how fast the news of your transition plan travels, even among a network outside of your own.

Using your network saves you time in a job search because you won't have to do such a hard sell to convince an employer about your character. Your network will have already sold you. Companies like to hire based on testimonials of people they already trust.

Networking Simplified

Networking is simply the act of establishing ties between people who share commonalities—hobbies, experiences, interests, careers, etc. It is the art of building alliances. Networking can be as simple as asking, "Hey, does anybody know the name of a good realtor?" It's those same kinds of questions and introductory conversations that serve as the networking lifelines for departing and retiring servicemembers.

The most important feature of networking is letting other people know what you want and need—especially when what you need is employment. Networking is quite possibly the *most important* step in a job seeker's success. Job seekers need a network of career contacts that can provide support, information, and job leads.

Networking is not contacting everyone you know at the end of your transition process and asking if they know of any job openings. Truthfully, networking starts long before your job search, and you probably don't even realize you've been doing it. You probably began networking long before your formal transition process started.

Your networking can be as formal and structured as informational interviews or as relaxed and casual as a conversation at the local gathering place for servicemembers and retirees. Networking can start by striking up a conversation while waiting in line at the Base Exchange or Post Exchange (BX/PX), or at the barbershop, or during a chance encounter in the parking lot.

For separatees and retirees, personal networking assistance can begin at the closest reserve center, recruiting station, or organization for former military. Many communities have welcome wagons or community centers, which function as networking hubs that can include military contacts. Let the coordinator know who or what you're looking for, and they can put you in contact.

To Network or Not to Network?

For many people, networking conjures an image of politicking, and is regarded in a negative light. They think of networking as a lot of insincere, ego-driven interactions. Sometimes that may be true; however, networking does have rewarding and positive aspects.

Regardless of how you feel about networking, the truth is that it's critical to a successful career transition and must be used effectively—not only in your initial career change but also throughout the remainder of your civilian working life. The bottom line is that networking is a good way to meet new people and look for what you need, whether it is a job or a good auto mechanic.

Why Should You Network?

Networking creates opportunities for job seekers to meet hiring managers or people who can put them in touch with hiring managers. Networking is also a means of gaining valuable information about a company and its employees that is not common knowledge nor available through the company's publications or website. Networking can yield critical information about personalities, employee morale, salary ranges, financial soundness, or other information of value that would be critical during an interview. That kind of privileged information would prove invaluable to helping you make a decision about whether or not you want to work for that company.

Networking can create opportunities for you to meet a potential employer's key players in an informal situation, which may also allow you to find out about job opportunities before they are advertised. An organization event may create a position for you, if you have the critical skills they need. One network often leads you to another network, which eventually leads you to a job. Think about this rationally. Why would any organization interview candidates for a job and hire an unknown person when, other things being equal, they know you and your professional and personal traits from a previous association. Why would an employer take a chance on an unknown when you are a known candidate with a proven track record?

Beyond looking for a job, you can use your network to learn about different careers and industries. Your contacts may be able to introduce you to specific companies. People are often hired by someone who knows someone who knows someone else. It is not uncommon for job seekers to be hired by someone in their network. Therefore, the more expansive your network, the better chance you have of getting the job or getting into the career field that you love.

When Should You Start?

Even if you are still in the military, you can start building a network to help you identify job leads and even obtain a job once you enter the civilian workforce. Your networking contacts will likely come in two different ways. First, you have been networking throughout your military career with people you worked with, for, or supervised. These associations have formed your reputation and you have very little control over them. They reflect your professional work skills, how you interact with others, and your moral and ethical character. Second, some within your networking system are contacts you intentionally developed through an association of friends and associates, professional and social clubs, or by seizing opportunities to meet people who may help you in the transition process.

How Do You Begin to Network?

To put your network into place, start reaching out to family, friends, neighbors, old classmates, military alumni, etc., to learn more about their careers and get a better understanding of their daily routines and responsibilities. Once your network begins to take shape, your contacts will probably refer you to helpful people with new ideas and perspectives. Soon, you could find yourself with a network of job resources you never dreamed possible.

Your network will be especially helpful in identifying potential civilian jobs that align with your interests and strengths. This can ultimately help you streamline your job search. As a result, you will end up with a more defined set of personal goals that can translate into a more focused resume and efficient search process.

After you have determined your post-military career focus—what you want to do and possibly where you want to do it—make a list of people and organizations in that field and start networking. In some instances, you will join a local chapter of the organization you have targeted. In other cases, you may want to join an organization simply to meet people who know other people, such as a social, civic, or advocacy organization.

Networking for Officers

As any servicemember can attest, the military and civilian worlds operate differently. Military officers who are networking should not expect that their rank will influence people in a civilian business capacity. A high military rank may help in certain contexts, but probably will not be the foundation of your network.

Although networking may be the single most important factor of a successful career transition, generally speaking, military officers are not trained to value it and therefore, don't care much about networking. Since making such connections was never a part of their career mobility, it was not a part of the military culture. Conversely, in the corporate world, having a strong network of friends, clubs, and business associates is critical to job competition and upward mobility.

Networking pays great dividends and should become the target of your energies during the transition process. It has been estimated that as many as

85% of all jobs are found through networking, so the majority of your energy should be directed to this area.

Networking outside your Service branch community can lead to multiple opportunities. For example, ACAP has a comprehensive job-hunting checklist, while the Department of the Navy (DoN) also offers a host of opportunities for meeting people and applying for DoN jobs.

Networking is a proven and effective way to help you gain access to information about the best jobs.

Seven Simple Rules for Networking

Wouldn't it be a great world if everyone had equal information and access to all of the jobs that are out there? It would be nice, but that's just not the way the job market works. The truth is, some of the best jobs out there are never publicly posted or listed in the classifieds. Networking is a proven and effective way to help you gain access to information about the best jobs. That's when it's time to put your military networking power into action!

The best place to start networking may be with the people you assume are going to be the least helpful. Have lunch with them or invite them out for coffee. By engaging with the people you assume will be the least helpful, you will not feel nervous or needy and will learn how you confidently express what you need.

So, how do you apply for jobs that aren't advertised anywhere but exist only in the minds of America's inaccessible employment movers and shakers? There are many ways to go about it.

- Talk to people who know people who can help you out.

- Contact people who can give insight into conducting a job search.

- Interview people who can help you pursue your career goal after your military transition.

- Converse with strangers at parties and social gatherings.

- E-mail, write, or cold-call people you've read about in the newspaper.

- Write cordial letters to community leaders.

- Volunteer to work at important civic or social events or gatherings that will expose you to people in your chosen career field.

- Cultivate an arsenal of contacts.

If the thought of networking makes you shiver, think of it as a game of sport or a personal challenge. The following seven guidelines for networking provide strategies for success:

1. Think of Everyone as a Networking Contact

Think of every person you know who could possibly serve as a contact. Be careful not to restrict your network to only the people you first identified as being able to help you out. Friendly, accessible people in unrelated fields often have contacts they would be happy to share with you—your next-door neighbor, the den mother for your son's Boy Scout troop, or even your aunt Elvira. Who knows? Aunt Elvira once may have been nanny to the most successful business family in town and keeps in contact with them frequently.

Keep in touch with the extroverts. People who maintain contact with a diverse crowd, either through work or volunteer activities, can be extremely helpful. To get you started with your list, here are some of the kinds of people and places that can help build your base network.

Alumni (high school, college, military school)
Business conferences
Business executives
Class reunions
Club meetings
Club members
Cocktail parties
Community groups and events
Community leaders
Continuing education classes
Conventions

Entrepreneurs

Family friends

Former coworkers and supervisors

Fundraisers

Hair stylists or barbers

Internet blogs, listservs, and social networking groups

Journalists

Neighbors

News media

Non-profit directors

Political events

Politicians

Postal carrier

Primary care physician

Professional associations

Professors

Relatives

Religious affiliations

Religious leaders

Volunteer opportunities

Voter education/registration events

2. Plan to Network Wherever You Go

While it's essential that you are honest and relaxed while networking, you should not go at it unprepared. Networking can be compared to a political campaign. Just as politicians think about what they need to accomplish when making an appearance or giving a speech, you should also have a definite approach to your networking opportunities. In other words, get a game plan. Before you charm your way into a business conference, cocktail party, or public event, do your homework. It's important to know who will be there (if you can obtain this information) and how each person can help you in your job search or career change. Determine whom you want to meet and why they are important to know. Then, once you have your golden opportunity to talk with a key resource person, don't waste that precious time—theirs or yours.

Know the information you want to walk away with. Determine what you want to convey to the people you meet. Finally, have a backup plan and be flexible. You might not meet the people you planned to talk with, but you might meet their executive assistant, immediate subordinate, or even their college-bound daughter that will open the door to an opportunity you hadn't planned.

3. Care about People and Relationships

Some people tend to approach career networking like trading stocks on the open market. The person networking has no interest in the companies or individuals behind those stocks. He just wants the profits that the trades will bring. A person who approaches networking like it is a profession takes full advantage of every encounter. He carefully listens to useful information that the contact gives him, until he no longer perceives the information as valuable to him. The contact is merely a commodity being traded.

The most effective networking calls for investing in relationships. Your best networking efforts mean building relationships with people and caring about their affiliated companies or industries. A strong network comes from ongoing encounters that are built through mutually beneficial contacts. For example, you may call or e-mail a new contact for advice or share a link to a website containing important information about the industry. Over time, this sharing leads to a relationship or strong association. You become members of one another's circle. You become acquaintances or friends for the sake of the relationship, not simply because you expect it will benefit you later.

Getting to know another person requires a time investment. This approach to networking and business, in general, reveals integrity, maturity, and patience. When you take the time to cultivate relationships—business, social, or professional, it demonstrates that you are a person who is worthy of trust. When people trust you, they sense that you are part of the same circle. Then, they will be glad to recommend you to others for a new position or opportunity.

People allow others into their circle when they perceive genuine interest. When you have the proper credentials, and a reputation among those in your network as one who truly cares about others, it enhances your marketability even more!

4. Remember, Networking Knows No Bounds

Anywhere and everywhere you go can be an opportunity to network. First, there are the usual events—cocktail parties, class reunions, corporate events, political gatherings, and social and civic affairs are all places where you expect to network and gather a few business cards, phone numbers, and e-mail addresses.

But there are many other places to network—simple, everyday encounters that can surprise you. Making your network work requires flexibility. But the reality is that some of the invaluable contacts we make and the once-in-a-lifetime opportunities we get often surprise us. Good networkers are flexible people who approach opportunities to connect as a free-flowing endeavor that extends far beyond hotel conference rooms and hiring managers and interviews.

You can never tell who you will meet walking on the indoor track at the gym or in the sauna. Conversations in long lines at the grocery store or the post office can yield valuable information for your job hunt.

Don't hesitate to network with someone who has no obvious connection to your ambitions. Your new contact may be able to give you relevant names of friends and colleagues who are directly connected to what you would like to do. The odds of chance can place you in an airline seat right next to someone who knows someone who wants to hire someone in your chosen field.

Don't overlook any opportunity that arises. Chalk these encounters up to pure dumb luck or karma, but your ability to be flexible and work with the situation can be the ticket to taking you where you want to be in your career. You can turn a chance meeting into a golden opportunity for success.

5. Make It Easy for Your Contacts

When you call, meet with, or write to a potential contact, make it as easy as possible for them to help you. Explain what you want specifically, and ask detail-oriented questions.

For example, "I'm looking for jobs in arts administration. Do you know anyone who works at the Arts Council? May I have their names and phone numbers? May I use your name when I introduce myself to them?" Another entrée into a productive conversation is to solicit career tips and advice from your contact. Most people love to talk about themselves. By asking your contact to offer valuable insight from his or her personal experiences and successes, he or she will feel important and respected. Who doesn't like to feel like an expert?

Be sure to avoid making general demands, such as, "Do you know of any jobs that would be good for me?" This sort of question is overwhelming and puts an undue burden on your contact.

6. Stay Connected

Have you ever had an old contact call you because he or she is job-hunting? After a couple of pleasantries, what could have been a casual, friendly conversation turns into a monologue spewed out by a motor-mouth who makes you wish you'd let the call go to voicemail. Out-of-the-blue contacts don't work well when they're made out of desperation.

When you make critical network connections, nurture them as best you can and keep them warm. Send a note or an e-mail thanking your contact for the specific way(s) that he or she helped you. Even powerful, top-level executives like to feel needed and appreciated. In fact, most people enjoy being able to offer help and encourage others along their career path.

By keeping in touch with your contacts, they are more likely to think of you when a career opportunity arises. They can probably help you get your foot in the door, and maybe even land the job. Try to find a way to stay on their radar screens without being pushy or invasive.

7. Organize Your Network

Whether you use a personal digital assistant (PDA), a computer database, or a simple spiral bound notepad, it's important to keep a record of your networking activities and contacts. Keep track of who each person is, how you met him or her, relevant associations, and how that person can help you in the future regarding your career options.

Even though you may still be in the military, you can start building a network that can help you identify and obtain a job once you are ready to enter the civilian workforce. You don't need to have a network of high-powered corporate types or military officers. Effective networking for your career transition can start by reaching out to friends, family, old schoolmates, neighbors, military alumni, etc. to learn more about their careers and get a better understanding of their daily routines and responsibilities. Use your network to learn about different careers and industries.

Once you have gone through these steps, you can use your network to identify potential civilian jobs that meet with your interests and strengths. This information can ultimately help you streamline your job search. As a result, you will end up with a more defined set of personal goals that can help you produce a more focused resume and efficient search process.

Another Side of the Networking Story...

I can't stress enough how important it is to network. Everyone I served with in the military knew that I wanted to retire in northern Georgia where contractor positions are abundant. One day, our deputy commander came to me and said, "I have a friend who is the senior vice president with a firm in Atlanta. Send your resume to him."

I did and received a call from the senior vice president later that same week and was hired from a phone interview. Now that I'm retired from the military, I have a great job with no deployment worries, and I'm making good money.

Ted B.
Former Army Lt. Colonel

• • • • • •

If you are separating or retiring from the military and plan on staying in the local area, start networking as soon as possible. If you intend on staying in the same line of work, start talking with your supervisors about continuing employment with that same organization as a civilian or federal employee. Your current or past supervisors know you best and know what you are capable of doing.

Sam K.
Retired Army Sergeant

• • • • • •

Having a good resume is important but networking is what really gets your foot in the door. It's never too late to work on your transition plan, and one of the best ways to do that is to take that HQ job, get on new programs, or take on responsibilities that will expose you to industry or the civilian world. Whenever you make contacts, keep their names, numbers, and e-mail addresses handy. Try to make contact with them a few times a year so they don't forget you.

Leon R.
Former USAF Senior Airman

ONLINE NETWORKING
RESOURCES

With the innovation of technology, taking advantage of the strengths of the military network is broadened through the Internet. Many online employment sites are targeted to veterans, some in specific career fields. A few of them are described next. You can find more information regarding online networking resources in Chapter Eight: Online Resources for Veterans.

American Association of People with Disabilities (AAPD) – Employment Opportunities (http://www.aapd-dc.org/employment/indexemploy.php)

An online job bank dedicated to persons with disabilities.

American Council of the Blind Job Connection (www.acb.org/acbjobs)

Lists job openings across the country for blind or visually impaired applicants.

AMVETS Career Center (http://careers.amvets.org)

Provides an online job bank for veterans seeking employment and for employers seeking qualified veteran applicants.

Army Civilian Personnel Vacancy Announcement Board (https://cpolwapp.belvoir.army.mil)

Offers civilian employment opportunities in the U.S. Army for former soldiers, marines, sailors, and airmen.

Career Command Post – Job Seekers Page (www.careercommandpost.com/ccp.cfm)

Includes a job bank, help with writing resumes, and other information for job seekers.

CareerOneStop — Job Search (www.careeronestop.org/JobSearch/JobSearch.aspx)

Offers resources and information regarding the job search, including state job banks and other resources.

Destiny Group (www.destinygrp.com)

Brings employers and military job seekers together. The site offers online job postings, resume searches, educational opportunities, and access to a large affiliate network, including NavySEALS.com, 101st Airborne Division Association, and the Air Force Association, to name a few.

State Job Bank (www.jobbankinfo.org)

Click on a state on the map to find information for job banks in your state that offer help finding and keeping employment.

GI Jobs (www.gijobs.net)

A civilian career guide for military job seekers. Provides an online job search tool, career fair calendar, employer listings, and articles on employment for veterans.

Helmets to Hard Hats (http://helmetstohardhats.org)

Career training and employment opportunities in the construction industry for transitioning active duty servicemembers. Offers information on how experience gained through military service can apply to civilian jobs.

Hire Heroes USA (www.hireheroesusa.org)

Helps military veterans who were wounded while serving in Afghanistan, Iraq, and other locations around the world find careers working in many types of jobs, especially the healthcare industry.

Hire Veterans (www.hireveterans.com)

Searchable job boards where employers hire veterans returning to civilian employment.

HireVetsFirst (www.hirevetsfirst.gov)

Offers information for veterans on searching for jobs through state One-Stop Career Centers.

Iraq War Veterans Organization — Employment (www.iraqwarveterans.org/employment.htm)

Provides links to numerous job banks and employment resources for veterans.

Job Opportunities for Disabled American Veterans (www.jofdav.com)

A free job board specifically for American veterans with disabilities to search for jobs or post resumes.

Jobs for Veterans (http://usvetsinc.destinygrp.com)

Job board focused on bringing transitioning military, former military, and spouses together with employers seeking employees with a military background.

Jobs for Vets Alpha (www.jobsforvetsalpha.org)

Provides a link between transitioning veterans and job listing sites of organizations looking for veteran applicants.

Joe's Jobs – Employment for Veterans (www.vajoe.com/jobs)

Whether you are just leaving the Service, or looking to change careers or move up in your current field, your military background will give you an edge with the employers listed in Joe's Jobs.

Military Exits (www.militaryexits.com)

Job assistance and employment opportunities for returning soldiers and their families. Helps soldiers and families make the transition from military to civilian life with relocation files for every base stateside and overseas, educational resources, and discounted products and services.

Military Family Network Employment Ads (www.emilitary.org/classifieds)

Job bank from an organization that supports military families.

Military Hire (www.militaryhire.com)

This site has been developed and maintained by a team of military veterans and corporate hiring authorities that have created a network where former military personnel can seek careers and utilize their professional skills.

Military Job Zone (www.militaryjobzone.com)

Assists transitioning military members and veterans in finding civilian careers. Site allows you to create and post military resumes, search military-friendly employers, and apply online to posted jobs.

Military Spouse Corporate Career Network (www.msccn.org)

Specializes in employment placement solutions for military spouses, war wounded, and caregivers of war wounded.

Military Stars—Browse Jobs (www.militarystars.com)

Helps transitioning military personnel and veterans find civilian jobs through job search tools, nationwide career expos, and placement services.

Military.com Job Search Information for Spouses (http://jobsearch.spouse.military.com)

Offers a job bank for military spouses. Includes a comprehensive listing of "military spouse-friendly" employers.

Military.com Veteran Job Board (www.military.com/careers/home)

Job board for veterans that offers job searches, resume building, networking with other veterans, salary calculator, information on career fairs, and more.

Navy's Civilian Human Resources — Job Search (https://chart.donhr.navy.mil)

Job listings for returning disabled and recently medically retired servicemembers and their spouses.

Operation Transition (www.dmdc.osd.mil/ot)

Provides job listings and other employment information for separating or retiring military and federal civilian personnel and their spouses.

RecruitMilitary.com (www.recruitmilitary.com)

Provides free comprehensive job search and career transition services for veterans, their spouses, and enlisted transitioning military personnel worldwide. The site also features listings of career fairs offered nationwide.

Still Serving Veterans—Job Listings (www.stillservingveterans.org)

List of job banks and other resources.

Troops to Teachers
(www.dantes.doded.mil/dantes or www.troopstoteachers/index.asp)

Provides referral assistance and placement services to military personnel interested in beginning a second career in public education as a teacher.

USAJOBS Job Search (http://jobsearch.usajobs.gov)

Job listings for veterans and others from the official job site of the U.S. federal government.

VA Careers—Job Search Tool (www.vacareers.va.gov)

Find open positions in the career fields and locations where you are looking for employment. The tool offers search options for the general public, VA employees, and status-eligible candidates. Includes information for those interested in healthcare careers.

Veteran Career Network (http://benefits.military.com/vcn/search.do)

Through the Veteran Career Network, you can get connected with over 600,000 veterans. Find veterans working in companies, government agencies, career fields, industries, or locations that interest you. A project of Military.com, the Veteran Career Network allows you to: use the power of networking to get ahead in your career; connect with members in specific companies, industries, or locations; view career profiles of others in the Network; and create your own profile for others to view.

VetCentral — Job Referrals for Veterans (www.jobcentral.com/vetcentral)

Provides links to career resources as well as a search function to locate jobs and employers.

VetJobs (www.jobbankinfo.org/govtJobBanks.aspx)

Job search site for transitioning servicemembers and veterans.

Veterans and Government Job Banks
(www.jobbankinfo.org/govtJobBanks.aspx)

Job banks designed specifically for veterans and servicemembers from CareerOneStop.com.

Wounded Warrior Project Job Postings
(https://wtow.woundedwarriorproject.org)

This site features a listing of career opportunities.

CAREER NETWORKING TIPS

Most job seekers begin their search in the job market by turning to the classifieds section of the newspaper or surfing the Internet's voluminous job postings. Some rely on headhunters and recruiters. Very few start their search where their efforts will produce the best results—directly with employers or companies where they would like to work. A critical part of establishing your career network begins with the diligence to infiltrate both the hidden and open job markets.

It's estimated that over 80% of job seekers report that their network helped them to land the job they wanted. But as many jobs as there are out there, in newspapers and online, resignations, new businesses, corporate expansions, unfilled positions, or jobs created for a viable candidate are all reasons employers may hire outside traditional advertising mediums. This hidden job market, though difficult to access, holds the greatest potential for job seekers and employers who are looking for the perfect match.

The importance of career networking shouldn't be discounted when you are in the midst of a job search or a career change. In fact, career networking should become a part of your daily work and career-related endeavors, even if you're not actively engaged in a search. Your career network should be in tact for whenever you need it, both for job searching and for moving along your career path. It's important to maintain an active career network because you never know when you might need it.

Networking contacts can help with more than just job leads. They can provide referrals or insider information about companies where you might be interested in working. Your network can provide information on career fields you might want to explore or what the job market is like in that field on the other side of the country. Your network contacts can advise you on where to look for jobs or even review your resume for its relevancy to your chosen career field. The possibilities are unlimited.

Who's in Your Career Network?

Your career network should include anyone who can help you with your transition from military service to civilian employment. Your contacts can include fellow servicemembers, officers, military family members, old school friends, club members, fellow parents at your child's school, acquaintances you meet through online networking services, and so forth. Your network can also include extended family members, neighbors, and anyone who might have a connection that will help you with your next career move.

Work Your Network

Your civilian career begins before you actually leave military service. Don't wait until you have already separated from military service and need a job to pay the bills to start getting in touch with your contacts. People are more willing to help when they know who you are. Keep in touch with key contacts in your network regularly, even if it's just an occasional e-mail to say hello and an update on news about the industry you are interested in. When networking with people you don't know, make sure that you know what you want. Are you looking for career or company information? Do you want to know about job opportunities with a particular company? Be specific in your requests.

Help Others in Your Career Network

Effective networking isn't a one-way street. If you find information about your chosen career path or a job listing that can help others, share it with your network. The point of having a career network is to have resources that can help; nevertheless, you should reciprocate when possible. Then, when you really need help, anyone you've helped in the past would feel honored to help you with your request.

Keep Track of Your Network

Keep track of your personal career network somewhere. Whether it's electronically or on paper, make sure you know who is who, where they work, and how to get in touch.

Online Career Networking

Online job searching and networking does work. Sites that specialize in military needs, as well as other sites like LinkedIn and a variety of other social networking websites can help you contact fellow military networkers, or networkers at specific companies, those with particular academic training or certification, or in a certain geographic area.

Networking Events

Face-to-face networking works extremely well. If you can, register for training conferences, and expand your network as you attend meetings and mixers. You'll find that many of the participants have the same goals you do and will be glad to exchange business cards.

The following examples show how even casual career networking can pay off in meaningful ways.

Patrick wanted to continue his career path as a diesel mechanic once he left the Marines. While walking to his car in a parking lot, he noticed a lady whose car would not start. He went over to help her. The problem turned out to be minor, and Patrick was able to get the car started again. The woman was very grateful and started asking how he knew so much about engines. As it turned out, she was the wife of a trucking company executive. She gave Patrick her husband's business card and told him she would make sure her husband talked to the hiring manager about a job for him once he got out.

· · · · · ·

Travis was interested in pursuing a career in medical technology. He mentioned his interest to an old Navy buddy whose father had done critical research in the field. The friend arranged a meeting between Travis and his dad. The medical researcher arranged for Travis to spend a day shadowing him in a laboratory and provided some excellent advice on medical career paths based on current trends.

· · · · · ·

Patsy was interested in moving from her rather unexciting career as an information officer in the Air Force to magazine publishing in the civilian world. Even though she had been out of college for more than a few years, she reached back and tapped her college network. One of her college sorority sisters was now a top executive at a major women's lifestyle magazine. In addition to being sent new job postings, her resume was personally delivered to the magazine's vice president of human resources. When Patsy found a position she wanted to apply for, she got the job and left the Air Force with no worries about where she would go or what she would do.

· · · · · ·

During a casual conversation at a parent's meeting in her child's elementary school, Colleen casually mentioned to another mother that she was taking classes in graphic design and would graduate shortly after her stint in the Army. The mother happened to be a media buyer for a Fortune 500 corporation. She set Colleen up with some important contacts with several advertising and design agencies, including one that led to a fantastic job with great pay.

Career networking really does work, and it pays off, so it's important to have a viable network in place as you plan your military career transition. As you take steps to exit military service and enter the civilian marketplace, use your network to your advantage when job searching or exploring career options.

Establish Your Product ID

As you prepare to access the civilian job market, both hidden and open, remember that each time you introduce yourself to someone, either in conversation or through correspondence, you have an opportunity to introduce your abilities, experience, and potential. This is when a Product ID comes in handy.

What is a Product ID? It's a 60- to 90-second sales pitch designed to introduce you, connect you to the contact through common interests, and present your key strengths, practical expertise, and personality. Your Product ID can also help you establish an agenda for sharing information with your contact.

Your Product ID is important, so don't wait until the last minute to develop it or improvise one during the encounter. Prepare your Product ID in advance and practice it well. When you speak comfortably about your experiences and accomplishments without hesitating or stiffly reciting personal facts, your confidence in who you are and what you can do shines through.

SECTION II

Best Careers for Veterans

- **CHAPTER SIX: Finding Your Right Career**

  Statistics indicate a serious shortage of available workers in the United States, especially in certain fields. As you discover the civilian careers that are best suited to your skills and training, you can also determine the best employment fields to position yourself for future job security and fulfillment.

What Other Vets Are Saying...

When Denise Crowe decided to leave her post as a captain in the Army Corps of Engineers in pursuit of a better-paying civilian job, she had an easy time landing a position.

But Greg Keller had a much different experience. After four years in the Navy as a journalist, it took him six months to land a job in his field. He found work doing public relations for a medium-sized non-profit agency. Greg blames his field, which tends to have few openings, the current job market, and some employers who did not look fondly on his military experience.

"Some interviewers shook my hand and thanked me for fighting in the Gulf War," he recalled, "while others took on a defensive posture that I could see their eyes and their body language." He observed, "I think maybe they were unsure that my military experience as a journalist had prepared me adequately for civilian work."

Earl Wilson, an ex-marine, remembers when things were different. He explained, "I remember back in the 1980s when ex-military had priority, even at the unemployment office. They would send vets on job interviews over other people. I know I got a job that way. I also remember seeing signs that said 'Hire a Vet.' Today, though, I have to conceal my military experience because it dates me. I don't want to be discriminated against because of my age."

CHAPTER SIX ||||||||||||||||||||||||||||||||||||||||||||||||

FINDING YOUR
RIGHT CAREER

Deciding what you will do after leaving the military is an important decision, considering that, depending on your age, you could spend tens of thousands of hours at your job. Don't you want to spend that time doing something you're good at and enjoy? Find out how you can take your personality, skills, and education and turn them into a successful career.

Over the last few years, the job market and the economy have had ups and downs. Announcements of the latest waves of layoffs seem to bombard the news daily. Amid this uncertainty, leaving the military may not seem like such a sound idea. But depending on how you approach your transition and accompanying job search, now may be the perfect time to enter the civilian market.

With so many choices, it might be hard to pinpoint exactly what you want to do for a career. It's a good idea to look at the careers that are predicted to grow in the near future, and find out how they best fit with your military skills and training. Or, if you want to pursue a new career, find out the skills, education, and training required.

There's no better time to be an American worker! Gone are the days when a person had one occupation, worked on the same job for 25 or 30 years, and then went home to retire with a gold watch. Today, careers can be more varied and exciting. Many people will have two, perhaps three careers in his or her lifetime.

According to the Bureau of Labor Statistics (BLS), the employment rate is expected to increase by 15.6 million jobs in the ten-year period between 2006 and 2016. Almost all of this growth is expected to occur in the service-providing sector, which will account for 75% of all jobs in 2016. The BLS projects (www. bls.gov/emp) that professional service occupations are expected to grow just as quickly, accounting for more than six of every ten new jobs acquired by 2016.

The best way to make a smooth transition from the service to the civilian job market is to translate the experience you gathered in the service into credit toward an academic degree. Through the DANTES programs, you can earn college credit based on some of your experience in the service. Read more about DANTES in Chapter Two. You can also choose to get degrees that will prepare you to work in some of today's fastest growing industries—including information technology, computer science, business, criminal justice, and graphic design. Even better, you can complete many of these degree programs online, using your tuition assistance benefits, including your GI Bill.

In today's knowledge-driven job market, the more you know, the more you're worth. Over a lifetime, the difference between having a college degree or not can be worth millions of dollars.

The General Employment Market

Our economy base and accompanying employment base is rapidly changing. But there are some careers that are generally considered good career fields by military veterans. Additionally, according to the Department of Labor's *2008-2009 Occupational Outlook Handbook*, the following career fields are among the best employment prospects through 2016.

Computer Science/Network Systems Management: The job requires a minimum of an associate's to a master's degree, depending on the position. The range of pay falls between $38,000 and $145,000 annually.

Health Care Administration: The job requires a minimum of an associate's to a master's degree, depending on the position. The range of pay falls between $45,000 and $128,000 annually.

Human Resource Management: The job requires a minimum of a bachelor's to master's degree, depending on the position. The range of pay falls between $51,000 and $98,000 annually.

Training and Education: The job requires a minimum of an associate's to a doctoral degree, depending on the position. The range of pay falls between $33,000 and $141,000 annually.

Law Enforcement: The job requires a minimum of a high school diploma to a master's degree. The annual range of pay falls between $27,000 and $104,000.

Computer Software Engineers: The position often requires a minimum of an associate's degree, with a bachelor's degree preferred. By 2016, growth in this career field is expected to escalate by nearly 50%. The salary for this position is over $45,000 annually.

Personal Financial Advisor: Jobs in this field are expected to grow by over 40%. Minimum training required is a bachelor's degree. Annual earnings average near $50,000.

Medical Assistant: These usually require only moderate on-the-job training, with a projected growth rate of 35%. Annual salaries for these positions range between $21,000 and $30,000.

Substance Abuse/Behavioral Disorder Counselor: This growing field is projected to increase by over one-third by the year 2016, according to DoL statistics. Salaries for these positions range between $30,630 and $46,300 for a bachelor's degree. Many positions pay higher for advanced degrees.

Veterinary Technologists/Technicians: These positions require less formal training, usually an associate's degree. Available positions are projected to increase by 40% by 2016. Position's pay varies from $21,260 to $30,560 annually.

Makeup Artists, Theatrical, and Performance: A nontraditional vocation, these positions are expected to increase by nearly 40%. Training requires a vocational degree and salaries range from $30,630 to $46,300 annually.

Trendy Careers

Cutting-edge careers are often exciting, and they tend to offer a strong job market. The flip side, however, is that these innovative careers often fizzle and flop rather than take off like a rocket ship. But some jobs, though relatively new, are viable career options that promise even further growth. According to the *US News and World Report*, the most promising careers stem from an increasingly global economy, digitization, and an increased worldwide concern for good environmental stewardship. Many of these positions compliment a number of MOSs, which can minimize the need for additional formal training.

Behavioral Geneticist: New and emerging philosophies toward human behaviors such as sexual orientation, alcoholism, intelligence, and the propensity for violence call for more researchers and clinicians who specialize in developing and implementing ethical gene-related therapies.

Data Miner: Data mining is a great career choice for people who enjoy working with statistics to unearth patterns in data and using software that continues to expand in its capability.

Emergency Planning Manager: Since the 9/11 attacks, the field of emergency planning has grown. And with another major terrorist attack considered inevitable, the growth will likely accelerate. The wave of natural disasters also factors into the need for persons trained to respond. While the federal jobs are more difficult to get, these types of positions are increasing in the private sector and local governments.

Global Business Development Specialist: More U.S. companies (corporate, government, nonprofit, large and small) are creating joint ventures, licensing arrangements, financing deals, and other transactions within global markets, especially Asian countries. People who can identify, assess, and facilitate such transactions will be increasingly in demand.

Green-Collar Consultant: Concern for global warming and its effects are causing a lot of companies to "go green." This push toward better environmental stewardship is creating a surge of specializations—industrial carbon footprint reduction, new green construction and retrofits, municipality strategic planning for sustainability, wetlands delineation and restoration, ecotourism, and "smart growth" land use planning.

Health Informatics Specialist: Hospitals, insurers, and regional health networks are switching to electronic medical records. As insurers require doctors and nurses to do more evidence-based medicine, the demand grows for computerized expert systems to guide their diagnoses and treatment recommendations. Health care providers are also collecting more data to evaluate quality of care.

Immigration Specialist: The immigration issue is a hot one in the United States, and the steady increase of immigrants over the last decade has given rise to unprecedented demand in all sectors for immigration specialists. Businesses are eager to figure out how to attach themselves to this new market segment. Public schools are struggling to meet the needs of the masses of children and parents who don't speak English. Hospitals, government agencies, the criminal justice system, and nonprofit advocacy organizations need language and cultural experts to serve a growing population of Americans.

Offshoring Manager: The digitization of business has American corporations and even small businesses turning to offshoring more than ever. Offshoring is challenging, and requires excellent managers with superb organizational, leadership, and multicultural communication skills—like those acquired in the military.

Patient Advocate: The U.S. healthcare system can be a beast to do battle with, and most patients don't have the skills or the energy to pick up a weapon big enough to fight back. Patient advocates do just what the job title says—give patients information about their condition, educate family members on how to provide support and care to the patient, and sort through the mountains of paperwork and bills to deal with healthcare providers and insurance companies.

Simulation Developer: It's fascinating to watch a simulation in action, whether it's for entertainment, training, education, or projecting future events. The use of simulations in training should increase due to the wide availability of broadband and mobile Internet access.

Wellness/Life Coach: Physical fitness trainers are trendy and popular, but more and more people now want the same kind of support in their efforts to eat less, break a bad habit like smoking or drinking, and reduce stress. People are more interested in quality of life and are seeking the services of wellness coaches. Individuals, employers, and even health insurers are soliciting such services as a likely cost-efficient employment perk.

Deceptive Careers

People should enjoy the work that they do because they will spend a good portion of their lives doing it. The old saying, *work like you don't need the money,* is definitely true because it adds to career fulfillment, if you are able to do it. But if you choose a career just for the money or job prestige alone, you probably will end up unfulfilled and disappointed.

No doubt, there are some great jobs out there. All of the court shows on television tend to glamorize the legal profession. However, attorneys often find their work to be more tedious than others would guess. Likewise, people enter careers like teaching or nonprofit management hoping to make a difference in the world, only to be frustrated by apathy and bureaucracy. People tend to admire the folks who branch out on their own and start a business. But many small business owners will tell you that it's much more difficult than they imagined to achieve others' storied success.

Even jobs that are prestigious can have drawbacks that career seekers are unaware of when considering those occupations.

Even jobs that are prestigious can have drawbacks that career seekers are unaware of when considering those occupations. The *U.S. News & World Report* has designated the following as being among the kinds of careers that are often overrated in terms of their job satisfaction.

Advertising Executive: It might look like fun to create funny and effective advertisements. Who wouldn't want to create commercials for the Super Bowl? The truer picture of an advertising career includes pressure to generate new clients and retain existing ones. The creative part is fun, but it may leave some wondering whether it really matters what brand of diet soda you buy. A more fulfilling option may be a social marketing position that will allow you to use your creativity, drive, and passion for a cause or organization you truly believe in.

Architect: The skylines of modern cities like Dallas, Seattle, and Atlanta boast creative architecture that surely must be fun to create. The pay isn't bad either. A career in architecture can still be a satisfying choice, but the flip side is that architects are often saddled with bringing the design choices of others to fruition.

Plus, the construction industry can be shaky with its ups and downs. While opportunities to use innovation and creativity can be scarce, a new concern toward building "green" architecture can still be an exciting venture. Consider a career in interior design as a viable medium for expressing creativity and design flair.

Attorney: High profile attorneys and court or crime television shows can make the legal profession seem quite attractive—so can boasts of huge settlements won from lawsuits. Truthfully, the legal profession demands a lot of detail, tedium, and paperwork. The most exciting and high profile cases include plenty of boring details that the public never sees. There is prestige, but also pressure to rack up billable hours. If you enjoy negotiations, a career in mediation can yield satisfaction that doesn't boggle you down in legal minutia.

Chef: You may imagine the "oohs and ahs" rolling off the tongues of clients drooling over your latest culinary creation. But usually, what's waiting for you back in the kitchen is a recipe book from a chain restaurant, leaving little or no room for creativity. The high-end chef positions at four- or five-star restaurants are few and far between. A more fulfilling career option could be working as a chef for a country club, exclusive health club, or as a personal chef for a group of well-to-do families or one wealthy family.

Clinical Psychologist: If you like listening to people talk and enjoy helping them work through their issues, you may think that a career as a therapist could be your calling. However, research reveals that many psychological problems have physiological roots, minimizing the potential impact on traditional psychotherapy. This trend, combined with the number of people who are turning to short-term therapy approaches, is causing some in the profession to question its merits. Instead, careers in personal life-coaching are steadily increasing, and the training required is much shorter.

Medical Scientist: It's wonderful to think of having a career that leads to improving the quality of life for humanity. Plus, it's impressive. But it's also a long haul to get there. The amount of school and preparation required will take years out of your life. Then, after you get a job in the field, you get to work long hours. There's also the profitability factor. It's not all about saving lives; raising revenues matters a lot too. If you love the medical profession, consider a career in pharmaceutical or medical library science.

Nonprofit Manager: People who want to make a difference gravitate toward careers in nonprofit agencies. Undoubtedly, millions of lives have been changed by the humanitarian efforts of nonprofit entities. Truthfully, there are probably few lives that have never been affected by a nonprofit agency, from the YMCA® to a local homeless shelter. Few experiences are more rewarding than helping improve the quality of someone's life, but there are many organizations out there striving for those program dollars. Salaries tend to be low, but pressure to raise money and keep funding going can be high. There must be constant concern for federal and grant regulation compliance and most agencies depend greatly on volunteers to do the task. Too often, nonprofit managers feel like lone rangers, fighting the battle alone. If you want to help humanity, you can work in a more lucrative field and donate to your favorite organizations

Police Officer: Cop shows are television staples because they afford the opportunity for lots of drama. Law enforcement has gone high tech. The days of old-fashioned legwork in shows like *Dragnet* hardly seem as exciting as today's *CSI*. A career as a police officer is a chance to help people up close and personal, and many find it fulfilling. But it's dangerous business if you're a street cop. Even from time to time, detectives find themselves in the line of danger. There are usually lots of paperwork and court appearances, not to mention long hours. Many police officers work security on the side to make ends meet. The stress of witnessing the horrors of criminal activity and fatal traffic accidents on a daily basis can take its toll after a while. The formation of the Department of Homeland Security has opened the field for positions in law enforcement as a career option that does not entail the same level of danger.

Real Estate Agent: Plenty of people have made a pile of money in the real estate game, but even tycoons like Donald Trump have had their real estate woes. It's enticing to get into real estate because you can make money if you have the clientele. The relative ease of obtaining a real estate license has flooded the market. Plus, a fledgling real estate and construction market has diminished its attractiveness, not to mention other options available today for buying and selling properties. Consider a career in sales that isn't so crowded or unstable.

Small Business Owner: Being your own boss is great! You make the decisions. You call the shots. You can enter a field you truly love and believe in. Plus, you position yourself to make the amount of money you want. It's all on you—but that works both ways. Being your own boss means coming up with your own salary, paying your own bills, and often working long nights and weekends. Before jumping off into your own business, try working for another small business to give you an idea of what will be required of you.

Teacher: The education field has a long-standing reputation for prestige, though a somewhat diminishing sense of job fulfillment. Most teachers have great job security, good benefits, and summers off. But many of today's teachers are frustrated by budget cuts, parental apathy, and seemingly unreasonable administrative mandates. Private school teachers, while usually paid less, often experience greater job satisfaction. Consider an alternative profession such as a GED instructor, trainer in a human resources department, training consultant, professional tutor, or educational placement training.

Post-Military Careers

A 2007 article by *CNN Money* ranked the best careers for veterans based on a variety of factors, including the ease of the transition from the service to the industry, the stability of the industry, the potential for job growth, and the total compensation package offered. Based on these facts, the concluding assessment was that jobs in network systems, business, intelligence analysis, logistics, and training are best suited for veterans ("Retired from the Military—Top 20 Jobs," *CNNMoney.com*). The positions include the following job titles:

Senior Training Manager: In the private sector, training managers are responsible for the development, evaluation, and oversight of corporate training programs. If you are or about to be a veteran who moved up in your military career, chances are good that you were entrusted with training enlisted personnel. Your experience, along with a bachelor's degree in a business or technical field, can equal a great job as a training manager that earns you a median salary of $83,500 annually.

Operations or Intelligence Analyst: Having a military security clearance is one of the easier transitions to civilian employment. Plus, it puts you well in front of the competition for these jobs. Securing an analyst position typically requires a bachelor's degree in an area such as business or information technology, and involves evaluating and improving the operations or security of a company. An analyst position pays a median salary of $68,900 a year. However, the pay can vary widely depending on the level of the position.

Information Technology/Network Systems Manager: The military is a great way to acquire hands-on training in certain kinds of software before the civilian world gets access to it. If you have at least five years of experience with computer operating systems, and a bachelor's degree in some form of information technology or management, you have the competitive edge in securing this career. An IT position pays a median of $73,600 and generally entails managing, maintaining, or developing a firm's computer systems.

Logistics Manager: From delivering inventory and raw materials to shipping finished goods, supply-chain management in the logistics field is a likely career prospect for many veterans. The old saying, *an army moves on its stomach*, refers to logistics. Logistics management is a fairly easy transition for ex-military with at least eight years of experience and a bachelor's degree in business logistics and operations. The average salary is $82,500 a year.

These previously mentioned positions require the experience you gathered in the service, along with a bachelor's degree. If you don't have a bachelor's degree, strongly consider using your military education benefits to further boost your post-military civilian career.

Other positions that have been cited as good career options for veterans include the following:

Behavioral disorder counselor
Computer software engineer
Computer systems analysts
Computer/systems software engineer
Database administrators
Dental assistant
Dental hygienist
Environmental science and protection technicians
Financial analyst
Forensic science technician
Gaming and Sports book writers and runners
Gaming surveillance officer/gaming investigators
Home health aides
Medical assistant
Mental health counselors
Mental health social workers
Personal and home care aide

Personal financial advisor
Physical therapist
Physical therapist assistants
Physician assistant
Social and human service assistant
Substance abuse and behavioral disorder counselors
Substance abuse social workers
Veterinarian
Veterinary technologist/technician

Health Care Jobs

According to the Bureau of Labor Statistics' current employment data, health care employment continues to grow and has become the largest industry in the United States, accounting for 13.5 million jobs. The BLS also projects that the health care sector will generate an additional three million new jobs by 2016, more than any other industry. Most of these new positions will require less than a traditional college education.

Nurses: Registered nurses are in great demand. This is an ideal career for you if your personality is nurturing and detail-oriented, and you are capable of staying calm in stressful situations. With a shortage of nearly 1.1 million nurses projected, the nursing field represents long-term job security. Demand is projected to be greatest for nurses in emergency rooms, operating rooms, intensive care, pediatrics, and labor and delivery rooms. Salaries for nurses average in the mid-$50,000 range. Nursing training programs vary from diplomas in nursing to master's level programs.

Health Information Technicians: It's difficult to be in the military without having good organizational skills and being detail-oriented, qualities which are essential to a career in health information technology. Health information technologists maintain the medical records for patients, including observations of their general health, medical history and symptoms, X-rays, diagnoses, surgeries, and treatments. If you prefer working quietly and keeping to yourself, this is one of the few careers in the healthcare field that can accommodate you. Excellent computer skills are essential in analyzing data, and most positions require an associate degree to qualify. Typically, earnings for these jobs hover at the $30,000 mark.

The shortage of workers who have chosen the professional trade path puts these skills in high demand.

Dental Hygienists: Though you might not think it, dental hygienists can earn a good living; plus, they get to help people maintain good oral health and hygiene. Many dental hygienists work part-time or arrange a work schedule that requires only two or three days each week. The average annual salary of $64,740 combined with the relatively quick training required—an associate degree or certificate from an accredited dental hygiene school and a state license—makes this career option a definite plus!

Health Care Administrators: The booming health-care business requires the skills of good managers who understand finance and accounting and are able to manage millions of dollars and hundreds of employees. A master's level degree in health services administration, public health, or business administration can command an annual salary of around $75,000, according to the BLS. A bachelor's degree can secure an entry-level job at a smaller health services facility.

Skilled Trade Jobs

A college education has long been valued as a strong employability asset that can positively affect your long-term income potential. But college is not for everyone and it's not the only solution. The shortage of workers who have chosen the professional trade path puts these skills in high demand.

A strong demand for power plants, oil refineries, and export goods has many manufacturers and construction contractors scrambling to find enough skilled workers to fill current and future shortages.

It is expected that a shortage of welders, pipe fitters, and other such high-demand workers is likely to worsen as more of them reach retirement age. In anticipation, unions, construction contractors, and other businesses are trying to determine how to attract younger workers to these fields. Consequently, they are turning to the military to find a pool of trainable workers.

One of their hurdles is overcoming the perception that blue-collar positions offer lower status, less money, and little opportunity for advancement in comparison to white-collar jobs that often require a college degree. In reality, some unionized craft workers can earn more than the average college graduate, without the burden of student loans.

Plus, there are a number of negatives associated with trade-type jobs that prevent some from pursuing such careers, mainly, the myth that vocational jobs are for people who don't have the intellect to pursue a professional career. There was a time when vocational or trade career training was viewed as inferior to a liberal arts education, but students opting for the trade career path today are smart, savvy, and practical. They want an educational experience that is focused and practical, and one that will not tie them up for years with seemingly irrelevant coursework.

There was a time when vocational or trade career training was viewed as inferior to a liberal arts education, but students opting for the trade career path today are smart, savvy, and practical.

There are a number of industries that require a high degree of intellect, training, and skill. Vocational jobs, like everything else, are becoming more technical. They require the kind of skills and training that are quite relevant to the MOS training of former servicemembers. Construction, welding, plumbing, electric, machinery, CNC (computer numerical control) programming, masonry, tool and die technicians, and HVAC (heating, ventilation and air conditioning) maintenance and assembly are highly marketable career fields whose workers are constantly sought by employers.

The energy industry is searching for workers who can make precision welds, fit pipes for pipelines and oil refineries, and understand the complex electrical wiring in modern power plants. One veteran, a 25-year-old union electrician in Portland, Oregon earns $34 an hour working on renewable energy projects. Meanwhile, some of his college-educated friends have been laid off and are having a hard time finding jobs.

Similarly, there is a short supply of workers trained in HVAC. It is estimated that an additional 20,000 technicians and installers are needed each year to work in the air conditioning, heating, refrigeration, and plumbing industries.

If you don't have the skills to enter one of these vocations, or if your skills need enhancing, there are a number of national, regional, state, local, and union-sponsored apprenticeship programs available.

If you don't have the skills to enter one of these vocations, or if your skills need enhancing, there are a number of national, regional, state, local, and union-sponsored apprenticeship programs available. What's more, you can use your military education benefits to help formalize your training and skills.

Veterans in the Federal Workforce

If you've ever wondered about the number of veterans who are employed in the federal government, know that veterans from all military service branches proudly make up a large segment of the federal workforce. In addition, it is anticipated that veterans will continue to maintain a strong and essential presence as employees of the federal government.

According to a Department of Labor report, *The Employment of Veterans in the Federal Government—FY 2003*, veterans comprise approximately 25% of the federal workforce, compared to the slightly less than 10% of our nation's civilian labor force. The federal government also employs five times more disabled veterans than any other entity.

Although veterans are not evenly distributed among the various categories of federal employment, they are a significant percentage of the occupational categories with higher salaries and opportunities for substantive careers and advancement.

Among federal workers, veterans represent about 14% of the professional category, which earns the largest average salary. Veterans represent 27% of the administrative category, which has the second highest average salary. As the largest occupational category in the federal government, many of the jobs in the administrative category represent positions with skill requirements comparable to the skills obtained in military occupations—logistics, administration, finance, and human resource management.

The skills many servicemembers acquire while serving in the military have many comparable civilian jobs in both the public and the private sector. The Avue MOS Translator™ can help you obtain information on federal government and private industry occupations equivalent to your military occupational specialty. It will also advise you regarding civilian employment through military services and a few other agencies, such as the FAA in the Department of Transportation and the Department of Veterans Affairs. These entities have the greatest number of jobs where military experience serves as outstanding preparation for a federal civilian career. To access the Translator, visit www.vetjobs.us and click on the link to use the Avue MOS Translator.

Finding the right career is an important life step, even if you've already enjoyed a successful career in the military. Stepping into a civilian career is an opportunity to do what you love and love what you do. You want a job that will challenge you, while maximizing your skills and experience. You want the best, and so do employers. Many corporations are ready to offer qualified veteran job seekers the opportunity to do their best and be challenged to stretch themselves to new levels of expertise. All you have to do is choose your direction!

● **VET VIP**

The Avue MOS Translator™ can help you obtain information on federal government and private industry occupations equivalent to your military occupational specialty.

To access the Translator, visit www. vetjobs.us and click on the link to use the Avue MOS Translator.

HIRING BENEFITS OF VETERANS' PREFERENCE

As a veteran, if you are disabled or served on active duty in the Armed Forces during a certain time period or military campaign, you are entitled to preference over others when you apply for federal civilian positions.

As early as the Civil War era, veterans of the Armed Forces have been given preference in appointments to federal jobs in recognition of their dedicated sacrifice to serving their country, and to help make up for the economic loss many veterans experienced as a result of their military service.

The Veterans' Preference Act of 1944 is an earned entitlement for certain military veterans who served their country honorably. By law, veterans who are disabled or served on active duty in the Armed Forces during a certain time period or military campaign are entitled to preference over others when an agency is hiring from a competitive list of candidates. If you are eligible for this preference, you will have additional points added to your passing score or rating when you apply for federal civilian positions.

Preference Categories

The statutory employment requirements associated with the Veterans' Preference Act can be found in Titles 5 and 38.

5-Point Preference Eligibility

Five points will be added to your passing examination score or rating if you served:

1. During any war; or

2. During the period of April 28, 1952 through July 1, 1955; or

3. For more than 180 consecutive days, any part of which occurred after January 31, 1955 and before October 15, 1976; (Note: active duty for training does not count); or

4. During the Gulf War from August 2, 1990, through January 2, 1992; or

5. For more than 180 consecutive days, any part of which occurred during the period beginning September 11, 2001 and ending on the date prescribed by presidential proclamation or by law as the last day of Operation Iraqi Freedom; or

6. In a campaign or expedition for which a campaign medal has been authorized. Any Armed Force Expeditionary medal or campaign badge, including El Salvador, Lebanon, Grenada, Panama, Southwest Asia, Somalia, and Haiti qualifies for preference.

Ten-Point Compensable Disability Preference (CP) Eligibility

Ten points will be added to your passing examination score or rating if you are a veteran who served at any time and who has a compensable service-connected disability rating of at least 10% but less than 30%.

Ten-Point/30% Compensable Disability Preference (CPS)

Ten points will be added to your passing examination score or rating if you served at any time and have a compensable service-connected disability rating of 30% or more.

Ten-Point Disability Preference (XP)

Ten points will be added to your passing examination score or rating if you are a veteran who served at any time and has a present service-connected disability or is receiving compensation, disability retirement benefits, or pension from the military or the Department of Veterans Affairs but does not qualify as a CP or CPS; or a veteran who received a Purple Heart.

Special Federal Hiring Authorities for Veterans

Several special authorities are available that provide for noncompetitive appointment of eligible veterans. Use of these special authorities, however, is entirely at an agency's discretion. While no one is entitled to one of these special appointments, it is important that you know of the existence of these authorities and the options they can provide as you search for opportunities to be considered for available federal positions.

Veteran's Recruitment Authority (VRA): The VRA is a special authority created so that eligible veterans can be appointed to positions in the federal government without competition.

Veteran's Employment Opportunity Act of 1998 (VEOA): The VEOA allows eligible veterans to apply and compete for federal employment under merit promotion procedures.

Other Special Appointing Authorities

If you are a veteran who wants to work for the federal government, be proactive and begin networking with local agencies, contacting listed resources, and aggressively seeking out all available federal employment opportunities.

The federal government's hiring options include excepted service special appointing authorities for people with disabilities. Although not developed exclusively for disabled veterans, they are eligible to apply if they meet the criteria. Federal employers are authorized to use these authorities when considering certain people with disabilities (those who have severe physical, cognitive, or psychiatric disabilities or who have a history of having such disabilities).

In addition, once you're hired, your agency can use certain hiring authority to provide assistance should your disability warrant it.

Filing Applications after the Announcement Closes

As a 10-point preference eligible, you can file an application at any time for any position where:

- A permanent appointment has been made in the preceding three years;
- A list currently exists of individuals who are eligible for a position that is closed to new applications; or
- A list is about to be established.

You should contact the agency that announced the position for further information.

Student Educational Employment Program (SEEP)

Many veterans, particularly those who are disabled, decide to return to school to gain training or education that will enhance their ability to pursue a successful career. The SEEP program provides employment opportunities to students who are pursuing education on at least a half-time basis.

The eligible school you wish to attend must be an accredited high school, technical school, vocational school, two- or four-year college or university, graduate, or professional school. There are no maximum age restrictions for this program, but you must be at least 16 years old to participate.

Employment Assistance

Today's military personnel are exceptionally qualified and capable of meeting the needs of the current and future civilian workforce. The process of seeking employment with the federal government is often an intricate process. The time between applying for a position, interviewing, and being selected can be several weeks or even months.

There are many websites dedicated to offering assistance for veterans in seeking employment opportunities with the federal government. The employment process can be rather lengthy so do not get discouraged during the job seeking process. Often the vacancies you apply for have a contact person that you can call or e-mail to update you on the status of the job for which you applied. Some agencies are quicker than others in moving the employment process along.

SOURCE:
U.S. Office of Personnel Management (www.opm.gov/veterans/html/vetsinfo.asp#Entitled)

VET-FRIENDLY COMPANIES

It's nice to work at a place where you are appreciated. The following companies are identified as being receptive, or even eager to hire veterans. Why? Transitioning military often require little on-the-job training. Military-friendly employers recognize that ex-military bring discipline, relevant skills, and a work ethic that are assets to their corporation. Plus, veterans are a renewable resource for companies that develop the right programs to attract them.

Companies are confirming that, as a rule, veterans are well disciplined, highly trained, and strongly motivated. They also are more likely to possess a broader range of technical and professional skills. Vets tend to be both goal- and task-oriented. Many speak more than one language. They tend to be more mature and responsible, are quick learners, and can remain flexible amid corporate changes like job transfers, overtime, and stressful deadlines. Veterans are confident, self-reliant, resourceful, and accustomed to working in environments that depend on high levels of teamwork to succeed. Overall, they are assets to the companies where they work.

In short, many employers are figuring out what military-friendly companies have known for a while—that veterans are a best choice, all other factors being equal.

For these reasons, and many more, the following companies have been identified by a number of veteran's advocacy organizations, as well as veterans themselves, as good employers.

Anheuser-Busch
Beverage Manufacturer
www.buschjobs.com

American Electric Power
Energy – Utilities
www.aep.com/careers

Applied Materials
Nanomanufacturing
www.appliedmaterials.com/careers

AT&T
Telecommunications
www.att.com

Bank of America
Financial Services
http://careers.bankofamerica.com

BearingPoint
Technology Consulting
www.bearingpoint.com/careers

BNSF Railway
Transportation – Railroad
www.bnsf.com/careers/military

Booz Allen Hamilton
Strategy & Technology Consulting
www.boozallen.com/careers

Brinks U.S.
Business – Security Services
www.brinksinc.com

California Prison Health Care Receivership
Corrections
www.changingprisonhealthcare.org

Capital One
Financial Services
www.capitalone.com

Central Intelligence Agency
National Security/Intelligence
www.cia.gov

Cintas
Uniforms – Business Services
www.cintas.com/hr/military.asp

COMTek
IT Managed Services
www.comtechnologies.com

Constellation Energy
Energy – Utilities
www.constellation.jobs

Cornell University
Education – Private University
www.cornell.edu

CSX Transportation
Transportation – Railroad
www.csx.com

DynCorp International
Technology – Professional Services
www.dyncorprecruiting.com

EDS
Business – Technology Consulting
www.edscareers.com

EG&G (Lear Siegler Services)
Engineering – Technical Services
www.egginc.com/careers

ENSCO International
Drilling
www.enscous.com

Freeport-McMoRan Copper & Gold
Mining
www.fcx.com/about/career.htm

General Electric
Energy, Finance & Healthcare
www.gecareers.com

Exxon Mobil
Energy – Petrochemical
www.exxonmobil.com

FirstEnergy Corporation
Electric Utility
www.firstenergycorp.com

Fluor
Construction – Government Services
www.fluor.com/career

FMC Technologies
Technology – Energy Services
www.fmctechnologies.com

General Dynamics Information Technology
Information Technology
www.anteon.com

Georgia-Pacific
Paper Manufacturer
www.gp.com

Health Net
Healthcare
www.careersathealthnet.com

Honeywell Technology Solutions Lab
Technology Manufacturer
www.honeywell.com

IAP Worldwide Services
Logistics
www.iapws.com

ISYS Technologies
IT and Engineering Services
www.isystechnologies.com

ITT Corporation
Engineering/Manufacturing
www.itt.com/careers

J. B. Hunt Transport
Transportation Logistics
www.jbhunt.jobs

Johnson Controls
Automotive, Building, and Power Products
www.johnsoncontrols.com

Kaiser Permanente
Healthcare Plans and Services
www.kaiserpermanente.org

L-3 Communications Intelligence Solutions
Communications
www.l-3com.com

Legacy Health Systems
Healthcare Plans and Services
www.legacyhealth.org

Lockheed Martin
Advanced Technology Systems Integrator
www.lockheedmartinjobs.com

Lowe's
Retail – Home Improvement
www.lowes.com

ManTech International
IT – Technical Services
www.mantech.com

Manpower Inc.
Employment Services
www.manpower.com

Mastec Advanced Technologies
Infrastructure Solutions
www.mastec.com

Merrill Lynch
Financial Services
www.ml.com/poa

Morgan Stanley
Financial Services
www.morganstanley.com/about/careers

Northrop Grumman
Global Defense and Technology
www.northropgrumman.com

Norfolk Southern
Transportation – Railroad
www.nscorp.com

NVR, Inc. (NV Homes/Ryan Homes)
Construction
www.nvrinc.com/careers

Pioneer Services
Financial Services
www.pioneerservices.com

Progress Energy
Energy – Utilities
www.progress-energy.com

Prudential
Insurance Products
www.prudential.com

Raytheon
Missile Defense/Intelligence
www.raytheon.com

SAIC
Scientific/Engineering/Technical
www.saic.com

Sears Holdings
Retail – Services
www.searsholdings.com/careers

Southwest Airlines
Transportation – Air
www.southwest.com

Schneider National
Transportation – Trucking & Logistics
www.schneiderjobs.com

Southern California Edison
Energy – Utilities
www.edisonjobs.com

Southern Company
Energy – Utilities
www.southerncompany.com/careers

Sprint Nextel
Telecommunications
www.sprint.com/hr/military

State Farm
Financial Services – Insurance
www.statefarm.com/careers

Sunbelt Rentals
Equipment Rental – Construction
www.sunbeltrentalscareers.com/gi

T-Mobile
Telecommunications
www.t-mobile.com/jobs

The Home Depot
Retail – Home Improvement
www.homedepot.com/careers

Travelers
Financial Services
www.travelers.com/careers

Transocean
Offshore Drilling
www.deepwater.com

Union Pacific
Transportation – Railroad
www.up.com/employment/military

United Parcel Service
Package Delivery
www.ups.com

U-Haul
Retail – Business Services
http://jobs.uhaul.com

USAA
Financial Services – Insurance
www.usaa.apply2jobs.com

Verizon Communications
Communications
www.verizon.com

Wachovia
Financial Services
www.wachovia.com/careers

Werner Enterprises
Transportation – Logistics
www.werner.com

Westinghouse
Energy – Professional Services
www.westinghousenuclear.com/careers

Xcel Energy
Energy – Utilities
www.xcelenergy.com

SOURCE:
1. Military.com (www.military.com)
2. GI Jobs Online (www.gijobs.net)

FROM MOS TO JOB

You know what your job and responsibilities were in the military, but how does that translate to a civilian career. With all of the job possibilities, what can you do? The following detailed listing includes actual positions advertised by employers looking to employ former servicemembers. Listed by branch of service, some of the jobs listed are civilian jobs within the military. Many others are with government agencies or companies that hold defense or military contracts.

While some of the job titles may seem out of place (i.e. an administrative assistant under an armament MOS), remember that corporations need all types of skills to run their businesses. So, if you have good administrative skills and experience with armament, you may easily qualify for an executive assistant position with a company that manufactures weaponry.

This list is by no means exhaustive of all MOS categories, but by examining it, you will know for certain that the jobs are out there. With a little legwork, determination, and a positive attitude you can soon be on your way to a meaningful civilian career!

AIR FORCE

CHAPLAIN ASSISTANT
Chaplain
Chaplain PRN
Chaplain Registry
Hospital Staff Chaplain
Staff Chaplain – PRN (Varied)

CIVIL ENGINEERING
Civil Affairs Operations Analyst
Civil Designer/Microstation Technician
Civil Engineers
Civil Engineers EITs, PEs
Electrical Engineers
Entry-Level Engineers (Mentor Program)

COMMUNICATIONS AND COMPUTER SYSTEMS
Aerospace Engineer
Aircraft Mechanic – Aerospace
Aircraft Mechanic – Service Mechanic
Hydraulic Specialist
Information Management Officer
Police Officer
Radio Operator

CONTRACTING
Acquisition Contract Manager
Business Developer Manager
Contracts Manager
Merchandise Assistant
Purchasing Agent
Purchasing Technician (OA)

DENTAL
Contracting Specialist
Dental Assistant
Dental Hygienist
Dental Lab Technician
Office Manager
Orthodontist
X-ray Lab Technician

FINANCIAL
Annex Supervisor (RET)
Department Manager

Military Account Manager – USAF
Senior Store Associate
Shift Manager (Retail/Gas)
Store Assistance
Store Associate

FUELS
Aircraft Pneudraulic Systems Mechanic
Auto Worker (Service Station)
AWACS Fuel System Instructor
AWACS Fuel System Technician
Fuel Distribution System Mechanic
Fuel Distribution Systems Worker
Shift Manager (Retail/Gas)

HISTORY
Assistant Professor of Modern
   European History
Foreign Military Sales Program Analyst
Military Analyst and War-Gaming Action
Military Order of Battle Analyst
Museum Specialist (History)
Personnel Specialist
Professor of Joint Military Operations
Senior Analyst, Military Order of Battle

INFORMATION MANAGEMENT
Air Force Program Manager
Information Management
Major Account Manager, U.S. Air Force
Materials Handler I
Personnel Specialist
Program Manager (Air Force Weapons)
Senior C2/Acquisition Analyst

LOGISTIC PLANS
Annex Supervisor (RET)
Collections Technician
Finance Specialist – Entry-Level
Logistics Assistant
Major Account Manager, U.S. Air Force
Program Manager (Air Force Weapons)
Senior C2/Acquisition Analyst/Air Force
Warehouse Worker Foreman

MAINTENANCE MANAGEMENT SYSTEMS
Assembler/Fitter
Cutting Operator
Quality Control Analyst
Silker
Switcher
Systems Enterprise Project Management
Technical Director
Unit Deployment Manager

MANPOWER
Air Force Program Manager
Food Activity Foreman
Food Service Worker (Supervisory)
Materials Handler I
Reorder Assistant
Store Assistant (Supervisory)
Warehouse Worker Foreman

MEDICAL
JIEDDO Subject Matter Expert
Pediatric Physician
Pharmacist, AF Base
Primary Care Sales
Security Technical Writer
Subject Matter Expert

MISSILE AND SPACE SYSTEMS MAINTENANCE
Air Force Program Manager
Air Operations Specialist
Annex Supervisor (RET)
Director, Exercises and Training
Equipment Specialist (Missile)
Warning Missile Warning Specialist
Realty Specialist
Supervisory Cost Analyst

MISSION SUPPORT
Human Resources Assistant
Human Resources Assistant (Military)
Human Resources Manager
Human Resources Specialist (Military)
Human Resources Technician

MUNITIONS AND WEAPONS
Air Support Operations Center
AWACS Air Surveillance Instructor

Director, Exercises and Training
Fire Equipment Dispatcher
Intelligence in Force Modernization
IO Force Development Support
Security Forces
Technical Trainer, Senior Professional

PARALEGAL
Administrative Officer – Entry-Level
Air Force Judge Advocate (JAG)
Finance Specialist – Entry-Level
Human Resources Specialist – Entry-Level
Information Management
Staff Instructor I-CONUS

PRECISION MEASUREMENT EQUIPMENT LABORATORY
Auto Worker
Carpenter
Intelligence in Force Modernization
Logistics Management Specialist
Management Analyst
Senior Staff Instructor – CONUS
Staff Instructor I – CONUS
Staff Instructor II – CONUS/OCONUS

PUBLIC AFFAIRS
Electronic System Security Assessment
Finance and Accounting Officer
Legislative and Public Affairs Liaison
Public Affairs
Public Affairs Officer
Public Affairs Specialist
Radio/Television Broadcasting Personality

SECURITY FORCES
Alcohol, Tobacco, Firearms, and
    Explosives Special Agent
Bomb Squad
Campus Security Officer
Central Intelligence Agency – Security
    Protective Officer
Computer Forensics
County Police Officer
Crime Scene Investigation Officer
Deputy Sheriff
Drug Enforcement Administration
    – Special Agent
Environmental Protection Agency
    – Special Agent

Federal Bureau of Investigation Special Agent
Homeland Securities – Border Patrol Agent
Immigration and Customs Special Agent
Inventory Control Analyst
Military Police
Police Detective
Police Officer
Police Records Technician
Polygraph Administrator
Professional Police Officer
Security Guard
Sex Crimes
State Bureau of Investigation Officer
State Highway Patrol
State Trooper
Store Detective

SERVICES

Commissary Contractor Monitor
Commissary Management Specialist CAO
Commissary Specialist Supervisor
Commissary Supervisor
Meatcutter Supervisor
Store Associate

SUPPLY

Finance Specialist – Entry-Level
Food Activity Foreman
Food Service Worker (Supervisory)
Laborer
Shift Supervisor
Supply Technician Air Cargo

TRANSPORTATION AND VEHICLE MAINTENANCE

Auto Worker (Service Station)
Automobile Sales Associate
Office Assistant
Quality Supervisor – Air Force
Staff Instructor I – CONUS
Warehouse Worker
Warehouse Worker Foreman

VISUAL INFORMATION

Information Assurance Officer
Senior Network Technician
Visual Designer
Visual/Media Specialist
Warehouse Worker
Web Content Management/Analyst
Web Developer

ARMY

ADMINISTRATIVE
Accounting Assistant
Accounting Clerk II
Accounting Technician I
Administrative Assistant
Administrative Assistant
Administrative Management Specialist
Administrative Services Technician
Administrative Support – Customer
Administrative Support Assistant
Administrative Support Clerk
Administrative Support Clerk
Administrative Support Specialist
Administrative Technician
Army and Air Force Exchange
    Service Intern (Generic)
ARMY Communications Systems Analysts
Army Project Officer
Chaplain Assistant
Customer Service Assistant
Human Resources Assistant
Human Resources Specialist
Maintenance Administrative Technician
Office Assistant
Reserve Health Care Administrative
Secretary
Secretary I
Senior Office Associate
Senior Office Associate
Staff Administrative Assistant
USAR Unit Administrative Technician
Warehouse Worker

ARMAMENT MAINTENANCE
Armament Repairer
Armorer
Component Repair (Drivetrain) Supervisor
Component Repair (Powerpack) Supervisor
Component Repair (RWS/Vectronics)
    Supervisor
Crane Operator
Electronic Integrated Systems Mechanic
Forward Repair Activity Manager (D Band)
General Dynamics LS – LEW
General Equipment Repairer
Heavy Mobile Equipment Mechanic
Heavy Mobile Equipment Repair Inspector
Industrial Specialist
Inventory Management Specialist
IT Specialist

Machine Tool Operator
Mechanical and Industrial Equipment
Production Specialist
Program Analyst
Program Support Assistant
Repair Technician A
SCA Electronic Technician Maintenance II
Secretary
Small Arms Repair Mechanic
Social Worker
Supervisor Logistics Management
Supervisory Contract Specialist
Supply Technician
Weapons Technician Senior Assistant
Welder

CHEMICAL OPERATIONS
Acquisition Program Manager
All Source Analyst
Anti-Terrorism Analyst
Anti-Terrorism/CIP Analyst
Business Development Analyst, Senior Staff
CBRN Command Post Operator
CBRN Instructor
CBRN Instructor with Security Clearance
CBRN Scientist
CBRN Senior Analyst
CBRN Trainer/Instructor
CBRNE/Consq Mgt FP Planner-3622
CBRNE CATS Analyst, MT
CBRNE Installation Preparedness Analyst
CBRNE/Consequence Management
    FP Planner
Emergency Management Branch Chief
Hazardous Materials Program Analyst
HAZMAT Program Analyst
    w/ Top Secret Clearance
Journeyman Technical Intelligence Analyst
Lead Plans Specialist
Medical Countermeasures Analyst (GTD)
Medical Countermeasures CBRN Analyst
Program Analyst, CBRNE
Project Manager
Radiation Equipment Calibration
Radiation Equipment Logistics Technician
Senior Analyst IV
Senior Analyst – CBRN
Senior CBRNE Scientist
Senior Communications Technician
Senior Program Analyst

Senior Scientist – CBRNE
Software Engineer III
Spectroscopist/Scientist
SW Engineer III
Technical Intelligence Analyst
Trainer – Chemical, Biological
Training Instructor (CBRN)
Warehouse Support Personnel

CIVIL AFFAIRS

Carpenter
Civil AutoCAD Drafter
Civil Engineer
Civil Engineer Hydraulic
Civil Engineer Structural
Civil/Structural Engineer
Commercial Plumber
Construction Materials Technician – Field
Engineering Technician (Civil)
Environmental Consultant – Air Quality
Environmental Scientist
GIS Analyst
GIS Analyst/Specialist
Intern Civil-Power Industry
Project Architect
Project Civil Engineer
Senior Civil-Highway Engineer
Senior Environmental, Civil, or Chemical
Simulation Engineer
Structural Engineers
Supervisory Civil Engineer
Supervisory Research Civil Engineer
Transportation Engineers

COMMUNICATIONS INTELLIGENCE

Analyst, Advanced Geospatial
ANSS – Counterintelligence Team Leader
ANSS – Counterintelligence Technical
Army Linguist, Cryptologic
Army Logistician
Army Project Officer
Budget Analyst
Chief Current Operations and Intelligence
Counterintelligence Analyst
Criminal Intelligence Analyst
CTDB Intelligence Analyst
Director, Business and Competitive
    Intelligence
Intelligence Analysis, Associate Manager
Intelligence Analyst
Intelligence Analyst Senior
Intelligence and Operations
Intelligence and Operations Specialist V

Intelligence Assistant
Intelligence Data Collector
Intelligence Document Writer
Intelligence Master
Intelligence Officer Training
    and Exercise SME
Intelligence Specialist
Intelligence Specialist Operations
Intelligence Specialist – GMI Analyst
Military Analyst
Network Architect
Occupational Health Nurse Senior
Senior Army Analyst – C2 Acquisitions
Supervisory Intelligence Specialist
Training Specialist Intelligence

COUNTER AND HUMAN INTELLIGENCE

All Source Counterterrorism
All Source Intelligence Analyst
Analyst/HUMINT Trainer
ANSS – Human Intelligence (HUMINT)
APA3 Intelligence Operations
CI/HUMINT Analyst
CMMA Intelligence Trainer
Collections Intelligence Analyst, Principal
    TS/SCI
Computer Technician
Counter Narcotics Intelligence Analyst
Counterintelligence Analyst
CTDB Intelligence Analyst
Database Analyst (SAP BI)
Financial Manager/Fiscal
Financial Manager/Fiscal
    Manager/Accountant
HUMINT Analyst
HUMINT Analyst/Trainer
HUMINT Collector – 4/5
HUMINT Instructor
HUMINT Intelligence Analyst
HUMINT Intelligence Analyst – 6/7
HUMINT Interrogation Instructor
HUMINT Operations Instructor/Developer
HUMINT Policy Technical Writer
HUMINT Statistical and
    Performance Analyst
Information Operations (IO) Plans Officer
Intelligence Analyst
Intelligence Analyst Team Chief
Intelligence Analyst, Principal – TS/SCI
Intelligence Collections Managers
Intelligence Community Analyst
Intelligence Reports Specialist
Senior Intelligence Analyst (HUMINT)
Senior Specialist, Training 35M

Senior Specialist, Training 35M HUMINT
SIGINT Intelligence Analyst, Mid
Social Network Intelligence Specialist

EXPLOSIVES AND AMMUNITION

Ammunition Supply Technician (Ammo
Supply)
Chemical Engineer
Computers & Information Technology
Contract Specialist
Design Engineering Manager
Direct Fire Weapons Integrator
Director of Ammunition Program
Electronic Security Systems (ESS) Technician
Explosives Maintenance Mechanic
Explosives Operator
General Machinist
Greek Language Instructor
Handler, Ammunition
Human Resources Spec (Military)
Lineman A
Machine Repairer
Marine Training Advisory Team Member
Munitions Handler (Motor Vehicle)
Munitions Handler (Motor Vehicles)
Observer/Trainer, 13M
Occupational Health Nurse Senior
Process Chemical Engineer
Program Manager II
Safety and Occupational Health
Safety Engineer
Senior Manager, Materials/Distribution
Senior Principal Systems
Shop Planner (carpentry)
Subject Matter Expert I (Mechanical)
Subject Matter Expert I (Mitigation)
Subject Matter Expert I (Neu EE Lasers)
Subject Matter Expert I (Physics)
Subject Matter Expert I (Sensors)
Subject Matter Expert I (Statistical)
Subject Matter Expert I (Systems)
Technology Project Manager
Training Ammunition Technician
Warfighter Ammunition
Warfighter Ammunition Information Team
Writer, Technical

ELECTRONIC MAINTENANCE

AC Equipment Mechanic
Business Development Specialist
Custodial Worker-Foreman
Data Warehouse/SQL Developer
Director, Facility Maintenance

Electrical Engineer
Electro Mechanical Technician
Electronic Game Room Technician
Electronic Industrial Controls Mechanic
Electronic Integrated Systems Mechanic
Electronics Engineer
Electronics Mechanic Supervisor
Electronics Worker
Embedded Control Software Engineer
Equipment Specialist (Electronics)
Field Service Engineer
Fuel Station Repair Technician
General Equipment Mechanic Supervisor
Industrial Maintenance Technician
Installation/Maintenance/Repair Technician
Interdisciplinary Social Worker
Maintenance Manager
Maintenance Mechanic
Maintenance Technician
Maintenance Worker
Manager I – Engineering Technical
Mobile Army S6 Training/Support
Office Assistant III
Plant Maintenance and Operations
Process Improvement Specialist
Reporting Solutions Analyst
Sandblaster
SCA Electronic Technician Maintenance 2
Sheet Metal Mechanic Supervisor
Support Maintenance Supervisor (SBCT 7)
Technical Supervisor (Equipment)
U.S. Field Service Technician Senior
Visual Information Equipment

ELECTRONIC WARFARE

Administrative Support Assistant
Army C4ISR Tactical Operations Analyst
Army Linguist, Cryptologic
Army Project Officer
Asset Group Manager
Aviation Electronic Warfare
Avionics/Electronic Technician
Director of Business Development II
Electrical Electronic Craftsworker
Electronic Industrial Control Mechanic
Electronic Integrated Systems Mechanic
Electronic Systems International Offset
Electronic Tech I (EMA-RM)
Electronic Technician (RF) (LINK436)
Electronic Technician I/II
Electronic Warfare (EW) Systems Engineer
Electronic Warfare Algorithm
Electronic Warfare Analyst
Electronic Warfare Analyst

Electronic Warfare Program Manager
Electronic Warfare Specialist
Electronic Warfare/Sonar/Radar Experts
Electronics Engineer
Electronics Technician
Engineer, Electronic
General Manager – Army Ammunition
International Business Development-
Production Control Planner II
Program Manager I (Electronic)
SCA Electronic Technician II
Senior Electronic Technician With TS
Senior Engineer (SE) Electronic
Senior Technician, Electronic
Supervisor, Army Community Services
Systems Engineering – Radar
Transmitter Electronic Technician III

FINANCE
Accounting/Finance/Tax/Controls
Accounting Technician I
Accounting/Office Clerk
Administrative/Customer Support
Army Acquisition and Finance SME
Asset Management Pal Financial Services
Associate Planned Giving Director
Chief Cashier
Collections Technician
Coordinator, Finance Operations –
    Chargebacks
Director of Finance
Director of Finance
Finance Analyst
Finance Analyst – Deductions
Finance Director
Finance Manager
Finance Manager – Accounts Receivable
Finance Manager – Accounts Receivable
Finance Manager – Economic Modeling
Finance Manager – Packaging
Finance Representative – Deductions
Finance Secretary
Finance Senior Manager
Finance Supervisor
Finance Technical Specialist
Finance, Insurance and Investment Sales
Functional Accountant
Human Resources Specialist
In-House Finance Attorney
Internal Auditor
Principal Specialist – Finance Analyst
Senior Analyst, Finance
Senior Financial Analyst – Supply
Senior Specialist – Finance

Senior Systems Engineer – Army
    Future Combat
Staff Accountant
Supervisor of Contract Funding

INTELLIGENCE
Afghanistan-Pakistan Senior
All Source Intelligence Analyst
Army Linguist, Cryptologic (35P)
Army Logistician
Army Project Officer
Budget Analyst
Chief Current Operations and
Combat Developer and Counter-IED
Counterintelligence Analyst
Counterterrorism/Intelligence Analyst
Criminal Intelligence Analyst
CTDB Intelligence Analyst
Financial Manager/Fiscal
Intelligence Assistant (OA)
Intelligence Collections Managers
Intelligence Community
Intelligence Operations (APA3)
Intelligence Reports Specialist
Intelligence Specialist
Intelligence Specialist GMI Analyst
Intelligence Specialist Operations
Intelligence Specialist Operations
Major Account Manager US Army
Occupational Health Nurse, Senior
OSINT/Intelligence Analyst
Senior Army Analyst-C2 Acquisitions
Social Network Intelligence Analyst
Supervisor Intelligence Specialist S and
Supervisory Intelligence Specialist
Training Specialist Intelligence
U.S. Army Intelligence Subject Matter

LAW ENFORCEMENT
Anti-Terrorism Specialist
Asset Protection Manager
Assistant Account Manager
Business Analyst Associate Professional
Business Systems Administrator – EAM
Computer Systems Security 2
Correctional Officer, P/T
Credit Card Processing Associate
Data Analyst Professional
Director of Security
Director, Construction Management
Emergency Communications Dispatcher
ICE FPS Security Assistant
Info Security Analyst

Information Assurance Analyst
Licensed Practical Nurse, P/T
Military Police
Network Security Analyst with Security
Police Officer
Police Officer Desk Sergeant
Principal Specialist – Intelligence
	and Operations
Project Architect
Project Manager
Public Affairs Specialist
Registered Nurse (Non-Exempt)
Registered Nurse, P/T
Security and Safety Officer
Security Manager
Technical Operations Officer
Technician, Help Desk
Victim Advocate
Victim Advocate, Sexual Assault

LEGAL SERVICES

Assistant Legal Counsel
Associate Director of Special Gifts
Attorney (General)
Attorney (Labor)
Attorney (Real Property)
Chief Operating Officer
Corporate M and A Paralegal
Corporate Paralegal
General Counsel
Healthcare Paralegal
In-House Finance Attorney
In-House Paralegal Corporate Generalist
JAG Corps Attorney/Lawyer
Legal Assistant
Legal Assistant (OA)
Legal Clerk
Legal Counsel
Legal Nurse
Legal Secretary
Legal Technician (OA)
Legal, Law Enforcement, and Security Analyst
Medical Records Technician
Paralegal Specialist
Paralegal/Legal Assistant II
Program Director
Secretary (OA)
Secretary II
Supervisor of Contract Funding
USAR Unit Administrative Technician

PSYCHOLOGICAL OPERATIONS

Intelligence Specialist (Operations)
MTT Trainer/Developer
Open Source Analyst
Principal Developer, Instructional

PUBLIC AFFAIRS

Academic Director – Audio Production
Account Supervisor – Public
Arabic Interpreter/Translator
Army Reserve Careers
Army Strategic Communications Associate
Arts, Media, and Music Opportunities
Combat Documentation/Production
Information Officer/Photographer
Information Receptionist
Interpreter
Interpreter/Translator
Legislative Public Affairs Specialist
Marketing/Public Affairs Specialist
Principal Strategic Communications Lead
Program Coordinator, Office of LGBTQI
Public Affairs Advisor
Public Affairs Assistant
Public Affairs Broadcast Specialist
Public Affairs Manager
Public Affairs Officer
Public Affairs Specialist
Public Affairs/Communications Director
Public Information Officer
Public Relations Specialist
Regulatory Affairs and Compliance
Senior Director, Public Affairs,
	and Speech Writer
Student Trainee (Public Affairs)
Supervisory Public Affairs Specialist

MEDICAL

Accounting/Office Clerk
Active Hospital Dietitian
Allied Health – Pharmaceutical Technician
Allied Health – Pharmacist
Certified Nurse Midwife
Health Care Coordinator-RN
Health System Assistant
Health System Specialist
Health Technician
Health Technician Paramedic
Health Technician-Ophthalmology
Nurse
Nurse Administrator
Nurse Anesthetist
Nurse Anesthetist (Reserve Duty)

Nurse Clinical Communications
    Occupational Health
Nurse Clinical Psychiatric
Nurse – Administrative
Nurse – Case Manager
Nurse – Clinical Ambulatory
Nurse – Clinical Medicine-Surgical
Nurse – Clinical OB/GYN
Nurse – Clinical Research Oncology
Occupational Health Nurse Senior
Practical Nurse
Practical Nurse – Occupational Health
Public Health Manager
Safety and Occupational Health Specialist
Supervisor Health Systems Specialist
Vocational Nurse – Emergency Room

RECRUITING AND RETENTION
Associate Vice President of
    Human Resources
CareFocus – Human Resources Assistant
Custodial Worker
Customer Service Assistant
Entry-Level Event Marketing
Food Activity/Operation Foreman
Global Communications and
    Public Affairs Manager
HR Technician I (Supervisor)
Human Resources
Human Resources Analyst
Human Resources Assistant
Human Resources Assistant – File Room
Human Resources Assistant (Military)
Human Resources Director
Human Resources Director – Distribution
Human Resources Generalist
Human Resources IT Specialist
Human Resources Manager
Human Resources Specialist (Military)
Multi-Functional HR Associate
Multi-Functional HR Manager
Regional Human Resources Manager
Regional Human Resources Manager, Sales
Senior Store Associate
Store Associate
Supervisor, Accounting Associates
Vice President of Human Resources
Warehouse Worker Foreman

RELIGIOUS SERVICES
Army Volunteer Cord/Army Family Team
Assistant Chaplain
Care Partner

Care Partner – PRN
Chaplain
Chaplain Palliative Medicine
Chaplain – Hospice
Chaplain, Staff
Community Liaison
Medical Receptionist
Office and Administrative Support
On-Call Victim Advocate
Part-Time Chaplain
Psychological Health Outreach Counselor
Psychological Health Support Team Member
Registered Nurse II-CC
U.S. On-Call Victim Advocate
Veterans' Chaplain
Victims' Advocate

SPECIAL EQUIPMENT
AH-64 Aircraft General Repair Mechanic
AH-64 Aircraft General Repair Mechanic
Aircraft Electrical Repair Mechanic
Aircraft Engine Repair Mechanic
Aircraft General Repair Mechanic
Aircraft Structural Repair Mechanic
CC Plant Senior Technician
CH-47 Aircraft General Repair Mechanic
Director, Turbine Generator Services
Engineer II – Tech Support AGT1500
Gas Turbine Systems Technician
Generator Mechanic (Vehicle/Equipment)
Generator Tech
Generator Technician – L-2
Generator Technician – L-3
Generator Technician II
Lead Generator
Line Mechanic-D-C-B-A
Power Generator Technician II
Power Plant Mechanic – F/A-18
Power Plant Technician – Electrical
Power Plant Technician – Mechanical
Power Systems Planning Consultant
Power Systems Planning Senior Staff
Programmer Analyst
Purchasing Specialist – Utility
Region Prod Support Supervisor
Rig Electrician
Senior Electric Power Modeler
Skilled Maintenance Technician
Technical Service Representative
UH-1 Aircraft Avionics/Electrical Repair
UH-60 Aircraft Electrical Repair
UH-60 Aircraft General Repair Mechanic
UH-60 Aircraft Mechanic

SUPPLY AND LOGISTICS

Acquisition Logistics Analyst
Acquisition Logistics, Senior
Administrative Services
Applications Administrator
Army Project Officer
Director of Logistics
General Supply Specialist
JIEDDO JTF PALADIN Logistics
Logistics Analyst
Logistics Analyst (132-08408)
Logistics Management Analysis Associate
    Manager
Logistics Management Analyst Staff
Logistics Management Analyst, Senior
Logistics Management Assistant
Logistics Management Specialist
Logistics Specialist – TS/SCI
Medical Supply Technician
R-Supply Subject Matter Experts
Senior Aviation Logistics Analyst
Senior Logistics Analyst
Senior Logistics Management
Senior Logistics Specialist II
Senior Logistics Technician
Senior Navy Supply Analyst
Senior Supply Analyst
Senior Technician, Supply
Staff Training Specialist
Supervisory Supply Specialist
Supply Chain Manager/Business
Supply Chain Project Engineer
Supply Management Specialist
Supply Technician
Supply Technician
Supply Technician
Supply Technician (OA)
Workstation Controller

TRANSPORTATION

Accounting Assistant
Annex Supervisor
Army Community Services Division Chief
Army Project Officer
Driver
Environmental Protection Specialist
Food Service Worker
HBCT Foreign Military Sales (PSA Sr.)
JLTV Foreign Military Sales (PSA Sr.)
Laborer
Logistics Management Specialist

Maintenance Supervisor
Marine Transportation Specialist
Materials Handler I
Military Analyst
Military Operations Analyst
Military Personnel Consultant
Occupational Health Nurse Senior
Operations Supervisor Trainee
Supervisory Supply Specialist
Supervisory Transportation Specialist
Transportation Assistant
Transportation Assistant (OA)
Transportation Captain
Transportation Functional Analyst
Transportation Management Specialist
Transportation Manager
Transportation Planner
Transportation Specialist
Transportation Technician
Vending Machine Attendant
Warehouse Worker (Stocker)
Warehouse Worker Foreman (Stocker)
Waste Management and Transportation

VEHICLE MAINTENANCE

Army Project Officer
Assistant Account Manager
Automotive Worker
Correctional Maintenance Officer
Field Service Technician Senior
Iraq Automotive Technician
Maintenance Finisher (Motor Vehicle)
Maintenance Finisher Motor Vehicle Operator
Maintenance Mechanic (Motor Vehicle)
Maintenance Mechanic Motor Vehicle
    Operator
Maintenance Test Pilot
Maintenance Worker
Maintenance Worker (MVO)
Manager, Vehicle Fleet Administrator I
Microwave Systems Operator
Motor Vehicle Inspector
Motor Vehicle Maintenance Supervision
Motor Vehicle Mechanic
Resident (Assistant) Manager - Military
Roofer (Motor Vehicle Operator)
Vehicle Maintenance Supervisor
Vehicle Mechanic
Vehicle Systems Technician I
Wheeled Vehicle Mechanic

MARINE CORPS

AMMUNITION AND EXPLOSIVE ORDINANCE DISPOSAL
Ammunition Handler
Ammunition Supply Technician
   (Ammo Supply)
Chemical Engineer Co-Op
Design Engineering Manager
Electronic Technician I
Environmental Technician
Explosives Maintenance Mechanic
Explosives Operator
Explosives Test Operator IV
Freight Rate Specialist
General Clerk – Ammunition (CIS)
Instructor/Developer
Lead Munitions Logistics Analyst
Munitions Technician
Procurement Coordinator
Truck Driver, Heavy (Lead) (Low Haz)
Truck Driver, Heavy (Low Haz)
Vehicle Systems Technician

AIR CONTROL, AIR SUPPORT, ANTI-AIR WARFARE, AIR TRAFFIC CONTROL
Community Analyst (OA)
Emergency Dispatcher
Firefighter (EMT)
Marine Machinery Mechanic
Navy/Marine Corps Business Development
Painter
Radio Operator
Supervisory Management Analyst

AIRCRAFT MAINTENANCE
Aeronautical Engineer
Aircraft Airframe Power Plant Mechanic
Aircraft Maintenance Technician
Aircraft Mechanic – Contract Field Teams
Aircraft Mechanic, PEN FL T39 A/F
Airframe and Power Plant Mechanics
Airframe and Power Plant Mechanic
Bell Helicopter Mechanic
Design Engineer
F-5 Airframe Mechanic
H-60 Power Plant Mechanic
Helicopter Parts Person
Instrumentation Technician – Flight Test
IT Service Manager II
Janitor
Maintenance Electronics Repairer

Manager, Purchasing – H1 Program
Master Data Senior System Analyst
Material Dispatcher
Mechanic, Aircraft IDIQ N.I. IMANN
Plant Protection Officer
Principal Test Specialist, NDE
Project Manager
Quality Analyst
Regulatory Specialist
Senior Engineering Specialist
Senior Field Engineer, MTS

AIRFIELD SERVICES
Administrative Assistant
Director of Operations
Information Operations (IO) Analyst
Joint Aviation Operations Analyst
Navy/DoD Financial Management Analyst
Senior Principal Analyst, Operations
Special Operations Analyst
USMC Liaison Officer

AVIONICS
Aviation/Avionics Technology Sales
   Representative
Avionics Comms Engineer 4
Avionics Comms Engineer 4 (w/Clearance)
Avionics Installer
Avionics Installer, Lead
Avionics Integration Engineer
Avionics Maintenance Specialist
Avionics Systems – Broad Area
Avionics Systems Engineer
Avionics Technician
Avionics Technician, Completions
Avionics Technician, Final Assembly
Avionics/Electronic Technician
Avionics/Electronic Technician (AVIM)
College Student Technician, Senior
Electronic Tech III/Avionics Tech
Electronics Engineer
Electronics Technician
Helicopter Avionics Bench Technician
Navy UCAS Demo Engineer
Senior Engineer (Systems Avionics)
Senior LAN Administrator
Skyhook Design and Analysis
Staff DMSMS Avionics Analyst II
Systems Acquisition Manager

AVIATION, LOGISTICS

Engineer, Logistics
Logistics Analyst III
Logistics Analyst, Senior Principal
Logistics Engineer – Navy ILS
Logistics Engineer III
Logistics Management Specialist
Logistics Specialist III (EMA-PC054)
Logistics Support Services
Logistics/Materials Handling Technician
Navy UCAS Demo Engineer
Navy/Marine Corps Business Development
Principal Engineer, Logistics
Project Manager
Project Manager I
Senior Logistics Analyst
Senior Principal Analyst, Operations
Senior Supply Analyst
SIAT MAGTF Certification Engineer
Software Engineer Associate
Supply Chain Coordinator
Systems Engineer II – Navy Training
Tactical Radios Systems Engineer III
USMC Liaison Officer

AVIATION, ORDNANCE

Criminal Investigator, Tedac
Equal Employment Manager
Explosive Ordnance Disposal Instructors
Explosive Ordnance Disposal Technician
Explosives Chemist
Explosives Operator
Field Service Engineer, Explosives
Fingerprint Specialist
Intelligence Research Specialist
Investigative Analyst
Learning Technologies Training
Mechanic, Aircraft 1 (Aviation
      Ordnance), CFT
Mechanical Engineer III (Ordnance)
NAVAIR Ordnance Training Analyst
Operator, Junior
Ordnance Equipment Repairer
Ordnance Loader
Ordnance Maintenance Analyst
Production Controller (Ordnance)
Program Analyst
Senior DoD Project Engineer
Senior Project Engineer
Senior Quality Assurance Engineer
Senior Quality Engineer (Ordnance)
Specialist – Explosives

COMMAND AND CONTROL SYSTEMS

Aerospace Engineer
Financial Management Analyst
Industrial Hygienist
Motor Vehicle Dispatcher
Production Control Supervisor (SBCT 2)
Production Controller
Program Plan Control Analyst Associate
Tactical Air Command/Control

DATA COMMUNICATIONS MAINTENANCE

Aircraft Maintenance Technician
Applications Analyst
BI Data Integration Specialist
C4ISRT Field Service Engineer – Electronics
C4ISRT Integration and Testing
      Engineer – HW/SW
C4ISRT Integration and Testing
      Engineer – Software
Configuration Data Technician
Data Analyst Senior Professional
Data Management Specialist
Data Warehouse/SQL Developer
Data Warehouse Developer
Electronic Data Interchange (EDI)
Enterprise Data Analyst
ETL/Data Integration Manager
Facilities and Maintenance Manager
Functional Analyst, Aviation Maintenance
Maintenance Technician
Manager Application Development
NGEN/MCNIS Acquisition
      Contracting Team
NGEN/MCNIS Acquisition
      Contracts Analyst
Project Manager
Regulatory Specialist
Senior Programmer – Data Warehouse
Systems Analyst (with Security Clearance)
Systems Integration Analyst IV
T & E Engineer
T & E Engineer 3/4

DATA SYSTEMS

Cashier/Sales Associate
Configuration Data Technician
Data Analyst Senior Professional
Data Clerk (Office Automation)
Data Technician
Database Administrator Senior Professional
Database Analyst
Electronic Data Interchange

Electronic Data Interchange Manager
Financial Analyst
Financial Systems Analyst
Food Management Systems Analyst
Human Resources Technician (MIL/OA)
Information Technology Specialist
IT Specialist (Data Management)
Lessons Learned Analyst/Pre-Deployment
Logistics Management Specialist
Marine Officer (Ground)
Office Automation Assistant
Oracle Database Administrator
Oracle PL/SQL Database Developer
Release Manager – Military Sealift
Remedy ARS Developer
Supervisory IT Specialist/Financial
System Analyst Professional
Worker's Comp Contact Representative

ELECTRONICS MAINTENANCE
Application Analyst – Electronic Medical
Boiler Technician
C4ISRT Field Service Engineer
C4ISRT Field Service Engineer – Software
C4ISRT Help Desk Engineer – Field
C4ISRT Help Desk Support Engineer
C4ISRT Integration & Testing
    Engineer – HW/SW
Communications Line Installer
Director, Facility Maintenance
Electrical Engineer
Electronic Data Interchange (EDI)
Electronic Gameroom Technician
Electronics Engineer
Engineer Technician – CENTRIXS
Field Service Engineer
Fuel Station Repair Technician
Industrial Maintenance Technician
Installation/Maintenance/Repair Worker
Machinist
Maintenance Mechanic
Maintenance Technician
Maintenance Worker
Ordnance Maintenance Analyst
SCA Electronic Technician Maintenance II
Technical Supervisor (Equipment)
Vehicle Electronics Systems Mechanic

ENGINEER, CONSTRUCTION, FACILITIES, AND EQUIPMENT
Architecture Construction Representative
Construction Inspector Aide
Construction Planner/Estimator

Construction Worker
COO Development Program/Associate
Director Facilities and Construction
Director, Facility Maintenance
Electrician – Construction
Electrician's Helper
Entry-Level Construction Inspector
Estimating Director
Facilities and Maintenance Manager
Facilities Equipment, and Lab Technician
Field Service Technician – Medical
Foreman
Heavy Equipment Operator
Inventory Control Specialist
Management Trainee Program
Manager, Quality and Food Safety
Mobile Facility Engineer
Occupational Health Nurse, Senior
ODC Disability Services Coordinator
Pier Technician
Project Manager I-FSC
Quality and Food Safety Manager
Quality Technician
Safety Manager
Senior Geographic Information Systems
Transportation Technician

EXCHANGE
Electronics Buyer
Prospect Manager
Retail Buyer
Retail Management
Retail Planogram Specialist
Retail Sales Clerk
Sales
Visual Merchandiser

FIELD ARTILLERY
Marine Officer (Ground)
Systems Integration Analyst II
Systems Safety Engineer
Tactical Air Command/Control
Track Vehicle Mechanic
Track Vehicle Mechanic (M2)

FINANCIAL MANAGEMENT
Contract Specialist
Financial Analyst
Financial Manager
Foreign Military Sales Financial
Head, Resource Management
IT Specialist/Financial Management
Supervisory IT Specialist, Financial

FOOD SERVICE

Au Pair (live-in Nanny)
Food Management Systems Analyst
Supervisory Management Analyst

INFANTRY

Infantry Weapons Equipment Specialist
Infantry Weapons Requirements Analyst
Infantry Weapons Senior
    Requirements Analyst
Infantry Weapons Specialist
Infantry Weapons Team Lead
Manpower and Training Analyst – Infantry
Marine Officer (Ground)

INTELLIGENCE (COUNTER-INTEL)

ANSS – Counterintelligence (CI) Doctrine
ANSS – Human Intelligence (HUMINT)
Associate Analyst, Operations
CI OPS Analyst, Lead TS/SCI
CMMA Intelligence Trainer
Counterintelligence Analyst
Counterintelligence Analyst, Principal
Counterintelligence Mid-Level Analyst
Counterintelligence Mid-Level Analyst
Counterintelligence Officer/CI
Counterintelligence Operations Analyst
Counterintelligence Senior Analyst
Counterintelligence Training Officer
Financial Systems Analyst
Geospatial Intelligence Analyst
Geospatial Intelligence Analyst (Security
    Clearance)
Intelligence Analyst (Finance) III
Intelligence Specialist
Modeling and Simulation Analyst for
Professional Technician (Non-Exempt with
    Security Clearance)
Senior Acquisition Analyst/USMC
Senior Counterintelligence (CI) Target
Senior Expert for Counterintelligence
Senior Intelligence/IT System
Senior Manager, Information Systems
SME – Marine Expeditionary Systems
Subject Matter Expert
Training Development Specialist III

LOGISTICS

Acquisition Logistics Process Analyst
Acquisition/Logistics Analyst
Customer Service Associate
IT Specialist (Systems Analyst/
    Customer Support)
Lead Logistics Support Analyst
Lead Munitions Logistics Analyst
Lead Technical Trainer
Logistics Analyst
Logistics Engineer – Navy ILS
Logistics Management Specialist
Logistics Manager
Logistics Program Analyst
Logistics Specialist III – (EMA #DL060)
Logistics Supervisor
Navy Radar Engineer
Navy UCAS Demo Engineer
Navy/Marine Corps Business Development
Production Controller
Sales/Navy – Broadband Solutions
Senior Principal Engineer, Logistics
Supervisor Logistics Management
Supply Logistics Analyst
WMS Support – Navy Yard

LEGAL SERVICES

Assistant Deputy Director, MWTC
Contract Administrator
Legal Administrative Specialist
Legal Assistant (OA)
Senior Principal Analyst, Research
Technical Manager for Marine Corp Weapon
Technician, Help Desk

LINGUIST

All Source Analyst/Arab
Arabic Linguist
Arabic Linguist Active TS SCI CI
Arabic Linguist with TS SCI
Bengali Linguist
General Editor/Linguist
Greek Linguist
Hindi Linguist
Malay Linguist
Pashto Linguist for Afghanistan
Portuguese Linguist
Somali Linguist
Spanish Linguist

MARINE AIR GROUND TASK FORCE (MAGTF) PLANS

IT Specialist (Security)
MAGTF/Joint Fires Analyst IV
Senior C2 Systems Engineer (USMC/USN)
SIAT MAGTF Certification Engineer
Statistician
System Administrator Professional
Training Development Specialist III

MILITARY POLICE AND CORRECTIONS

Certified Police Officer
Correctional Counselor III
Correctional Officer
Correctional Officer IV
Corrections Supervisor I – (SR-24)
Deputy I – Corrections
Health Program Manager III
K-9 Handler – Explosive Detection
Library Technical Assistant (Safety)
Military Police
Military Police (no experience)
Parole Agent II, Adult Parole
Police Officer
Professional Police Officer
Program Director
Records Technician – Police
Special Police Officer, Armed
Staff Information Systems Analyst

MOTOR TRANSPORT

AC Equipment Mechanic
Anti-Armor Motor Vehicle Transport
Armor Equipment Operator
Drill Instructor
Engineering Equipment Operator
Fork Lift Operator
Logistics Management Analyst, Senior Staff
Master Supply Technician
Motor Transport Operator
Motor Vehicle Dispatcher
Motor Vehicle Mechanic
Motor Vehicle Operator
PR Electrical Engineer
Property Book Team Chief
Reports Coordinator/Warehouse Manager
USMC Anti-Armor Equipment Operator
Vehicle Modification Team Member

MUSIC

Church Musician
ETL Developer
Musician/Accompanist
QA Manager
Religious Educator/Musician
Sales, Customer Service Representative

NAVIGATION OFFICER

Air Crewmen
Aircraft Mechanic – Aerospace
Airframe and Power Plant Mechanic

NUCLEAR, BIOLOGICAL, AND CHEMICAL

CBRN Command Post Operator
CBRN Instructor
CBRN Instructor with Security Clearance
CBRN Officer
CBRN Senior Analyst
CBRN Training Instructor
CBRN Training Instructor
Combat Development/Material Systems
Human Resources Specialist (Military)
Medical Countermeasures Analyst (GTD)
Medical Countermeasures CBRN Analyst
Project Manager
SW Engineer III
Systems Administrator
Warehouse Support Personnel

OPERATIONAL COMMUNICATIONS

Allied Health – Clinical Psychology/Mental
CMMA Intelligence Trainer
Communications Analyst
Deputy Project Manager (Marine Corp)
Financial Manager
Hospital Corpsman
Lane Controller Assistant Project
Logistics Analyst
Logistics Analyst (8EOS-055)
Logistics Specialist III (EMA-DL050)
MAGTFC4I Systems Tester
Military Analyst and War Gaming Action
Monitoring Technician
MRAP Operations and Business Manager
Multimedia Design Engineer
Multimedia Design Engineer Associate
Plans Support Analyst – CFS
Project Manager I (PDS Installation Team)
Release Management Process Lead
Release Manager – Military Sealift
Senior Communications Engineer
Senior Principal Systems
Senior Technical Editor/Writer
Site Survey IT – Information Systems Security
Supervisory Budget Analyst
System Analyst Professional
System Analyst Senior Professional
System Engineer – C4I
System Engineer – C4I (CS8055)
    with Clearance
USMC Communications and
    Computer Systems

ORDNANCE

C4I Test Development Specialist
Engineering Technician
Explosive Ordnance Disposal Instructor
Explosive Ordnance Disposal Technician
Instructor/Developer
Logistics Engineer Senior Staff
Logistics Management Analyst
Mechanic, Aircraft 1 Ordnance CFT LMC
Mechanic, Aircraft 1/Aviation Ordnance CFT
NAVAIR Ordnance Training Analyst
NAVAIR Ordnance Training Analyst
News and Media Personality
Ordnance Equipment Mechanic Helper
Ordnance Equipment Repairer
Ordnance Loader
Ordnance Maintenance Analyst
Ordnance Mechanic Associate
Ordnance Packager
Ordnance Professionals
Ordnance Test Technician
Principal Software Safety Engineer
Principal Software Safety Engineer
    with Clearance
Production Controller (Ordnance)
Senior Software Systems Safety Engineer
Social Scientist
Software Systems Safety Engineer II
Systems Safety Engineer II
Test Manager
Training Development Specialist III

PUBLIC AFFAIRS

Communications Specialist
Communications Specialist – Public
Communications, Senior Professional
Community and Business Relations Liaison
Diabetic Nurse Educator
Entry-Level Public Affairs
Information Technology Specialist
Legislative Public Affairs Specialist
Manager, Regional
Mid-Level Public Affairs/Public
Military Analyst II – COIN Analyst
Military Analyst II – COIN Operations
Military Analyst-Action Officer
Nurse Officer of the Day (NOD) RN
Program Management, Principal Leader
Public Affairs Broadcast Specialist
Public Affairs Professional
Public Affairs Specialist
Public Affairs Specialist – PEO Carriers
Public Affairs/Public Relations Specialist
Public Utilities Analyst I

Radio Producer
Security Engineer (CISSP)
Senior Military Analyst
Student Trainee (Public Affairs)
Supervisory Social Worker (Vet Center)

PERSONNEL ADMINISTRATION

Administrative Support Assistant (OA)
Deputy Project Manager (Marine Corp)
Legal Assistant (OA)
Personnel Program Manager
Regional School Liaison Specialist
Supervisory Management Analyst
Supervisory Management and
    Program Analyst
Supply Technician

SIGNALS INTELLIGENCE/GROUND ELECTRONIC WARFARE

Director of Engineering – SIGINT
DoD/SIGINT Account Executive
Electronic Warfare-Action Officer
Electronic Warfare (EW) Systems Engineer
EW Field Service Engineer, Regional
EW Systems Engineer
Field Service Engineer – EW
ISR/Electrical Engineer (Entry-Level)
Lead Engineer – Systems (SIGINT)
Manager, Business Development – Land
Manager, Naval and Missile Defense
Principal Systems Engineer,
    SIGINT C4 Systems
Senior SIGINT/EW Systems
Senior SIGINT/EW Systems Engineer
    with Clearance
Sensor Systems Design Engineer V
Senior SIGINT Engineer
Senior Technical Experts – SIGINT
Senior Technical Program Manager
SIGINT Analyst
SIGINT Intelligence Analyst, Mid
Software Engineer/SIGINT
Staff Systems Engineer – SIGINT
Technical Project Manager

SUPPLY ADMINISTRATION AND OPERATIONS

Assistant Deputy Director, MWTC
Equipment Specialist
Financial Technician (OA)
Inventory Planner (Retail)

IT Specialist (System Analysis)
Logistics Management Specialist
Mail Clerk
Material Expediter
MRAP Supply
Navy FMS Financial Analyst
Procurement Technician (OA)
Purchasing, Procurement and Supply
Recreation Specialist (Sports
Sales/Navy – Broadband Solutions
Senior Navy Supply Analyst
Senior Supply Analyst
Senior Supply Analyst with Security
Supervisory Navy Supply Support Analyst
Supply Chain Specialist
Supply Logistics Analyst
Supply Representative
Supply Technician (OA)
VMS Integration Lead Engineer –
   Navy UCAS
WMS Support – Navy Yard

TANK AND ASSAULT AMPHIBIOUS VEHICLE

Contract Administrator
Crane Operator
Electronic Integrated Systems Mechanic
Engineer – Mechanical – Survivability
Engineer – Mechanical Assoc – Weapons
General Equipment Repairer
General Maintenance Worker
Heavy Mobile Equipment Mechanic
Heavy Mobile Equipment Repair Inspector
Human Systems Interface Engineer – IT
Industrial Specialist
Intelligence Specialist
Machine Tool Operator
Manufacturing Engineering Specialist (E)
Marine Pump/Tank Cleaners
Mechanical Engineer (Family)
Program Analyst
Project Engineer
Quality Program Lead Manager (QPLM)
Secretary (OA)
Senior Systems Engineer for Weight
Supply Technician
Systems Engineer II (EMA-BM018)
Tank Mechanic
Tank Systems Technician
Tank Systems Technician, Senior
Welder
Wildfire/CAD Design Engineer

TRAFFIC MANAGEMENT

Acquisition Logistics Analyst
Acquisition Logistics Process Analyst
Contract Specialist
Department of Transportation Qualified
Heavy Mobile Equipment Mechanic
Heavy Mobile Equipment Mechanic
Industrial Engineer
IPT Lead – Navy Platforms
Logistics Engineer – Navy ILS
Marine Cargo Specialist
Marine Transportation Specialist
Motor Vehicle Dispatcher
MRAP Operations and Business Manager
Program/Project Manager – Kuwait
Project Engineer, Structures
Senior Optical Scientist
Senior Systems Engineer – Mechanical
Subject Matter Expert
Supervisory Navy Supply Support Analyst
Systems Engineer VI
Transportation Assistant
Transportation Assistant (Personal)
Transportation Specialist
USMC Anti-Armor Equipment Maintainer
USMC Anti-Armor Equipment Operator
WMS Support – Navy Yard

UTILITIES

Acquisition/Logistics Analyst
General Maintenance Worker
HVAC/Refrigeration Specialist
Laborer
Logistics Analyst
Recreation Specialist (Sports)
Retail MCX Buyer
Senior Project Manager

VISUAL INFORMATION

Military Analyst Lead
Software Engineer

WEATHER SERVICE

Aerographer Mate
Meteorologist (Intern)
Meteorologist Senior Forecaster
Operational Meteorologist
Weather Anchor
Weather Forecaster Trainer

NAVY

ADVANCED ELECTRONICS COMPUTER FIELD

Associate Technician, Electronics
Biomedical Electronics Technician II
C4ISRT Field Service Engineer
CEC Operation and Maintenance Technician
Customer Support Engineer
Electronic Field Service Engineer
Electronics Engineer III
Electronics Field Technician
Electronics Technician
Electronics Technician A, Range
Electronics Technician II, Blue Sky
Electronics Technician II, Lab Services
Electronics Technician/Field Service
Engineering Technician IV
Engineering Technician IV (U1656)
Field Service Engineer
Field Service Specialist
Field Service Tech I – Medical Equipment
Field Service Technician
Field Service Technician II, Medical
Field Service Technician, Senior
Lead Technician, Electronics
Senior Field Service Technician
Technical Field Service Representative
Technician
Technician – Calibration/Electronics/Metro
Technician, Electro-Optics Depot
Test Technician
Weapons Technician Senior Assistant

AIR

Aircrew Aviation Scheduling/Dispatch
Aircrew Mission Specialist
Aircrew TD Instructor
Aircrew – Weapon System
Aircrew – Weapon System Officer
Aircrew – Weapon System Officer-
    Engineer IV
AWACS Aircrew Training Devices
AWACS Instructor Navigator
Data Manager
Engineer IV – Air Vehicle Operator
Engineer IV with Security Clearance
FE Simulator Instructor
Ground Service Representative
Health Technician (Optometry)
Helicopter Mechanic/Aircrew
Military Analyst, Senior

Mission Manager I
Mission Planner IV
Mission Planner IV with Security Clearance
Part 135 Helicopter Dispatch Center
Payload Operator III
Payload Operator III with Security
Software Engineer II – F15C Aircrew
System Administrator II (IA Specialist)
Test Pilot Manager L

AIR TRAFFIC CONTROLMAN

Air Safety Officer, P-4
Air Traffic Control Position
Air Traffic Control Specialist
Air Traffic Control Specialist Station
Air Traffic Control Subsystem Manager
Air Traffic Controller
Air Traffic Manager
Air Traffic Services Maintenance Senior Radar
Air Traffic Specialist
ATC Air Traffic Controller
Counter Desk Attendant/Equipment
Junior/Mid-Level Software Engineer
Manager, Air Traffic Control
On-Air Promotion Coordinator
On-Air TV Traffic Reporter
SCA Air Traffic Control Specialist
Senior Integration and Test Engineer
Senior Software Engineer for Air Traffic
Traffic Administrator
Traffic Administrator, Senior
Traffic Reporter/Producer
Traffic Specialist

AVIATION

Aircraft Electrician
Aircraft Functional Test Electrician
Aviation Electrician, Senior
Aviation Electricians
DC Control Electrician
Electrical Design Intern
Electrical Engineering Tech
Electrical Supervisor
Electrical/Mechanical Product
    Support Specialist
Electrician
Electrician Assistant
Electrician, Maintenance
F18 Maintenance Subject Matter Expert

Field Service Technician, Senior
Field Technician
Final Assembly Electrician
Industrial Electrician
Jet Bridge Electrician
Journeyman Electrician
Lighting Service Technician
Maintenance Electrician I
Maintenance Technician
Medical Equipment Delivery and Service
Plant Electrician
Supervisor Service
Surgical Technologist I

AVIATION AEROGRAPHY
Administrative Assistant
Anchor/Reporter
Construction – Concrete Work/Equipment
General Assignment Reporter
Maintenance Technician II
    (Stone Mason) –MDC
Meteorologist
On-Air Host/Reporter
On-Air TV Traffic Reporter
Public Relations Intern
Reporter
Reporter/Weather
Snow Reporter
Street Outreach Counselor
VJ/Reporter
Weather Anchor
Weathercaster
Weekend Meteorologist
Weekend Meteorologist/Weather Anchor

AVIATION BOATSWAIN
American R-40 Derrick Operator
Analyst, Business Applications
Assistant Fire Chief
Assistant Fire Chief of Operations
Barge Foreman
Chief Engineer/DDE Unlimited
Crewing Manager
Director, Commercial Marine Risk
Emergency Manager Operations Officer
Field Network Engineer – Baseband CFSR
Firefighter
Hospital Security Specialist
Inland Pipeline/Construction Barge
Instructional System Designer/Technician
Instructor Technical Trainer
Instructor Technical Training I
JNN Instructor/Developer

Lead Munitions Logistics Analyst
Manager, Marine Operations
Manager, Project-Salvage
Marine Buyer
Marine Engineer
NetOps Instructor/Developer
Personnel Manager
Property Claims Representative
Purchasing Manager
Safety Coordinator
SATCOM Field Network Engineer
Senior Marine Surveyor
Specialist, Credit & Collections
Staff Accountant
Station Chief
WINT Inc I Instructor

AVIATION ORDNANCEMAN
Aerospace Ordnance Engineering Technical
Criminal Investigator, Tedac
Equal Employment Manager
Explosive Ordnance Disposal Instructor
Explosive Ordnance Disposal Technician
Explosives Chemist
Explosives Engineering Manager
Explosives Maintenance Mechanic
Explosives Operator
Field Service Engineer, Explosives
Fingerprint Specialist
Hazard Classification/Explosives Safety
Intelligence Research Specialist
Learning Technologies Training Specialist
Management Assistant, Office Automation
Mechanic, Aircraft I Ordnance CFT LMC
Mechanic, Aircraft I/Aviation Ordnance CFT
NAVAIR Ordnance Training Analyst
Occupational Health Nurse, Senior
Operator, Junior
Ordnance Assembler
Ordnance Equipment Mechanic Helper
Ordnance Equipment Repairer
Ordnance Handler – Associate
Ordnance Loader
Ordnance Mechanic, Associate
Ordnance Packager
Ordnance Professionals
Ordnance Test Technician
Production Controller (Ordnance)
Program Analyst
Safety Specialist (Chemistry/Explosives)
Secretary (OA)
Specialist, Explosives
Unexploded Ordnance Technician I
Unexploded Ordnance/Remediation

AVIATION ELECTRONICS

Associate Technician, Electronics
Biomedical Electronics Technician II
C4ISRT Field Service Engineer
CEC Operation and Maintenance Technician
Customer Support Engineer
Electronic Field Service Engineer
Electronics Engineer III
Electronics Field Technician
Electronics Technician
Electronics Technician A, Range
Electronics Technician II, Blue Sky
Electronics Technician II, Lab Services
Electronics Technician/Field Service
Engineering Technician IV
Engineering Technician IV (U1656)
Field Service Engineer
Field Service Specialist
Field Service Tech I, Medical Equipment
Field Service Tech II – Medical
Field Service Technician
Field Service Technician, Senior
Lead Technician, Electronics
Senior Field Service Technicians
Technical Field Service Representative
Technician
Technician – Calibration/Electronics/Metro
Technician, Electro-Optics Depot
Test Technician
Weapons Technician Senior Assistant

AVIATION MAINTENANCE ADMINISTRATION

A & P Mechanic (CASA 212/King Air)
A&P Mechanic
A&P Mechanics (General Aviation)
AMSEC – Senior Consulting Manager
AMSEC – Ship Design Manager
Automotive Service Center Manager
Aviation Maintenance
Aviation Maintenance Systems Analyst
Aviation Maintenance, Training
Aviation Maintenance/Quality Control
Aviation Sheetmetal Mechanics
Director of Maintenance
E-Business/Business Intelligence
Electronic Data Interchange
Functional Analyst, Aviation Maintenance
IT Project Manager
Maintenance Controller (Aviation)
Maintenance Electrician
Maintenance Engineer
Maintenance Manager

Maintenance Technician
Marketing Manager – Navy Programs
Master Maintenance Mechanic
Navy Surface Ship Combat Systems Analyst
Office and Administrative Support
Operations Manager
Program Manager
Project Manager
QA Manager – GCP/GLP
Regulatory Specialist
SCA Electronic Technician, Maintenance II
Senior Accountant
Technical Development Manager
Tooling & Material Analyst
UH-60 Aircraft Mechanic

AVIATION MACHINIST MATE

CNC Machinist
CNC Machinist/Programmer
CNC Mill Machinist
CNC Turning, Lathe Machinist
EDM Field Technician/Machinist
Electrician/Machinist
Field Machinist
Field Service Machinist
Journeyman Machinist
Machinist
Machinist/Fabricator
Machinist I
Machinist II
Machinist, CNC Machining Centers
Machinist/Gears/CNC
Machinist/Maintenance Mechanic
Manual Machinist
Master Machinist (Gear Grinding)
Mechanic-Machinist, Field Service
Pump/Motor Service Senior Machinist
Shop Supervisor/Machinist
Tool and Die/Machinist

AVIATION STRUCTURAL MECHANIC

A&P Mechanic
Aircraft Structural Mechanic
Aircraft Structural Repair Mechanic
Aviation Sheetmetal Mechanics
Aviation Structures Mechanic
Cabin Mechanic
Commercial Aviation – Apprentice
Instructor, Aviation Structural Mechanic
Maintenance Mechanic
Project Manager
Sheet Metal/Structural Mechanic
Sheetmetal Mechanic

Structures Mechanic
UH-60 Aircraft Mechanic

AVIONICS TECHNICIAN
AV-8 Electronics Tech
Avionics & Maintenance Inspector
Avionics Assembly Breakdown Analyst
Avionics Engineer IV
Avionics Install Technicians
Avionics Installer, Lead
Avionics Repairman
Avionics Systems Technician, Broad Area
Avionics Technician
Avionics Technician (MRO Tech)
Avionics Technician, Completions
Avionics Troubleshooter
Avionics/Electronic Technician (AVIM)
College Student Technician, Senior
Contracts Manager
Electronic Tech III/Avionics Tech
Electronics Engineer
Electronics Technician
Engineer III
HM&E Navy Systems Engineering
Logistics Management Specialist
Navy UCAS Demo Engineer
P-8A Avionics Test Requirement Specialist
Senior Avionics Leader
Senior LAN Administrator
Senior Software Engineer
Staff DMSMS Avionics Analyst II
Systems Acquisition Manager – Avionics
Technical Writer – Avionics

AVIATION WARFARE SYSTEMS
Acquisition Attorney
Aviation Electronic Warfare
Biologist
Business Development Manager
Company Grade O/T – Manager, Military
Computer Scientist
Computer Scientist, Supervisor
Editorial Assistant
Electronic Warfare Analyst
Electronics Technician
Financial Analyst
Head, Communications And Information
Human Resources Specialist
Information Technology Specialist
Intelligence Analyst, Senior
Intelligence Specialist
International Business Development

IT Specialist, Project Management, Systems Analysis
IT Specialist, Supervisor
Mid-Level Air Warfare Analyst
Military Analyst, Lead
Military Analyst, Senior
Military Operations Analyst
Navy Analyst
Navy Deck Test and Evaluation Team
Physicist
Program Analyst
Program Analyst
Research Analyst, Naval Warfare
SCA Engineering Tech III
Senior Analyst
Senior Military Analyst
Senior Staff Analyst, Level V
Special Operations Forces (SOF)
Sports Medicine Program Manager
Statistician
Systems Engineer, Radar
Technical Writer – Editor

BOATSWAIN'S MATE
Assembly Worker
Athletic Field/Turf Maintenance
Banquet Set-Up, Director
Bartender
Boat Engineer
Boat Maintenance and Repair
Boat Yard Worker
Building Operations Coordinator
CAD Operator
CDL Truck Driver
Deck Seamanship Maintenance Technician
Delta Boat Tour Guide
Dock Worker
Driver Apprentice
Engine/Machinery Maintenance Technician
Fiberglass, Paint & Gelcote Technician
Forklift Operator
General Laborers
Maintenance Mechanic
Maintenance Shop Laborer
Marina Dockhand/Maintenance Technician
Marina Yard Worker
Operations Supervisor II
Project Manager
Public Area Cleaner
Senior Maintenance Technician
Service Manager I – Dock Hub
Skilled Maintenance Technician
Supplemental Dock Worker
Supplemental Field Office

Warehouse Manager
Warehouse Worker
Welder, MIG & TIG

BUILDER

Bricklayers
Carpenter
Carpenter Journeyman
Concrete Finishers
Construction Foreman
Construction Worker
General/Misc
Journeyman Cement Masons/Helpers
Lead Carpenter
Masonry Foreman Bricklayer
Operations Manager, SAP
Rocklayer
Senior Software Developer – CS
Staging/Scenic Carpenter
Stone Mason

CONSTRUCTION ELECTRICIAN

Apprentice Construction Electrician
Construction Oil Field Worker
Construction Worker
Electrical Construction
Electrician
Electrician Construction Field
Electrician Specialist – Plant
Electrician's Helper
Industrial Electrician
Junior Electrician
Lighting Service Technician
Plant Electrician
PT&I Specialist/Electrician, Certified
Senior Field Service Technician
Trades Service Electrician

COUNSELOR

Corporate Generalist
Customer Service Representative
District Sales Manager
Employment/HR ERISA/Employment
     Benefits
Human Resources Assistant
Human Resources Director
Human Resources Manager
Human Resources Representative
Litigation Case Manager
Regional Human Resources Manager
Restaurant Management

Retail Sales Representative
Store Host
Tax Professional
Teacher's Assistant

CULINARY SPECIALIST

Catering Services Consultant
Catering Supplies Manager
Chef
Executive Chef II
Food Sales Representative
Manager II – Food Production
Manager II – Food Service
Pantry Worker
Restaurant Manager
Short Order Cook

CRYPTOLOGIC TECHNICIAN

Budget/Program Analyst w/ Security
     Clearance
Cryptologic and IO SME
Cryptologic Language Instructor II
DPOC-E Tier 4 Network Administrator
ESSO Analyst IV
Language Professional – Africa
Language Professional – Arab/Persia
Linguist – Dari
Linguist – Pashto
Multimedia Instruction Developer
Multimedia Instruction Developer
Native Cryptologic Albanian Linguist
Native Cryptologic Arabic Linguist
Native Cryptologic Farsi Linguist
Native Cryptologic Urdu Linguist
Native Cryptologic Yoruba Linguist
Naval Cryptologic Systems Target Analyst
Operations Researcher/Mathematician
Professional Cryptologic Arabic Linguist
Professional Cryptologic Chinese
Professional Cryptologic Farsi Linguist
Professional Cryptologic Russian
Senior Cryptologic Farsi Linguist
Senior Cryptologic Indonesian Linguist
Senior Multimedia Instruction Developer
Senior Multimedia Specialist
Senior Training Specialist
System Engineer
System Engineer 4/5 with Security Clearance
Telecommunications Analyst IV
Telecommunications Analyst IV
Veteran Cryptologic Kurdish Linguist

DAMAGE CONTROL
Certified Mine Foreman
Claims Adjuster II
Firefighter
Firefighter, Oilers
Inland Marine Underwriting Director
Internal Audit Specialist
Program Underwriting Account Manager
Territory Sales Director

DENTAL TECHNICIAN
Administrative Assistant I
Assistant Manager
Assistant Manager – Retail Sales
Assistant Manager – Dental Services
Assistant Office Manager
Care Management Assistant
Certified Nurse Technician
Certified Occupational Therapy Assistant
Corporate Generalist
Customer Service Representative
Dental Assistant
Dental Hygienist
District Sales Manager
Employment/HR ERISA/Employment
    Benefits
Full-Time, OTR Driver, Class A
Litigation Case Manager
Medical Assistant
Physical Therapy Assistant
Restaurant Management
Retail Sales Representative
Store Host
Tax Professional
Teacher's Assistant

DISBURSING CLERK
Accounting Clerk III
Accounts Payable Clerk
Bookkeeper
Bookkeeper/Administrator
General Office Clerk
Inventory Clerk
Warehouse Supervisor

DIVER
Aqua Theater Diver Technician
Aquatics Director
Assistant Operations Manager
Boat Captain FT/PT. USCG
Business Analyst – Contract
Business Analyst – Marketing and Channel
Business Analyst – Marketing and Sales

Certified Diver/Field Service
Contracts Administrator
Counsel
Deckhand
Director of Diving
Diver
Diver I
Diver III
Diving Estimator
Diving Operations Manager
Facility Director
Field Manager
Fish Laboratory Coordinator
HI-LO Diver
Husbandry Assistant II (Diver)
Life Sciences Diver
Manager, Data Operations
Maritime – Engineer Diver
Office Support Technician (Estimates)
Principal Subsea Pipeline Engineer
Professional Engineer/Diver
Project Coordinator
Senior Warfare Test and Evaluation
Staff Accountant
Supervisor, Data Operations

ELECTRONICS TECHNICIAN
Biomedical Electronics Technician II
Branch Operations Specialist III
Clinical Application Project Manager
Component Engineer Aerospace Electronics
Customer Support Engineer
Data Warehouse/SQL Developer
District Manager
Electro Mechanical Technician
Electronics Assembler
Electronics Engineer
Electronics Engineer – Entry-Level T1/T2
Electronics Engineer III
Electronics Engineer, Senior
Electronics Technician
Electronics Technician Senior
Engineering Specialist
Field Service Engineer
Field Service Engineer, Senior
Field Service Printer Technician
Field Service Representative, Operating Room
Field Service Technician, Senior
Field Technician
Lead Technician, Electronics
Lighting Service Technician
Operations Manager
Personal Nurse
Principal Electronics Hardware Engineer

Product Support Specialist
Program Coordinator
Project Manager
Reporting Solutions Analyst
RF Test Digital/Analog Technician
SCA Electronic Technician, Maintenance II
Senior Accountant
Senior Electronics Test Technician

ENGINEERING AIDE

Construction Surveyor
Land Surveyor/Project Manager
Professional Land Surveyor
Quantity Surveyor
Surveyor
Surveyor – Construction

EXPLOSIVE ORDNANCE DISPOSAL

EIC/EOD Instructors
EIC/EOD Specialists
Explosive Ordnance Disposal Instructor
Explosive Ordnance Disposal Logistics
Explosive Ordnance Disposal Operations
Explosive Ordnance Disposal Program
Explosive Ordnance Disposal Program Analyst
Explosive Ordnance Disposal Technician
Explosive Ordnance Disposal Training
Explosive Ordnance Disposal/Improvised
Explosives Test Operator IV
Human Resources Specialist (Military)
Information Analyst
Information Assurance Engineer
Senior Linux System Administrator
Staff Scientist
System Administrator
Training Development Specialist III
Unexploded Ordnance Technician I

ELECTRICIAN'S MATE

Avionics Technician
Career Education
Commissioning Engineer/Spec IV
    (Mechanical)
Conduit Bender
Construction Positions
Designer – Mechanical/Electrical/AutoCad
Director of Electrical Engineering
Electrical and Instrumentation Technician
Electrical Construction
Electrical Designer
Electrical Technician, Nuclear
Electrical/Mechanical Field Service

Electrical/Mechanical Specialist II
Electrician
Electrician's Helper
Electrician/PM Mechanic Sheraton Music
Electricians and Apprentices
Electro Mechanical Technician-Conveyor
Electro-Mechanical Assembler
Industrial Maintenance
Industrial Mechanical
Journeyman Electrician
Lighting Service Technician
Maintenance Mechanic
Maintenance Technician
Master Electrician
Mechanical/Electrical Technician
Motors – Drives Commodity Specialist
Service Technician
Supply Chain Manager – Model S Body

ENGINEMAN

Apprentice Diesel Electrician
Construction Equip
Diesel and Small Engine Mechanic
Diesel Engine Engineer OEM Applications
Diesel Generator/HVAC Certified
Diesel Mechanic
Diesel Mechanic/HVAC Tech
Diesel Shop Manager-Mechanic
Diesel Truck Fleet Service
Director of Finance
Electrician Diesel Engine – Locomotive
Engine Machinist
Express Employment Professionals
Field Service Technician, Generator
Generator Field Technician
Generator Set Technician
Generator Supervisor
Generator Technician
Generator Technician II
Global Account Executive
Heavy Duty Truck/Diesel Engine
Heavy Duty/Diesel Mechanic
Hydraulic Engineer
Locomotive Electronic Technician, Diesel
Mechanic, Diesel Engine
Mechanical Express Specialist
PM Technician
Power Generator Technician II
Preventive Maintenance Technician
Product Support Salesperson
Project Engineer (Diesel Engine)
Senior Engineer Diesel Engine Fuel
Technician – Light /Medium /Heavy
Vehicle Mechanic Journeyman

EQUIPMENT OPERATOR
Crane Operator
Heavy Equipment Operator
Heavy Equipment Operator I
Heavy Equipment Operator/Driver

FIRE CONTROLMAN
Advanced Telecom Technician – Submarine
Army C4ISR Tactical Operations Analyst
Assembler/Fitter
Assistant Account Executive
Associate Technician, Electronics
CEC Operation and Maintenance Technician
Computer Repair Technician
Digital Design Engineer
Digital Design Engineer
E-Business/Business Intelligence
Electronic Apprentices
Electronic Data Interchange
Electronic Systems Technician
Electronic Technician B (T-4)
Electronic Technician C (T-3) EW/LATR
Electronic Technician C (T-3) Range
Electronics Technician A, Range
Electronics Technician II, Lab Services
Engineer, Mechanical-Survivability
Engineer, Senior-Quality
Joint Fire Support Command
Lead Technician, Electronics
Machinist
Maintenance Electrician
Maintenance Mechanic I
Maintenance Technician
Master Maintenance Mechanic
Missile Technician
Motor Vehicle Mechanic
Navy Submarine Configuration Management
Pipe Fitter Surface Ship Platforms and
Plant Maintenance & Operations
Product Line Support Specialist
Program Analyst with Anti-Submarine
Shipfitter (Level III) Surface and Submarine
Submarine Acquisition Analyst
Submarine Design Systems Engineer
Submarine Engineering Technician
Submarine Planner (003063:CAP)
Submarine Program Manager (002887:CAP)
Submarine Quality Engineer (001951:CAP)
Submarine Trainer Maintenance Planning
Submarine Training Analyst
Submarine Training Analyst (Security
    Clearance)
Systems Analyst II/SWSMIN Administrator
Technical Specialist – Submarine/Fire
Technician – Submarine/Fire
Torpedo Maintenance Trainer, Senior

GAS TURBINE SYSTEMS
Accountant II
Business Underwriter
Debt Originator (Project Financing)
Director Business Development/Sales
Field Service Representative
Field Service Technician III
Finance Intern
Gas Production
Gas Turbine Coatings
Gas Turbine Controls Engineer
Gas Turbine Development and Verification
Gas Turbine Engineer II
Gas Turbine Field Solutions Manager
Gas Turbine Mechanical Program
Gas Turbine Repair Manager
Gas Turbine Systems Technician
Gas Turbine Test Technician
Industrial Systems Engineering Manager
Information Technology Analyst
IT Analyst
IT Intern
Manager – Safety/Power/Gas Turbine
Marketing Manager – Oil and Gas Onshore
Mechanical/Aerospace Engineer
NDE Field Service Technician
Plant Engineer
Power Services Internal Technical
Repair and Overhaul Engineer – Gas Turbine
Safety Manager – Safety/Power/Gas
System Measurement Leader

GUNNER'S MATE
Component Repair (Drivetrain) Supervisor
Component Repair (Power Pack) Supervisor
Electronic Engineer
Embedded Software Engineer
Forward Repair Activity Manager (D Band)
Image Processing Engineer
Industrial Engineer
Infrared and Optical Electrical Systems
Mechanical Design Engineer
Mechanical Engineer
Missile Guidance Engineer
Product Repair/MOD Technician
Product Repair/MOD Technician SMC
Product Repair/Modification Technician
SCA Aircraft Mechanic II, Armament
    Weapons
SCA Aircraft Worker Armament Weapons

SCA Electronic Technician Maintenance II
Small Arms Repair Mechanic
Software Development
Software Engineers – Imagery
Weapons Technician Senior Assistant

HOSPITAL CORPSMAN
Allied Health – Mental Health Technician
BPR Emergency Dept Technician
Burn Technician
Certified Nurse Technician
Clinical Care Technician
Clinical Care Technician/CNA 4th Med Card
Clinical Technician, Advanced
Dental Assistant
ED Technician
Emergency Room Technician
Emergency Services Technician
Family Nurse Practitioner
Health Unit
Licensed Practical Nurse
Medical Assistant
Nurse Extern, Student
Nurse Licensed Practical Nurse
Nurse Practitioner
Nurse Research Coordinator
Nursing Care Partner
Nursing Specialty Tech
Patient Care Technician II
Psychiatric Nurse
Registered Nurse
Registered Nurse – Critical Care
Registered Nurse – Physical
Trauma Technician
Utilization Registered Nurse

INFORMATION SYSTEMS
Administrative Assistant – Legal
Associate – Technical Support
Consulting SQL Database Administrator
Desktop Architect
Desktop Technician
Director, Information Technology
Electrical Engineering Technician
Engineer
Field Service Printer Technician
Help Desk Support Analyst
Information Assurance
Information Assurance Security
Information Technology Technician
Infrastructure Senior Project Manager
Infrastructure Services Consultant
Inside Sales Representative III

IT Desktop Support Technician
Lead Technician, Mechanical
Manager – Information Systems
Navy FMS Financial Analyst
Navy Radar Engineer
Navy Tomahawk Technical
NetIQ Systems Engineer
Network Engineer
Program Manager – Navy Programs
Risk Manager
Senior Analyst, Program
Senior Navy Supply Analyst
Senior Technology Consultant
SMS System Administrator II – HCAPS
Stock Plan Administrator
Supervisor, Computer Scientist
System Administrator (Network)
Technician I
Technician, Help Desk
WMS Support Specialist

LEGAL
Assistant Legal Counsel
BLO Litigation/SAE Paralegal
Contract Attorney
Contract Corporate Paralegal
Contract Paralegal
Corporate Attorney
Corporate Paralegal
General Counsel
Healthcare Paralegal
In-House Paralegal Corporate Generalist
In-House Paralegal Investor Relations
In-House Finance Attorney
IP Manager/Paralegal
Legal Assistant
Legal Assistant (OA)
Legal Counsel
Legal Nurse
Legal Secretary
Paralegal
Paralegal Specialist
Senior Paralegal – (26380)
Workers Compensation Paralegal

HULL TECHNICIAN
Advanced Sheet Metal Fabricator
Aircraft Structures Technician
Assembly Worker
CNC Operator/Machinist
Dock Workers
Estimator – Precision Sheet Metal
Experienced Sheet Metal

Forklift Operator
General Laborer
Machinist
Master Sheet Metal, Structural Aircraft
Millwright TIG Welders
Sheet Metal Fabricator
Sheet Metal Mechanic
Sheet Metal Mechanic (Fabricator)
Sheet Metal Structure Technician
Sheet Metal Worker
Sheet Metal, Structural Aircraft
Sheet Metal, Structural Mechanic
Structures Technician
Warehouse Worker
Welder – MIG TIG
Welder – Precision Metal Fabricator
Welder – TIG

INTELLIGENCE SPECIALIST
Business Lead, Financial Planning and
Civilian Naval Intelligence Analyst
Cyber Intelligence Analyst
Intelligence Analyst, Senior
Intelligence Information Management
Intelligence Specialist
Naval Intelligence Analyst, Senior
Navy FMS Financial Analyst

INTERIOR COMMUNICATIONS
A&P Mechanics
Aircraft Maintenance Technician
Biomedical Equipment Technician
Biomedical Equipment Repair Technician
Brake & Turret Press Set-Up Operators
Calibration/Metrology Technician
Chief Engineer (Laundry/Linen Services)
CNC Press Brake Operator
CNC Turret Operator
CNC Turret Punch Press Operator
CNC Turret Punch Press Operator/Set-Up
Director, Facility Maintenance
Distribution Technician
Electro Mechanical Technician
Electronic Field Technologist
Electronic Maintenance Technician
Electronic Technician IV
Express Employment Professionals
Facility Maintenance Technician
Field Service Engineer
Field Service Printer Technician
Field Service Representative, Operating Room
Field Service Technician, Senior
Field Technician

Field Technician
Field Technician II
Franklin, TN – HCA Healthcare
HLA Electronic Assembly Technician
Interactive Marketing Manager
Lighting Service Technician
Maintenance – Building and Machine
Maintenance Engineer
Maintenance Field Supervisor
Maintenance Mechanic
Maintenance Technician
Manufacturing Process Engineer
Mobile Facility Engineer
Nurse Practitioner
O&M Generalist I
Press Brake/Turret Machinist
Product Support Specialist
Product Support Specialist
Public Information Officer
Radiology Registered Nurse II-CC
Registered Nurse II-CC
Reporting Solutions Analyst
Service Crewman
Supervisor Area Housing Maintenance
System Lead/Electronic Technician
Tank Turret Mechanic (Security)
Turret CNC Programmer
Turret Lift Driver
Turret Mechanic
Turret Press Operator
Turret Press Programmer
Turret Punch Operator
Turret Punch Setup Operator
Turret/Press Brake Operator
Warranty Manager

MACHINERY REPAIRMAN
A&P Mechanics
Cabinet Builder/Benchman
CNC Machine Sales
Locksmith/Sign Maker
Maintenance Mechanic
Maintenance Worker
Millwrights TIG Welders
Service Technician, Machine Tool

MASS COMMUNICATION SPECIALIST
Academic Director – Audio Production
Manager, Public Affairs
Program Coordinator
Public Affairs Officer
Public Affairs Specialist
Regulatory Affairs and Compliance

MACHINIST MATE
- Air Quality Field Technician
- Air Testing Lead/Manager
- Biomed Equipment Technician
- Electro Mechanical Technician
- Environmental Technician I
- Field Customer Service Technician with
- Field Service Technician-Senior
- Field Service/Maintenance Technician
- Field Services Representative
- Field Technician
- Gas Field Technologist
- General Machinist
- Industrial Plant Maintenance
- IT Representative
- Machinist
- Maintenance Mechanic
- Mechanic/Machinist
- Nurse Practitioner
- Nurse Practitioner (Radiology)
- Radiology Registered Nurse II-CC
- Registered Nurse II-CC
- Supervisor Area Housing Maintenance
- Supervisor Service

MASTER AT ARMS
- Assistant Account Manager
- Assistant Account Manager-Recruiter
- Business Analyst Associate Professional
- Chief of Security
- ICE FPS Security Assistant
- Security Officer
- Security Director
- Security Manager

MISSILE TECHNICIAN
- Logistics/Materials Handling Technician
- Missile Technician
- Robotic Technician
- Technical Trainer

MINEMAN
- EIC/EOD Specialists/Instructors
- Explosive Ordnance Disposal Instructor
- Explosive Ordnance Disposal Logistics
- Explosive Ordnance Disposal Training
- Ordnance Handler-Associate
- Ordnance Packager
- Unexploded Ordnance Tech I

MUSICIAN
- Church Musician
- Music Sales, Customer Service
- Musician
- Musician/Accompanist

NUKE, NUCLEAR, INTERIOR COMMUNICATIONS ELECTRICIAN, ELECTRICIAN'S MATE
- Apprentice – Nuclear Plant Equipment
- Business Manager (Nuclear)
- Chemistry Technician – Nuclear
- Director, Nuclear Communications
- Electrical Technician – Nuclear
- Emergency Management Specialist
- Engineer – Systems/Power/Nuclear
- I &C Technician – Nuclear
- Major Project Account Manager – Nuclear
- Manager, BWR Reactor Services
- Manager, Nuclear Steam Supply
- Mechanical Designer for Operating
- Mechanical Engineering Technician
- Naval Architect
- Navy Technician (ET, IT, MM)
- Navy Engineer
- Navy/Nuclear Design Engineer, Senior
- Navy/Nuclear Product Engineer, Senior
- Non-Destructive Testing Inspector
- Nuclear Chemistry Technician
- Nuclear Design Engineering
- Nuclear Engineer
- Nuclear Licensing Engineers
- Nuclear Operations Instructor
- Nuclear Plant Equipment Operator
- Nuclear Ship Systems Test Engineer
- Operator, Nuclear Auxiliary I
- Power Plant Project Procurement
- Project Manager – Power Plant Control
- Project Manager at Nuclear Power Plant
- Radiation Protection Specialist
- Requal Training Supervisor – Nuclear
- Senior Mechanical Engineer – Nuclear Plant
- Senior/Staff Nuclear Consultant – Beaver
- Supervisor Nuclear Plant
- Welder – Nuclear

OPERATIONS SPECIALIST
- Business Operations Specialist, Senior
- CMB Specialist
- Management and Acquisition Support Specialist
- Operation Specialist, Recruitment
- Operations Systems Security Specialist, Senior
- Senior Modeling and Simulation Analyst
- Senior SIGINT Analyst
- Senior Training Specialist
- Senior Warfare Test and Evaluation Specialist

PERSONNELMAN
- Administrative Support
- Administrative Specialist I

Environmental Policy Analyst
Office Support Assistant

POSTAL CLERK

Administrative Assistant
ATS Mail Agent
Care Management Assistant
Correspondence Agent
Credentialing Coordinator
Customer Service/Copy, Mail, Shipping
Dialysis Collections Representative
Driver II
Electronic Technician
Entry-Level Account Manager
FHIG Consultant
Floating Customer Service
Mail Clerk
Mail Handlers
Mail Order Specialty Pharmacist
Mail Services Clerk I
Mailroom Supervisor
Maintenance Mechanic, Mail Processing
Maintenance Technician III
Network Architecture Manager, IT
Part-Time Collection Services
Patient Service Representative I
Postal Administration Clerk
Postal Clerk I
Postal Manager
Postal Operations
Postal Specialist
Product Support Specialist
Property Administrator
Reinvestigation Specialist
Senior Customer Service/Mail Services
Warehouse Manager

RELIGIOUS PROGRAM
SPECIFICATION/ CHAPLAIN

Associate University Chaplain
Chaplain
Chaplain & CNA Positions
Hospice Chaplain
Social Worker (MSW) and Chaplain

QUARTERMASTER

Boat Captain
Boat Operator-Small Engine Mechanic
Delivery – Route Sales Representative
Equipment Specialists – Propulsion
Field Operation Coordinator
Government Analyst II
Manager I – Retail
Manager II – Food Service

Manager, Retail/Restaurant Operations
Michigan – Continental Services
New Yacht Owner Experience Managers
Regional Business Manager – Vending
Retail Manager
Route Driver
Route Sales Associate
Ship's Serviceman
Technical Training Associate Manager

STEELWORKER

Custom Steel Fabrication Worker
Fabrication Specialist
Millwright/TIG Welder
Steel Fabrication Project Manager
Steel Fabrication Welding Supervisor
Steel Plate Fabrication Estimator
Structural Steel Detailer
Structural Steel Estimator

STOREKEEPER

Accounting Manager
Administrative Support Staff
AP/Purchasing/Inventory Control
Area Retail Supervisor
Assistant Store Manager
Branch Manager III
Director, Event Technology II
Executive Chef
Executive Chef II
Hotel Controller
Inventory Control Manager – Publishing
Inventory Control Specialist
Inventory Specialist
Manager-in-Training
Medical Lab Tech
Medical Review Nurse
MV Parts Manager
Research Analyst I
Retail Store Manager
Senior Financial Analyst – Supply
Senior Manager, Channel Optimization
Tech II, Health Systems, Pharmacy

SONAR TECHNICIAN

Actionscript Programmer
Computer Engineer
Computer Scientist
Digital Design Engineer T3/T4
Electronic Engineer
Electronic Technician I
Electronic Warfare/Sonar/Radar Expert
Electronics Test Technician
Electronics Worker
Engineering Scientist Associate – Sonar

Engineering Technician
Engineering Technician IV
Engineering Technician V
Field Engineer – Radar
Field Engineer – Sonar
Lab Technician
Manager, Embedded SW Engineering
Mechanical Engineer
Mid-Level Electronic Technician
Offshore Survey Technician
Senior Lead Engineer, Sonar Systems
Senior Technical Editor/Writer
Software Engineers
Sonar Dome Pressurization
Sonar Engineer
Sonar Instructor
Sonar Technician
Submarine Training Analyst
Systems Engineer
Technical Editor/Writer II
Technologist, Entry-Level

SEAL

All Source Intelligence Analyst
Bank Marketing Analyst
Business and Data Process Engineering
Configuration Analyst 3/4
Data Mgmt Analyst II
Facility Operations Analyst
Facility Operations Analyst, Senior
Functional Military
GIS Analyst III
Imagery Analyst with Security Clearance
Intelligence Analyst III
Intelligence Assistant (OA)
Lead Analyst
Manager – Operations Cells/Switch
Military Analyst
Military Analyst, Lessons Learned
Military Engineer
Military Operations Analyst
Military Operations Analyst with
    Security Clearance
N3JOD Analyst IV with Security Clearance
Operations Manager
Operations Officer – Current Military
Operations Research Analyst
Operations Research Analyst II
Operations Researcher
Operations Researcher, Senior

Personnel Security Customer Relations
Senior Collections Risk Analyst
Senior Operations Research Analyst
Special Operations Forces (SOF) Subject
UH-60 Aircraft Mechanic
Work Area Commander Special Purpose

TORPEDOMAN

Accelerator/Nuclear Detection
Assembly Supervisor
Engineering Fellow – Accelerator
Engineering Technician
Engineering Technician – Torpedoes
Engineering Technician III
Explosive Ordnance Disposal Instructor
Industrial Measurement Technician I
Maintenance Technician
Mechanic, Aircraft I/Aviation Ordnance CFT
Mechanical Engineer I
Mechanical Engineer I with Security
Mechanical Engineer III – Ordnance
NAVAIR Ordnance Training Analyst
Ordnance Equipment Logistician
Ordnance Equipment Mechanic Helper
Ordnance Equipment Repairer
Ordnance Loader
Ordnance Maintenance Analyst
Ordnance Professionals
Principal Electrical/Analog Engineer
Principal Electrical/Digital Engineer
Process Chemical Engineer
Production Controller Ordnance
Senior DoD Project Engineer
Senior Mechanical Engineer I
Senior Program Cost Schedule & Control
Senior Project Engineer
Senior Quality Assurance Engineer
System Safety Engineer
Torpedo Assembly Supervisor
Torpedo Maintenance Trainer Senior
Weapons Technician Senior Assistant

YEOMAN

Administrative Assistant, Sales
Administrative Support
Charge Entry
Credentialing/Purchasing Coordinator
Legal Secretary
Operations Assistant
Operations Support Analyst
Purchasing Coordinator

SOURCE:
www.militaryjobhunts.com

SECTION III
Resources and Information

• **CHAPTER SEVEN: Working USERRA**

The Uniformed Services Employment and Reemployment Rights Act (USERRA) provides certain employment protections and rights for members of the uniformed services, including National Guard and Reserve members. It pays to know the benefits and protections provided to you under the law.

• **CHAPTER EIGHT: Online and In-Print Resources for Veterans**

The Internet offers a wealth of information to help veterans with transitioning, education, employment, and building social networks.

A Practical Look at USERRA...

To be eligible for reemployment, the uniformed service protected under USERRA must be rendered under the authority of the military. In other words, the absences must be connected to actual military service. In *Leisek v. Brightwood Corporation*, John C. Leisek, a former employee of Brightwood Corporation and a member of the National Guard, sued after he was denied reemployment following his absence to participate in National Guard activities.

Leisek, a quality-assurance inspector for Brightwood, owned a hot-air balloon with National Guard insignia that he used to promote the Guard. Leisek received written orders from the National Guard in 1996 to perform temporary duty at ballooning events in Idaho and Wisconsin, but not at a Colorado event.

The Brightwood Corporation informed Leisek that the company would consider him to have resigned if he attended the Colorado event, but he attended anyway. Consequently, the company terminated him and refused reemployment.

Leisek sued, claiming Brightwood had violated USERRA, which "prohibits discrimination against persons because of their service in the uniformed services."

The court concluded that Leisek had no right to be reemployed as he was not engaged in "uniformed service" at the time of his absence from his employer. Prior to his absence for the Guard, Leisek indicated that he would be engaged in Guard duties at various locations and various dates, and asked for time off accordingly. He eventually did receive military orders for some of the dates and locations, but not for all of them. The court held that he was not serving in the "uniformed services" as to those dates for which he was not under orders to serve.

CHAPTER SEVEN

WORKING USERRA

Our government recognizes that when you devote a portion of your life to military service, you should receive certain benefits and protections for that service. Congress has acted to provide job security in your civilian life so that you do not have to choose between serving your country and your community.

Over 60 years ago, Congress enacted laws to protect employees "called to the colors" from being penalized for absences from their civilian jobs. First passed as the Selective Training and Service Act of 1940, federal veterans employment laws were modified several times until October 1994, when President Bill Clinton signed into law a comprehensive revision known as the Uniformed Services Employment and Reemployment Rights Act of 1994.

Like its predecessors, USERRA guarantees the rights of military servicemembers to take a leave of absence from their civilian jobs for active military service and to return to their jobs with accrued seniority and other employment protections.

USSERA is the primary legislation designed to protect veterans and encourages non-career uniformed service so that America can enjoy the protection of those services, staffed by qualified people, while maintaining a balance with the needs of private and public employers who also depend on these same individuals.

Today, the protections offered under USERRA and other protective laws are needed more than ever. Reserve and National Guard (RC/NG) forces are no longer only a strategic reserve. Since 1992, they have become an operational force. Over 630,000 Reserve and Guard members have been mobilized and deployed since September 11, 2005. Additionally, these men and women are deploying for longer periods, performing nontraditional missions, and returning from deployments as veterans. Since the trend will likely continue, USERRA will ensure job protection for these loyal Americans.

USERRA is intended to minimize the disadvantages individuals might incur when they need to be absent from their civilian employment to serve in this country's uniformed services.

Overview of USERRA

The Uniformed Services Employment and Reemployment Rights Act was signed into law on October 13, 1994. USERRA clarifies and strengthens the Veterans' Reemployment Rights (VRR) statute. The Act itself can be found in the United States Code at Chapter 43, Part III, Title 38.

The Department of Labor has issued regulations that clarify its position on the rights of returning servicemembers to family and medical leave under USERRA. See 20 CFR Part 1002.210.

USERRA is intended to minimize the disadvantages individuals might incur when they need to be absent from their civilian employment to serve in this country's uniformed services. USERRA makes major improvements in protecting servicemembers' rights and benefits by clarifying the law and improving enforcement mechanisms. It also provides employees with Department of Labor assistance in processing claims.

USERRA covers virtually every individual in the country who currently serves in or has served in the uniformed services and applies to all employers in the public and private sectors, including federal employers.

The law seeks to ensure that those who serve their country can retain their civilian employment and benefits and seek employment free from discrimination because of their service.

USERRA provides protection for disabled veterans, requiring employers to make reasonable efforts to accommodate the disability. USERRA is administered by the United States Department of Labor, through the Veterans' Employment and Training Service (VETS).

VETS provides assistance to those persons experiencing service-connected problems with their civilian employment and information about USERRA to employers. VETS also assists veterans who have questions regarding Veterans' Preference.

The Uniformed Services Employment and Reemployment Rights Act also protects workers across the country who wish to make a military commitment. The Act was established in 1994 in order to replace the Veterans Reemployment Rights Act. According to the provisions of USERRA, employees may make a military commitment at any time. Further, an employer may not discriminate against the employee who wishes to make a military commitment for any reason based on that military service.

When an employee takes time away from work for military service, that employee should be able to return to work and have the same or equivalent job. The employee should also receive the same benefits and salary that he or she had been receiving before taking the time off. However, the employee must not take off more than five years, total, if he or she wishes to continue to receive USERRA coverage.

Employees may leave work in order to serve in a variety of military branches, including:

- Armed Forces
- Coast Guard

USERRA provides protection for disabled veterans, requiring employers to make reasonable efforts to accommodate the disability.

- National Guard
- Public Health Service
- Reserves

Employees must also be able to leave work for a variety of reasons, including the following:

- active or inactive duty
- active or inactive duty for training
- voluntary or involuntary duty
- voluntary or involuntary duty for training
- full-time guard duty

When an employee takes time away from work in order to serve, the employee must return within a period of time based on the amount of time the employee was serving. These time frames are as follows:

When service lasts up to 30 days, the employee should return to work within one business day after returning home from service.

When service lasts between 31 and 180 days, the employee needs to return to work within 14 days after returning home from service.

When service lasts more than 181 days, the employee needs to return to work within 90 days after returning home from service.

Discrimination

USERRA protects all members of the uniformed services from discrimination in employment, regardless of whether their uniformed service was in the past, present, or future. For example, a Vietnam-era veteran remains protected against discriminatory employment actions based on that service even though that person's uniformed service preceded an employment relationship by many years. If that person is subsequently denied a benefit of employment, motivated even in part by that service in the uniformed services, then that person may have rights under USERRA.

The discrimination provisions of USERRA address problems regarding initial employment, reemployment, retention in employment, promotion, or any other benefit of employment. This chapter provides more information on the effect of uniformed services on benefits or general workplace issues.

Limitations of USERRA

USERRA establishes a floor, not a ceiling, for the employment and reemployment rights and benefits of those it protects. In other words, an employer may provide greater rights and benefits than USERRA requires, but no employer can refuse to provide any right or benefit guaranteed by USERRA.

- USERRA supersedes any state law (including any local law or ordinance), contract, agreement, policy, plan, practice, or other matter that reduces, limits, or eliminates in any manner any right or benefit provided by USERRA, including the establishment of additional prerequisites to the exercise of any USERRA right or the receipt of any USERRA benefit. For example, an employment contract that determines seniority based only on actual days of work in the place of employment would be superseded by USERRA, which requires that seniority credit be given for periods of absence from work due to service in the uniformed services.

- USERRA does not supersede, nullify, or diminish any federal or state law (including any local law or ordinance), contract, agreement, policy, plan, practice, or other matter that establishes an employment right or benefit that is more beneficial than, or is in addition to, a right or benefit provided under the Act. For example, although USERRA does not require an employer to pay an employee for time away from work to perform service, an employer policy, plan, or practice that provides such a benefit is permissible under USERRA.

If an employer provides a benefit that exceeds USERRA's requirements in one area, it cannot reduce or limit other rights or benefits provided by USERRA. For example, even though USERRA does not require it, an employer may provide a fixed number of days of paid military leave per year to employees who are members of the National Guard or Reserve. The fact that it provides such a benefit, however, does not permit an employer to refuse to provide an unpaid leave of absence to an employee to perform service in the uniformed services in excess of the number of days of paid military leave.

USERRA does not require the employer to return employees to the exact same position that they occupied before leaving for military service. The manner that the employer places the employees back into the workforce is

A common concern for reservists, activated and deployed, is the impact their absence from their civilian job will have on employer-provided health benefits.

structured according to the amount of time the employees were on military leave. If the employees were absent for one to 90 days, they must be promptly reemployed in the position that they would have occupied had they remained in continuous employment, provided they are qualified for that position or can become qualified after a relatively short training period.

If the employees are not qualified for that position, then they must be placed in a position closest to the position described above for which they are able to perform. In other words, the deployed-reservist employees progress as if they had remained in continuous employment.

USERRA does not require employers to pay employees wages during any period of military leave. An employer, of course, may choose to do so, or may opt to pay, for example, the difference between the military pay and the employee's regular salary.

A common concern for reservists, activated and deployed, is the impact their absence from their civilian job will have on employer-provided health benefits. Generally, if the period of leave is 30 days or less, the employer's health insurance benefits remain intact. If the leave is more than 30 days, employees and their dependants should be covered by military-provided healthcare benefits. In addition, other federal provisions offer reservists protection by enabling them to continue their healthcare insurance.

The Consolidated Omnibus Budget Reconciliation Act (COBRA) and USERRA allow for healthcare coverage rights to employees after an event in employment such as a reduction in hours worked due to military deployment. This extended coverage is good for a period of up to 18 months.

In addition, the Health Insurance Portability and Accountability Act (HIPAA) also recognizes the ability of some individuals to enroll in another health insurance plan, if one is available. For example, spouses may have a health insurance plan available through their employer that they may wish to take advantage of during the time of deployment. HIPAA allows for access to this plan regardless of the existence of set enrollment periods.

HIPAA includes protections for coverage under group health plans that limit exclusions for preexisting conditions; prohibit discrimination against employees and dependents based on their health status; and allow a special opportunity to enroll in a new plan to individuals in certain circumstances. HIPAA may also give you a right to purchase individual coverage if you have no group health plan coverage available, and have exhausted COBRA or other continuation coverage.

For more information about health rights under HIPAA, visit the Department of Health and Human Services website at www.hhs.gov/ocr/hipaa.

USERRA Time Limits on Service

To qualify for reemployment, the cumulative service generally cannot exceed five years. However, exceptions to this five-year prohibition exist and include the following:

- Situations where the servicemember cannot obtain a release through no fault of their own.

- Involuntary service during a domestic emergency or national security crisis.

- Service pursuant to an order to remain on active duty because of war or national emergency.

- Active duty by volunteers supporting "operational missions" for which members of the Select Reserve have been ordered to active duty without their consent.

- Service by volunteers in support of a "critical mission."

- Federal service by members of the National Guard called into service to suppress insurrection.

- Service connected to training.

USERRA and the Department of Labor

The Department of Labor, through the Veterans' Employment and Training Service, provides assistance to all persons having claims under USERRA. The Act also clarifies and strengthens the Veterans' Reemployment Rights statute.

USERRA protects civilian job rights and benefits for veterans and members of Reserve components and makes major improvements in protecting servicemember rights and benefits by clarifying the law, improving enforcement mechanisms, and including federal government employees in the class of employees eligible to receive Department of Labor assistance in processing claims.

USERRA establishes the cumulative length of time that an individual may be absent from work for military duty and retain reemployment rights to five years (the previous law provided four years of active duty, plus an additional year if it was for the convenience of the government).

There are important exceptions to the five-year limit, including initial enlistments lasting more than five years, periodic National Guard and Reserve training duty, and involuntary active duty extensions and recalls, especially during a time of national emergency. USERRA clearly establishes that reemployment protection does not depend on the timing, frequency, duration, or nature of an individual's service as long as the basic eligibility criteria are met.

USERRA provides protection for disabled veterans, requiring employers to make reasonable efforts to accommodate the disability. Servicemembers convalescing from injuries received during service or training may have up to two years from the date of completion of service to return to their jobs or apply for reemployment.

USERRA provides that returning servicemembers are reemployed in the job that they would have attained had they not been absent for military service (the long-standing "escalator" principle), with the same seniority, status, and pay, as well as other rights and benefits determined by seniority.

USERRA also requires that reasonable efforts (such as training or retraining) be made to enable returning servicemembers to refresh or upgrade their skills to help them qualify for reemployment. The law clearly provides for alternative reemployment positions if the servicemember cannot qualify for the "escalator" position.

USERRA also provides that while an individual is performing military service, he or she is deemed to be on a furlough or leave of absence and is entitled to the non-seniority rights accorded other individuals on nonmilitary leaves of absence.

Health and pension plan coverage for servicemembers is provided by USERRA. Individuals performing military duty of more than 30 days may elect to continue employer-sponsored healthcare for up to 24 months; however, they may be required to pay up to 102% of the full premium. For military service of less than 31 days, healthcare coverage is provided as if the servicemember had remained employed. USERRA clarifies pension plan coverage by making it explicit that all pension plans are protected.

The period where an individual has to make an application for reemployment or report back to work after military service is based on the time spent on military duty. For service of less than 31 days, the service member must return at the beginning of the next regularly scheduled work period on the first full day after release from service, taking into account safe travel home plus an eight-hour rest period.

For service of more than 30 days but less than 181 days, the servicemember must submit an application for reemployment within 14 days of release from service. For service of more than 180 days, an application for reemployment must be submitted within 90 days of release from service.

USERRA also requires that servicemembers provide advance written or verbal notice to their employers for all military duty unless giving notice is impossible, unreasonable, or precluded by military necessity. An employee should provide notice as far in advance as is reasonable under the circumstances. Additionally, servicemembers are able (but are not required) to use accrued vacation or annual leave while performing military duty.

The period where an individual has to make an application for reemployment or report back to work after military service is based on the time spent on military duty.

The Department of Labor, through the Veterans' Employment and Training Service, provides assistance to all persons having claims under USERRA, including federal and Postal Service employees.

If resolution is unsuccessful following an investigation, the servicemember may have his or her claim referred to the Department of Justice for consideration of representation in the appropriate District Court, at no cost to the claimant. Federal and Postal Service employees may have their claims referred to the Office of Special Counsel for consideration of representation before the Merit Systems Protection Board (MSPB). If violations under USERRA are shown to be willful, the court may award liquidated damages. Individuals, who pursue their own claims in court or before the MSPB, may be awarded reasonable attorney and expert witness fees if they prevail.

Servicemember employees of intelligence agencies are provided similar assistance through the agency's Inspector General.

For more information about U.S. Department of Labor employment and training programs for veterans, contact the Veterans' Employment and Training Service office nearest you, listed in the phone book under the U.S. Department of Labor or visit the DoL website at www.dol.gov/vets/aboutvets/contacts/main.htm.

Veterans Benefits Improvement Act

In 2004, Congress passed the Veterans Benefits Improvement Act (VBIA), which amended USERRA by adding a requirement that employers provide notice of the rights, privileges, and obligations of employees and employers under USERRA. In 2005, the Department of Labor published an interim final rule, setting forth language to be used by employers to comply with the notice requirement. Generally, the notice includes a description of the reemployment rights of those who voluntarily or involuntarily leave employment for military service, as well as the prohibition against discrimination on the basis of military service and the right to be free from retaliation for seeking enforcement of USERRA. The notice also contains a brief summary on the health benefits attendant to military deployment and a description of the enforcement mechanism.

Veterans' Employment Opportunities Act of 1998 (Amended)

When an agency accepts applications from outside its own workforce, the Veterans' Employment Opportunities Act of 1998 (VEOA) allows preference eligibles or veterans to compete for these vacancies under merit promotion procedures. Veterans who are selected are given career or career conditional appointments. Veterans are those who have been separated under honorable conditions from the armed forces with three or more years of continuous active service.

Purpose of the Law

Improve Access: The intent of the law is to open up opportunities to veterans that might otherwise be closed because agencies were increasingly limiting announcements just to "status" candidates (i.e., those who were already civil-service employees). This law requires an agency to allow eligible veterans to apply when the agency will accept applications from individuals outside its own workforce. In this context, "agency" means the parent agency, for example, the Department of Defense, not Department of the Army. Veterans' preference, however, does not apply to selections made under merit promotion procedures.

Improve Redress: The VEOA also allows a preference-eligible, who believes an agency has violated any of his or her rights under the veterans' preference laws or regulations, to file a formal complaint with the Department of Labor's Veterans Employment and Training Service. If VETS is unable to resolve the complaint within 60 days, the veteran may appeal to the Merit Systems Protection Board. The law also makes a willful violation of veterans' preference a prohibited personnel practice under law.

Who Is Eligible?

To be eligible for a VEOA appointment, a veteran must be honorably separated and either a preference eligible or have substantially completed three or more years of active service. ("Active service" under this law means active duty in a uniformed service and includes full-time training duty, annual training duty, full-time National Guard duty, and attendance, while in the active service, at a school designated as a service school by law or by the secretary concerned). A veteran who is released under honorable conditions shortly before completing a three-year tour is also eligible.

How to Apply

Agency announcements will say when veterans eligible under this law may apply. The veterans will be rated and ranked with other merit promotion eligibles. Those who are among the best qualified may be selected by the appointing official, but veterans' preference is not a factor. If selected, the veteran will be given a career or career conditional appointment, as appropriate.

A Practical Look at USERRA...

The new rules required by the Jobs for Veterans Act were designed to overhaul the last major veterans' jobs law—the Vietnam Era Veterans' Readjustment Assistance Act of 1974—and to prepare federal contractors for the influx of hundreds of thousands of job applicants who are veterans of the wars in Afghanistan and Iraq.

The new law requires that contractors doing business with the federal government give priority status to veterans for almost any job available on contracts of $100,000 were entered or modified after December 1, 2003.

The only jobs exempted from the new rules are executive or management openings, jobs that will be filled from within, or temporary jobs lasting fewer than three days.

Government contracts larger than $25,000 and older than the December 1, 2003 effective date will continue to follow the rules of the earlier 1974 veterans law.

Jobs for Veterans Act

The Jobs for Veterans Act (JVA), enacted into Public Law 107–288 on November 7, 2002 made a number of amendments to encourage veterans access to services within an integrated one-stop service delivery system. A new section of the law established a priority of service requirements applicable to all Department of Labor programs offering employment and training related services. (Public Law107–288, Section 4215 (b))

New reporting requirements to account for veterans' representation in programs in proportion to their representation in the labor market were also enacted. The secretary of labor was directed to evaluate whether veterans and other covered persons are receiving priority of services and are being fully served. (Public Law 107–288, Section 4215 (c))

The document provides policy for workforce development councils regarding these new requirements. A draft training and employment guidance letter has been distributed for implementing the Jobs for Veterans Act and has provided guidance for the policy section of this document. The Departments of Labor and Veterans Affairs continue to have discussions on implementation issues related to passage of the law.

Policy

A covered person is entitled to priority of service under all Workforce Investment Act (WIA) Title I funded programs—for example, adult, youth, dislocated workers, 10% funded projects, and National Emergency Grants (NEG). For purposes of this policy, the term *veterans priority of service* means that a covered person shall be given priority over nonveterans for the receipt of employment, training, and placement services provided under that program, notwithstanding any other provision of law.

Veterans and other covered persons must first meet the WIA program's eligibility requirements. A covered person who is determined eligible for WIA services shall receive priority over nonveterans, except for the priority of service established by law for the WIA adult program. Within WIA Title IB, the adult program is the only program to have a priority provision established by law, and therefore is considered a mandatory priority. Veterans are to be served within the context of giving priority to public assistance and low-income persons for intensive and training services. Refer to Policy No. 3640, *Revision 1: Eligibility and Priority for Services for the WIA Title IB Adult Employment and Training*, for more specific guidance and requirements regarding veterans priority of service under the WIA adult program.

Other targeting provisions for any WIA Title I funded programs, whether established by the governor or by regulation (but not by law), are considered discretionary or optional priorities. In these cases, veterans would receive priority in advance of the opportunities and services provided to the targeted population group.

The veterans' priority is not intended to displace the core function of the WIA program. The exact manner in which the veterans' priority will be applied may vary depending upon the construct of the program and the services offered. In a sequential service delivery model, when services are limited due to available funding, priority of services should be applied. For example, if there was only sufficient money to provide services to one individual and a veteran is in the pool, the veteran must receive priority.

Other Provisions for Veterans: Federal Contracting Program Reporting

The Federal Contractor Program requires that any contractor receiving a contract before December 1, 2003 from the federal government in the amount of $25,000 or more, or any subcontractor receiving a contract in the amount of $25,000 or more from such a covered contractor, must file a VETS-100 Report on an annual basis. In addition, a federal contractor or subcontractor is also required to take affirmative action to hire and promote qualified special disabled veterans, veterans of the Vietnam-era, and veterans who served on active duty during a war or in a campaign or expedition for which a campaign badge has been authorized.

Prior to amendment by the Jobs for Veterans Act, the Vietnam Era Veterans' Readjustment Assistance Act (VEVRAA), and its implementing regulations at 41 CFR 61.250 required all contractors and subcontractors with federal contracts in excess of $25,000 to report their efforts toward hiring and employing veterans in four specified categories: veterans of the Vietnam-era, special disabled veterans, other protected veterans, and recently separated veterans. JVA raised the VETS-100 reporting threshold from $25,000 to $100,000 for contracts awarded on or after December 1, 2003, and modified the report categories of veterans to disabled veterans, other protected veterans, Armed Forces service medal veterans, and recently separated veterans (41 CFR 61.300 in clearance). Additionally, JVA will require federal contractors and subcontractors to report the total number of all current employees in each job category and at each hiring location.

Why Veterans Get Federal Preference

Since the Civil War, veterans of the United States Armed Forces have been given some degree of preference in appointments to federal jobs. Recognizing their sacrifice, Congress enacted laws to prevent veterans seeking federal employment from being penalized for their time in military service. Veterans' preference recognizes the economic loss suffered by citizens who have served their country in uniform, restores veterans to a favorable competitive position for government employment, and acknowledges the larger obligation owed to disabled veterans.

Veterans' preference, in its present form, comes from the Veterans' Preference Act of 1944, as amended, and is now codified in various provisions of Title 5 of the United States Code. By law, veterans who are disabled or who served on active duty in the Armed Forces during certain specified time periods or in military campaigns, are entitled to preference over others in hiring from competitive lists of eligibles and also in retention during reductions in force.

Veterans' preference recognizes the economic loss suffered by citizens who have served their country in uniform, restores veterans to a favorable competitive position for government employment, and acknowledges the larger obligation owed to disabled veterans.

In addition to receiving preference in competitive appointments, veterans may be considered for special non-competitive appointments for which only they are eligible.

When Preference Applies

Veterans' preference does not require an agency to use any particular appointment process.

Agencies have broad authority under law to hire from any appropriate source of eligibles, including special appointing authorities.

Preference in hiring applies to permanent and temporary positions in the competitive and excepted services of the executive branch. Preference does not apply to positions in the senior executive Service or to executive branch positions for which Senate confirmation is required. The legislative and judicial branches of the federal government also are exempt from the Veterans' Preference Act unless the positions are in the competitive service (United States Government Printing Office, for example) or have been made subject to the Act by another law.

Preference in hiring applies to civil service examinations conducted by the Office of Personnel Management and agencies under delegated examining authority, for most excepted service jobs, including Veterans Recruitment Appointments (VRA), and when agencies make temporary, term, and overseas limited appointments. Veterans' preference does not apply to promotion, reassignment, change to lower grade, transfer, or reinstatement.

Veterans' preference does not require an agency to use any particular appointment process. Agencies have broad authority under law to hire from any appropriate source of eligibles, including special appointing authorities. An agency may consider candidates already in the civil service from an agency-developed merit promotion list or it may reassign a current employee, transfer an employee from another agency, or reinstate a former federal employee. In addition, agencies are required to give priority to displaced employees before using civil service examinations and similar hiring methods.

A PRACTICAL LOOK AT USERRA...

USERRA's definition of *employer* is quite different and much broader than other types of protective legislation. USERRA imposes liability for violations upon "any person. . . [who]. . . has control over employment opportunities," including "a person. . . to whom the employer" has "delegated the performance of employment-related responsibilities."

Several servicemembers have prevailed in defending their employment rights and a number of legal precedents have been sent through the courts. Many of these cases established that individual defendants (rather than the entire company) can be held liable under the provisions of USERRA.

Brandasse v. City of Suffolk, VA (1999)—Both a city, as a police officer's direct employer, and its director of personnel, who had authority over hiring and firing for the city, were subject to liability as employers under USERRA.

Jones v. Wolf Camera, Inc. (1997)—Individual supervisors could be liable under USERRA as persons with control over hiring and firing and to whom the employer has delegated the performance of employment-related responsibilities.

Satterfield v. Borough of Schuylkill Haven (1998)—Plaintiff could not bring an action under USERRA against individual members of a borough council, alleging that the council terminated him because of his military status, because such members did not have any individual power over the plaintiff and the plaintiff was not required to report to them individually.

Brooks v. Fiore (2001)—Supervisor was not covered by USERRA because he did not have the power to hire and fire the plaintiff.

Thus, courts have construed USERRA's definition of *employer* as including supervisors and managers in appropriate cases. Those courts that have found no individual liability have done so not because the language of the statute precludes it, but rather because the facts and circumstances of the case do not warrant the imposition of individual liability. Based on these considerations, the Department declines to adopt the position that individual supervisors and managers should be excluded from the regulatory definition of *employer* under USERRA.

UNDERSTANDING
USERRA TERMINOLOGY

Attorney General

The Attorney General of the United States or any person designated by the Attorney General to carry out a responsibility of the Attorney General under this chapter.

Benefit, Benefit of Employment, or Rights and Benefits

Any advantage, profit, privilege, gain, status, account, or interest (other than wages or salary for work performed) that accrues by reason of an employment contract or agreement or an employer policy, plan, or practice and includes rights and benefits under a pension plan, a health plan, an employee stock ownership plan, insurance coverage and awards, bonuses, severance pay, supplemental unemployment benefits, vacations, and the opportunity to select work hours or location of employment.

Employee

Any person employed by an employer. Such term includes any person who is a citizen or national or permanent resident alien of the United States employed in a workplace in a foreign country by an employer that is an entity incorporated or otherwise organized in the United States or that is controlled by an entity organized in the United States.

Except as noted below, the term *employer* means any person, institution, organization, or other entity that pays salary or wages for work performed or that has control over employment opportunities, including:

- a person, institution, organization, or other entity to whom the employer has delegated the performance of employment-related responsibilities;
- the federal government;
- a state;
- any successor in interest to a person, institution, organization, or other entity referred to in this subparagraph; and
- a person, institution, organization, or other entity that has denied initial employment.

Also, in the case of a National Guard technician employed under Section 709 of Title 32, the term *employer* means the adjutant general of the State in which the technician is employed.

In addition, except as an actual employer of employees, an employee pension benefit plan described in the Employee Retirement Income Security Act of 1974 (29 U.S.C. 1002(2)) shall be deemed to be an employer only with respect to the obligation to provide benefits.

Federal Executive Agency

Includes the United States Postal Service, the Postal Rate Commission, any non-appropriated fund instrumentality of the United States, any Executive agency, and any military department with respect to the civilian employees of that department.

Federal Government

Applies to any Federal executive agency, the legislative branch of the United States, and the judicial branch of the United States.

Health Plan

An insurance policy or contract, medical or hospital service agreement, membership or subscription contract, or other arrangement under which health services for individuals are provided or the expenses of such services are paid.

Notice

Any written or verbal notification of an obligation or intention to perform service in the uniformed services provided to an employer by the employee who will perform such service or by the uniformed service in which such service is to be performed.

Qualified

With respect to an employment position, means having the ability to perform the essential tasks of the position.

Reasonable Efforts

In the case of actions required of an employer under this chapter, the actions, including training provided by an employer, are those that do not place an undue hardship on the employer.

Secretary

Refers to the Secretary of Labor or any person designated by such Secretary to carry out an activity under this chapter.

Seniority

Longevity in employment together with any benefit of employment that accrues with, or is determined by, longevity in employment.

Service in the Uniformed Services

The performance of duty on a voluntary or involuntary basis in a uniformed service under competent authority. Includes active duty, active duty for training, initial active duty for training, inactive duty training, full-time National Guard duty, a period for which such person is absent from a position of employment for the purpose of an examination to determine the fitness of the person to perform any such duty, and a period for which a person is absent from a position of employment for the purpose of performing funeral honors duty.

State

Each of the several states of the United States, the District of Columbia, the Commonwealth of Puerto Rico, Guam, the Virgin Islands, and other territories of the United States (including the agencies and political subdivisions thereof).

Undue Hardship

In the case of actions taken by an employer, this means actions requiring significant difficulty or expense when considered in light of:

- the nature and cost of the action needed under this chapter;

- the overall financial resources of the facility or facilities involved in the provision of the action; the number of persons employed at such facility; the effect on expenses and resources, or the impact otherwise of such action upon the operation of the facility;

- the overall financial resources of the employer; the overall size of the business of an employer with respect to the number of its employees; the number, type, and location of its facilities; and

- the type of operation or operations of the employer, including the composition, structure, and functions of the workforce of such employer; the geographic separateness, administrative, or fiscal relationship of the facility or facilities in question to the employer.

Uniformed Services

The Armed Forces, the Army National Guard, and the Air National Guard when engaged in active duty for training, inactive duty training, or full-time National Guard duty, the commissioned corps of the Public Health Service, and any other category of persons designated by the president in time of war or national emergency.

SOURCE:
Military.com (www.military.com/benefits/legal-matters/userra/terms-and-definitions)

TYPES OF PREFERENCE
IN FEDERAL HIRING

To receive preference, a veteran must have been discharged or released from active duty in the Armed Forces under honorable conditions (i.e., with an honorable or general discharge). As defined in 5 U.S.C. 2101(2), "Armed Forces" means the Army, Navy, Air Force, Marine Corps and Coast Guard. The veteran must also be eligible under one of the preference categories below (also shown on the Standard Form (SF) 50, *Notification of Personnel Action*).

Military retirees at the rank of major, lieutenant commander, or higher are not eligible for preference in appointment unless they are disabled. (This does not apply to reservists who will not begin drawing military retired pay until age 60.)

For nondisabled users, active duty for training by National Guard or Reserve soldiers does not qualify as "active duty" for preference.

For disabled veterans, active duty includes training service in the Reserves or National Guard, per the Merit Systems Protection Board decision in *Hesse v. Department of the Army*, 104 M.S.P.R.647 (2007).

"War" is defined as only those armed conflicts declared by Congress as war and includes World War II, which covers the period from December 7, 1941, to April 28, 1952.

When applying for federal jobs, eligible veterans should claim preference on their application or resume. Applicants claiming 10-point preference must complete Standard Form (SF) 15, *Application for 10-Point Veteran Preference*, and submit the requested documentation.

The following preference categories and points are based on 5 U.S.C. 2108 and 3309 as modified by a length of service requirement in 38 U.S.C. 5303A(d). (The letters following each category, e.g., "TP," are shorthand references used by OPM in competitive examinations.)

5-Point Preference (TP)

Five points are added to the passing examination score or rating of a veteran who served:

- During a war; or

- During the period April 28, 1952 through July 1, 1955; or

- For more than 180 consecutive days, other than for training, any part of which occurred after January 31, 1955, and before October 15, 1976; or

- During the Gulf War from August 2, 1990, through January 2, 1992; or

- For more than 180 consecutive days, other than for training, any part of which occurred during the period beginning September 11, 2001, and ending on the date prescribed by presidential proclamation or by law as the last day of Operation Iraqi Freedom; or

- In a campaign or expedition for which a campaign medal has been authorized. Any Armed Forces Expeditionary medal or campaign badge, including El Salvador, Lebanon, Grenada, Panama, Southwest Asia, Somalia, and Haiti, qualifies for preference.

A campaign medal holder or Gulf War veteran who originally enlisted after September 7, 1980, (or began active duty on or after October 14, 1982, and has not previously completed 24 months of continuous active duty) must have served continuously for 24 months or the full period called or ordered to active duty. The 24-month service requirement does not apply to 10-point preference eligibles separated for disability incurred or aggravated in the line of duty, or to veterans separated for hardship or other reasons under 10 U.S.C. 1171 or 1173.

Gulf War Preference

The Defense Authorization Act of Fiscal Year 1998 (Public Law 105-85) of November 18, 1997, contains a provision (Section 1102 of Title XI) which accords veterans' preference to *everyone* who served on active duty during the period beginning August 2, 1990, and ending January 2, 1992, provided, of course, the veteran is otherwise eligible.

This means that anyone who served on active duty during the Gulf War, regardless or where or for how long, is entitled to preference if otherwise eligible (i.e., have been separated under honorable conditions and served continuously for a minimum of 24 months or the full period for which called or ordered to active duty). This applies not only to candidates seeking employment, but to federal employees who may be affected by reduction in force, as well.

SOURCE:
U.S. Office of Personnel Management (www.opm.gov/veterans/html/vetguide.asp)

FEDERAL HIRING AND THE VETERANS EMPLOYMENT OPPORTUNITIES ACT OF 1998

The Veterans Employment Opportunities Act of 1998, as amended by Section 511 of the Veterans Millennium Healthcare Act (Pub. Law 106-117) of November 30, 1999, provides that agencies must allow eligible veterans to apply for positions announced under merit promotion procedures when the agency is recruiting from outside its own workforce. ("Agency," in this context, means the parent agency, for example, the Treasury, not the Internal Revenue Service, the Department of Defense, nor Department of the Army.) A VEOA eligible who competes under merit promotion procedures and is selected will be given a career or career conditional appointment. Veterans' preference is not a factor in these appointments.

Eligibility Requirements

To be eligible for a VEOA appointment, a veteran must be a preference eligible or veteran separated after three or more years of continuous active service performed under honorable conditions. Veterans who were released shortly before completing a three-year tour are considered to be eligible.

("Active service" defined in Title 37, United States Code, means active duty in the uniformed services and includes full-time training duty, annual training duty, full-time National Guard duty, and attendance, while in the active service, at a school designated as a service school by law or by the secretary concerned.)

Terms and Conditions of Employment

Veterans who were appointed before the 1999 amendments to the VEOA were given Schedule B appointments in the excepted service. Those veterans who actually competed under merit promotion procedures will be converted to career conditional appointments retroactive to the date of their original VEOA appointments. Those who did not compete and were appointed noncompetitively will remain under Schedule B until they do compete. While under Schedule B, these employees may be promoted, demoted, or reassigned at their agency's discretion and may compete for jobs (whether in their own or other agencies) under the terms and conditions of the VEOA authority (i.e., they may apply when the agency has issued a merit promotion announcement open to candidates outside the agency). If selected, they, too, will be given career conditional appointments.

All employees appointed under the VEOA are subject to a probationary period and to the requirements of their agency's merit promotion plan.

Agencies should use ZBA-Public Law 106-117, Section 511 as the legal authority for any new appointments under the VEOA. This new authority code is effective December 1, 1999 and may be used with nature of action codes 100, 101, 500, and 501.

Appeal Rights

Employees who are appointed in the competitive service have the appeal rights of competitive service employees. Those under Schedule B have the appeal rights of excepted service employees.

A Word About VEOA

The VEOA gives preference eligibles or veterans access and opportunity to apply for positions for which the agency is accepting applications beyond its own workforce under merit promotion procedures. Access and opportunity are not an entitlement to the position and it is not a guarantee for selection.

VEOA eligibles are rated and ranked with other merit promotion candidates under the same assessment criteria such as a crediting plan, but veterans' preference is not applied. The appointing official may select any candidate from those who are among the best qualified. If selected, the VEOA eligible is given a career or career-conditional appointment, as appropriate.

SOURCE:
U.S. Office of Personnel Management (www.opm.gov/veterans/html/vetguide.asp)

FEDERAL HIRING AND VETERANS RECRUITMENT APPOINTMENT (VRA) AUTHORITY

The VRA is a special authority by which agencies can, if they wish, appoint eligible veterans without competition to positions at any grade level through General Schedule (GS)-11 or equivalent. (The promotion potential of the position is not a factor.) VRA appointees are hired under excepted appointments to positions that are otherwise in the competitive service. There is no limitation to the number of VRA appointments an individual may receive, provided the individual is otherwise eligible.

If the agency has more than one VRA candidate for the same job and one (or more) is a preference eligible, the agency must apply the veterans' preference procedures prescribed in 5 CFR Part 302 in making VRA appointments. A veteran who is eligible for a VRA appointment is not automatically eligible for Veterans' preference.

After two years of satisfactory service, the agency must convert the veteran to career or career-conditional appointment, as appropriate.

Eligibility Criteria

The Jobs for Veterans Act, Public Law 107-288, amended Title 38 U.S.C. 4214 by making a major change in the eligibility criteria for obtaining a Veterans Recruitment Appointment. Those who are eligible:

- Disabled veterans; or

- Veterans who served on active duty in the Armed Forces during a war, or in a campaign or expedition for which a campaign badge has been authorized; or

- Veterans who, while serving on active duty in the Armed Forces, participated in a United States military operation for which an Armed Forces Service Medal was awarded; or

- Recently separated veterans.

- Veterans claiming eligibility on the basis of service in a campaign or expedition for which a medal was awarded must be in receipt of the campaign badge or medal.

In addition to meeting the criteria above, eligible veterans must have been separated under honorable conditions (i.e., the individual must have received either an honorable or general discharge).

Note: Under the eligibility criteria, not all 5-point preference eligible veterans may be eligible for a VRA appointment. For example, a veteran who served during the Vietnam era (i.e., for more than 180 consecutive days, after January 31, 1955, and before October 15, 1976) but did not receive a service-connected disability or an Armed Forces Service Medal or campaign or expeditionary medal would be entitled to 5-point veterans' preference. This veteran, however, would not be eligible for a VRA appointment under the aforementioned criteria.

As another example, a veteran who served during the Gulf War from August 2, 1990, through January 2, 1992 would be eligible for veterans' preference solely on the basis of that service. However, service during that time period, in and of itself, does not confer VRA eligibility on the veteran unless one of the aforementioned VRA eligibility criteria is met.

Lastly, if an agency has two or more VRA candidates and one or more is a preference eligible, the agency must apply veterans' preference. For example, one applicant is VRA eligible on the basis of receiving an Armed Forces Service Medal (this medal does not confer veterans' preference eligibility). The second applicant is VRA eligible on the basis of being a disabled veteran (which does confer veterans' preference eligibility). In this example, both individuals are VRA eligible but only one of them is eligible for veterans' preference. As a result, agencies must apply the procedures of 5 CFR 302 when considering VRA candidates for appointment.

Making Appointments

Ordinarily, an agency may simply appoint any VRA eligible who meets the basic qualifications requirements for the position to be filled without having to announce the job or rate and rank applicants. However, as noted, veterans' preference applies in making appointments under the VRA authority. This means that if an agency has two or more VRA candidates and one or more is a preference eligible, the agency must apply veterans' preference. Furthermore, an agency must consider all VRA candidates on file who are qualified for the position and could reasonably expect to be considered for the opportunity; it cannot place VRA candidates in separate groups or consider them as separate sources in order to avoid applying preference or to reach a favored candidate.

Terms and Conditions of Employment

A VRA appointee may be promoted, demoted, reassigned, or transferred in the same way as a career employee. As with other competitive service employees, the time in grade requirement applies to the promotion of VRAs. If a VRA-eligible employee is qualified for a higher grade, an agency may, at its discretion, give the employee a new VRA appointment at a higher grade up through GS-11 (or equivalent) without regard to time-in-grade.

Agencies must establish a training or education program for any VRA appointee who has less than 15 years of education. This program should meet the needs of both the agency and the employee.

Appeal Rights

During their first year of employment, VRA appointees have the same limited appeal rights as competitive service probationers, but otherwise they have the appeal rights of excepted service employees. This means that VRA employees who are preference eligibles have adverse action protections after one year. VRAs who are not preference eligibles do not get this protection until they have completed two years of current continuous employment in the same or similar position.

Non-Permanent Appointment Based on VRA Eligibility

Agencies may make a noncompetitive temporary or term appointment based on an individual's eligibility for VRA appointment. The temporary or term appointment must be at the grades authorized for VRA appointment but is not a VRA appointment itself and does not lead to conversion to career-conditional appointment.

Thirty Percent or More Disabled Veterans

An agency may give a noncompetitive temporary appointment of more than 60 days or a term appointment to any veteran retired from active military service with a disability rating of 30% or more; or rated by the Department of Veterans Affairs since 1991 or later to include disability determinations from a branch of the Armed Forces at any time, as having a compensable service-connected disability of 30% or more.

There is no grade-level limitation for this authority, but the appointee must meet all qualification requirements, including any written test requirement.

The agency may convert the employee, without a break in service, to a career or career-conditional appointment at any time during the employee's temporary or term appointment.

SOURCE:
US Office of Personnel Management
(www.opm.gov/veterans/dvaap/2007/DVAAP-FY2007.pdf)

VETERANS WITH SERVICE-CONNECTED DISABILITIES IN THE WORKPLACE AND THE AMERICANS WITH DISABILITIES ACT (ADA)

According to government statistics, between October 2001 and February 2008, more than 30,000 veterans serving in Iraq, Afghanistan, and surrounding duty stations have been wounded in action. (Visit www. eeoc.gov/facts/veterans-disabilities-employers.html for more information.) Many of them have lost a hand or limb or have been severely burned or blinded. Others have been diagnosed with hearing loss, post-traumatic stress disorder (PTSD), traumatic brain injuries (TBIs), and other service-connected disabilities. Despite their injuries, many veterans who leave active duty are able to work.

This guide answers questions that veterans with service-connected disabilities may have about the protections they are entitled to when they seek to return to their former jobs or look to find their first, or new, civilian jobs. It also explains changes or adjustments that veterans may need, because of their injuries, to apply for, or perform a job, or to enjoy equal access to the workplace. Finally, this guide includes resources on where veterans can find more information about the employment rights of individuals with disabilities.

1. Are there any laws that protect veterans with service-connected disabilities?

Yes. At least two federal laws provide important protections for veterans with disabilities. The Uniformed Services Employment and Reemployment Rights Act has requirements for reemploying veterans with and without service-connected disabilities. The U.S. Department of Labor enforces USERRA. In addition, Title I of the Americans with Disabilities Act (ADA) prohibits private and state and local government employers with 15 or more employees from discriminating against individuals on the basis of disability. Title I of the ADA also generally requires covered employers to make reasonable accommodations in the workplace or in the way things are usually done to provide individuals with disabilities equal employment opportunities. The U.S. Equal Employment Opportunity Commission (EEOC) enforces Title I of the ADA. Finally, Section 501 of the Rehabilitation Act applies the same standards of non-discrimination and reasonable accommodation as the ADA to Federal Executive Branch agencies and the United States Postal Service.

2. How does USERRA differ from the ADA?

USERRA prohibits employers from discriminating against employees or applicants for employment on the basis of their military status or military obligations. It also protects the reemployment rights of those who leave their civilian jobs (whether voluntarily or involuntarily) to serve in the uniformed services, including the U.S. Reserve forces and state, District of Columbia, and territory (e.g., Guam) National Guards.

Both USERRA and the ADA include reasonable accommodation obligations; however, USERRA requires employers to go further than the ADA by making reasonable efforts to assist a veteran who is returning to employment in becoming qualified for a job. The employer must help the veteran become qualified to perform the duties of the position whether or not the veteran has a service-connected disability requiring reasonable accommodation. This could include providing training or retraining for the position. (See 38 U.S. Code ß 4313; 20 C.F.R. ßß 1002.198, 1002.225 -.226.) Additionally, reasonable accommodations may be available under USERRA for individuals whose service-connected disabilities may not necessarily meet the ADA's definition of *disability*. USERRA also applies to all employers, regardless of size. Information on the reemployment rights of uniformed service personnel can be found on the Department of Labor's website at www.dol.gov/vets.

Title I of the ADA prohibits employers from discriminating against qualified individuals with disabilities with respect to hiring, promotion, termination, and other terms, conditions, and privileges of employment. The ADA also prohibits disability-based harassment and provides that, absent undue hardship (significant difficulty or expense to the employer), applicants and employees with disabilities are entitled to reasonable accommodation to apply for jobs, to perform their jobs, and to enjoy equal benefits and privileges of employment (e.g., access to the parts of an employer's facility available to all employees and access to employer-sponsored training and social events). Under the ADA, an individual may ask for a reasonable accommodation at any time during the application process or during employment. It is best to request a reasonable accommodation as soon as possible after recognizing that one is needed. Additionally, an employer may have to provide someone who has been given one type of reasonable accommodation with a different or additional one (e.g., if the nature of the disability or the job changes, or if another type of accommodation becomes available). Documents explaining Title I of the ADA can be found on EEOC's website at www.eeoc.gov.

3. I was severely injured during active duty but don't think of myself as "disabled." How do I know if I am protected by the ADA?

You are protected if you meet the ADA's definition of disability. The ADA defines an "individual with a disability" as a person who (1) has a physical or mental impairment that substantially limits one or more major life activities (e.g., hearing, seeing, speaking, sitting, standing, walking, concentrating, or performing manual tasks); (2) has a record of such an impairment (i.e. was substantially limited in the past, such as prior to undergoing rehabilitation); or (3) is regarded, or treated by an employer, as having a substantially limiting impairment, even if no substantial limitation exists.

The ADA covers more than just individuals who were born with disabilities. It also covers individuals who use wheelchairs, were blinded, or became deaf because of an accident or injury and individuals who are diagnosed with medical conditions such as traumatic brain injury, major depression, and PTSD at any point in their lives.

The ADA does not require that someone be completely unable to work or perform other major life activities. In fact, the law recognizes that many people with physical or mental impairments are capable of working and protects them from discrimination that results from employer misperceptions or from the failure to make what are often simple workplace modifications.

4. I have been found to have a service-connected disability for purposes of receiving benefits related to my military service. Does this mean I am covered by the ADA?

It depends. The definition of *disability* under the ADA may differ from the definition used in other laws. For example, you may be considered a *disabled veteran* if you served on active duty in the armed forces, were honorably discharged, and have a service-connected disability, or are receiving compensation, disability retirement benefits, or pension because of a public statute administered by the Department of Veterans Affairs or a military department. (See 5 U.S.C.A. ß 2108.) It is possible that you may be a *disabled veteran*, but not covered under the ADA. For example, if you receive benefits based on a 10 % disability rating for service-connected tinnitus (which causes ringing in the ear), but are not substantially limited in hearing or some other major life activity, do not have a record of a substantial limitation, and are not treated by an employer as if you are substantially limited, then you do not have a disability under the ADA. However, it is certainly possible that you will meet both the definition of "disabled veteran" and the ADA's definition of *individual with a disability*. For example, if you have a complete loss of vision due to a combat-related injury, you are a *disabled veteran* entitled to military benefits and also an individual with a disability under the ADA.

5. Is an employer required to hire me over other applicants because I have a service-connected disability?

In most cases, it is not required. The ADA prohibits discrimination "against a qualified individual with a disability because of the disability of such individual." This means that if you are qualified for a job, an employer cannot refuse to hire you because you have a disability or because you may need a reasonable accommodation to perform the job. You are considered qualified under the ADA if you are able to meet the employer's requirements for the job, such as education, training, employment experience, skills, or licenses and are able to perform the job's essential or fundamental duties with or without reasonable accommodation. Even if you are qualified for a job, however, an employer may choose another applicant without a disability because that individual is better qualified.

Though it is not *required* to do so, an employer may *decide* to give a veteran with a service-connected disability a preference in hiring. In fact, federal agencies may use specific rules and regulations, called *special hiring authorities*, to hire individuals with disabilities outside the normal competitive hiring process, and sometimes may even be required to give preferential treatment to veterans, including disabled veterans, in making hiring, promotion, or other employment decisions. See the U.S. Office of Personnel Management's question-and-answer guide, *Excepted Service: Appointment of Persons with Disabilities and Career and Career-Conditional Appointments* at www.opm.gov/disability/appointment_disabilities.asp and Vet Guide at www.opm.gov/veterans/html/vetguide.asp. See also OPM's Disabled Veterans Affirmative Action Program at www.opm.gov/veterans/dvaap.asp.

6. During a job interview, may an employer ask about my missing arm, why I am in a wheelchair, or how I sustained any other injury I may have?

No. Even if your disability is obvious, an employer cannot ask questions about when, where, or how you were injured. However, where it seems likely that you will need a reasonable accommodation to do the job, an employer may ask you if an accommodation is needed and, if so, what type. In addition, an employer may ask you to describe or demonstrate how you would perform the job with or without an accommodation. For example, if the job requires that you lift objects weighing up to 50 pounds, the employer can ask whether you will need assistance or ask you to demonstrate how you will perform this task. Similarly, if you voluntarily reveal that you have an injury or illness and an employer reasonably believes that you will need an accommodation, he or she may ask what accommodation you need to do the job.

7. Do I have to disclose an injury or illness that is not obvious during an interview or indicate on a job application that I have a disability?

No. The ADA does not require you to disclose that you have any medical conditions on a job application or during an interview, unless you will need a reasonable accommodation to participate in the application process, such as more time to take a test or permission to provide oral instead of written responses. Some veterans with service-connected disabilities, however, may choose to disclose that they have medical conditions, such as PTSD or a TBI, because of symptoms they experience or because they will need a reasonable accommodation at work. Once an employer makes a job offer, he or she may ask you questions about your medical conditions, and perhaps even require you to take a medical examination, as long as it requires everyone else in the same job to answer the same questions and/or take the same medical examination before starting work.

8. Some applications ask me to indicate whether I am a disabled veteran. Is this legal?

Yes, if the information is being requested for affirmative action purposes. See EEOC's *Enforcement Guidance: Pre-employment Disability-Related Questions and Medical Examinations Under the Americans with Disabilities Act of 1990* (1995) at www.eeoc.gov/policy/docs/preemp.html. An employer may ask applicants to voluntarily self-identify as individuals with disabilities or disabled veterans when the employer is: (1) undertaking affirmative action because of a federal, state, or local law (including a veterans' preference law) that requires affirmative action for individuals with disabilities; or (2) voluntarily using the information to benefit individuals with disabilities, including veterans with service-connected disabilities.

If an employer invites you to voluntarily self-identify as a disabled veteran, he or she must clearly inform you in writing (or orally, if no written questionnaire is used) that: (1) the information is being requested as part of the employer's affirmative action program; (2) providing the information is voluntary; (3) failure to provide it will not subject you to any adverse treatment; and (4) the information will be kept confidential and only used in a way that complies with the ADA.

9. What types of reasonable accommodations may I request for the application process or on the job?

The following are examples of types of accommodations that may be needed for the application process or while on the job:

- written materials in accessible formats, such as large print, Braille, or on computer disk
- extra time to complete a test for a person who has difficulty concentrating or has a learning disability or traumatic brain injury

- recruitment fairs, interviews, tests, and training held in accessible locations

- modified equipment or devices (e.g., assistive technology that would allow a blind person to use a computer or someone who is deaf or hard of hearing to use a telephone; a glare guard for a computer monitor used by a person with a TBI; a one-handed keyboard for a person missing an arm or hand)

- physical modifications to the workplace (e.g., reconfiguring a workspace, including adjusting the height of a desk or shelves for a person in a wheelchair)

- permission to work from home

- leave for treatment, recuperation, or training related to the disability

- modified or part-time work schedules

- a job coach who could assist an employee who initially has some difficulty learning or remembering job tasks

- reassignment to a vacant position where a disability prevents performance of an employee's current position or where any reasonable accommodation in the current position would result in undue hardship (i.e., significant difficulty or expense)

10. How do I ask for a reasonable accommodation?

You simply have to indicate orally or in writing that you need an adjustment or change in the application process or at work for a reason related to a medical condition. For example, if you have a vision loss and cannot read standard print, you would need to inform the employer that you need the application materials in some other format (e.g., large print or on computer disk) or read to you. You do not have to mention the ADA or use the term *reasonable accommodation*. Someone acting on your behalf, such as a family member, rehabilitation counselor, health professional, or other representative, can also make the request.

11. What happens after I request a reasonable accommodation?

A *request for reasonable accommodation* is the first step in an informal interactive process between you and the employer.

The process will involve determining whether you have a disability as defined by the ADA (where this is not obvious or already known) and identifying accommodation solutions. An employer may also ask if you know what accommodation you need that will help you apply for or do the job. There are extensive public and private resources to help identify reasonable accommodations for applicants and employees with particular disabilities. For example, the website for the Job Accommodation Network (JAN) provides a practical guide for individuals with disabilities on requesting and discussing reasonable accommodations and on finding the right job. Visit JAN's website at www.jan.wvu.edu/portals/individuals.htm.

12. I am not sure whether I will need a reasonable accommodation. If I don't ask for one before I start working, can I still ask for one later?

Yes. You can request an accommodation at any time during the application process or when you start working even if you did not ask for one when applying for a job or after receiving a job offer. Generally, you should request an accommodation when you know that there is a workplace barrier that is preventing you from competing for or performing a job or having equal access to the benefits of employment. As a practical matter, it is better to request a reasonable accommodation before your job performance suffers.

13. Where can I find more information on USERRA and the ADA?

This guide includes resources on where to find information on your employment rights under both laws and provides a list of public and private organizations that can assist veterans with service-connected disabilities who are seeking employment. It also includes resources on reasonable accommodation.

SOURCE:
The U.S. Equal Employment Opportunity Commission
(www.eeoc.gov/facts/veterans-disabilities.html)

What Other Vets Are Saying...

I retired from the Army with no clue as to what I was going to do. I already knew where I was going to retire, so finding a place to live was my first concern.

Once we got settled into our new home, I started my job search. I decided to invest in a professional resume writing service, which for me was a good idea. After searching the old-fashioned way, I finally decided to start putting my resume online. During this period of adjustment, I went through some mild depression and really missed the military way of life.

I was so used to doing things a certain way for 22 years. Then, I got a call from one of the companies that advertised a job online. They put me through three interviews before I was hired.

I was pretty nervous during the first interview, but then I realized it was not different than the senior officers I'd dealt with while in the military. In the end, I was hired into a much higher position than the one I had originally found online.

The early weeks of the transition was difficult, but I just had to get used to the change. Today, I have a great job that uses the skills I spent 22 years cultivating in the service.

David Kemp
Retired Army

CHAPTER EIGHT

ONLINE AND IN-PRINT RESOURCES FOR VETERANS

A generation ago, job-hunting consisted of cruising the classified ads in the newspaper, visiting unemployment offices, and making cold calls or visits to potential employers. But today's veterans in the civilian job market, especially younger ones, are finding help online.

The number of online resources connecting veterans to jobs has mushroomed in the past few years. Veterans looking for jobs or who need help getting ready for a job search can get help at their fingertips. The federal government hosts many sites, while employment agencies, nonprofit organizations, and even veterans themselves host others.

Through the Internet, departing and former servicemembers can find help with resume building, interviewing tips, military-friendly companies, upcoming career fairs, and understanding more about employment-related rights as a veteran. The list is endless as more sites are being added every day.

The listings in this chapter are provided as resources for your information purposes only. It is not an indication of endorsement; therefore, when surfing these resources, as with all online activities, be careful in accessing the services offered. Check out sites carefully. Find out who sponsors the site. Stick with known and reputable companies or organizations.

You may want to begin your search with the Department of Veterans Affairs website at www.va.gov. In addition to post-military employment help and links, the VA site provides a wealth of information about all aspects of life following your military service. Another government site that is helpful to veterans is FirstGov at www.firstgov.gov. This site is the official web portal of the United States government, and its veteran's page includes links to many useful sites.

Another site worth investigating is the Veterans Resource Network Association at www.vrna.org. This site's stated goal is to educate veterans about the benefits and programs they are entitled to, provide a network through which veterans can support one another, and generally enhance the lives of those who have risked their lives for their country. The site offers useful links and discount programs for veterans.

Finally, you may want to take a look at the National Coalition for Homeless Veterans website at www.nchv.org. Dedicated to eradicating veteran homelessness, the site shows how to get back on your feet if you are a veteran who is experiencing difficult times, and how to help veterans in need, whether you are a veteran yourself or simply a concerned citizen.

Each of these sites provides links to additional resources, as well as to the other sites listed in this chapter. You are not alone. A number of online resources are available to offer you support, assistance, and information.

General Information Sites for Veterans

US Department of Veteran's Affairs
www.va.gov
The official website of the Veteran's Administration, which offers a wide range of benefits for the nation's veterans, servicemembers, and their families.

Military Spot
www.militaryspot.com
A private military website offering an array of resources for military people: military news, daily photos and videos, and interactive features (forums, photo and video uploads, and a military social networking community) where users actively participate, contribute, and share.

Military.com
www.military.com

Owned by Monster®, Military.com's free membership connects servicemembers, military families, and veterans to all the benefits of service—government benefits, scholarships, discounts, lifelong friends, mentors, great stories of military life or missions, and much more.

TurboTAP.org™
www.transitionassistanceprogram.com

A department of Defense-sponsored website of transition assistance resources for servicemembers (separatees and retirees) about to depart from military service, including online access to the DoD's *Pre-separation Guide* and the *Transition Guide* for Guard and Reserve servicemembers.

DoD TRANSPORTAL
www.dodtransportal.dod.mil

This site is designed specifically to assist servicemembers leaving active duty, including transition assistance, pre-separation and transition guides, an online booklet for transitioning members of the National Guard and Reserve, and a mini-course on conducting a successful job search campaign.

Civilian Personnel Management Service
www.cpms.osd.mil

This is the official website for information about civilian personnel programs, systems, policies, and guidance at the Department of Defense.

Employer Support of the Guard and Reserve (ESGR)
http://esgr.org

A DoD-sponsored site that helps to promote the work of ESGR, established to promote cooperation and understanding between Reserve component members and their civilian employers and to assist in the resolution of conflicts arising from an employee's military commitment.

Department of Defense
www.defenselink.mil

The official website for the Department of Defense and the starting point for finding U.S. military information online.

Today's Military
www.todaysmilitary.com

This DoD-sponsored site is intended to inform students, parents, and educators as they discuss the military as a career option, including reservist duty.

Department of Veterans Affairs
www.vetsuccess.gov

The purpose of this Department of Veterans Affairs website is to present information about the services that the Vocational Rehabilitation and Employment (VR&E) program provides to veterans with service-connected disabilities. It also provides information about vocational counseling available to active duty servicemembers, and veterans who have recently separated from active duty.

Veterans Today
www.veteranstoday.com

A website for veterans.

GovBenefits
www.govbenefits.gov

GovBenefits is a partnership of federal agencies with a shared vision to provide improved, personalized access to government assistance programs.

Vet Friends
www.vetfriends.com

A web portal for ex-military, featuring information on many aspects of military and veteran life.

Leatherneck
www.leatherneck.com

An online community for information sharing and exchange for marine veterans.

Education Sites

In addition to the following sites, conduct a keyword search on "veterans education" for more information about education opportunities and benefits.

American Council on Education
www.acenet.edu

ACE is the major coordinating body for all of the nation's higher education institutions, including providing oversight for granting academic credit for military training and service.

Creating Futures
www.creatingfutures.us

Sponsored by the Computing Technology Industry Association (CompTIA), Creating Futures strives to give transitioning veterans, individuals with disabilities, youths-at-risk, and dislocated workers the opportunity to achieve careers in the Internet technology field.

University World
www.university-world.com

An education portal of links to all colleges, schools, and universities in the United States, Canada, and Europe offering either undergraduate or graduate programs.

Careers and Education
www.careersandeducation.com

CareersandEducation.com is an educational resource center where individuals can find information on college degrees, certificates, high school diplomas, and more.

GI Bill
www.gibill.va.gov

This government site offers information and resources related to veterans' education rights.

The Fund for Veterans' Education
www.veteransfund.org

The Fund for Veterans' Education was established to provide scholarships to veterans from all branches of the U.S. Armed Forces who served in Afghanistan or Iraq since September 11, 2001 and who are now enrolled in college or vocational-technical school.

Financial Aid
www.finaid.org

The site provides information on financial aid available to veteran's pursing higher education.

Employment-Related Services

Baseops
www.baseops.net/transition
A selection of articles and books to help guide former military personnel in transitioning to civilian job searching.

O*NET
http://online.onetcenter.org/crosswalk
Maintained on behalf of the Department of Labor's Employment and Training Administration, site-users can enter a code or title from the CIP, MOC, RAPIDS, DOT, or SOC to find matching O*NET-SOC occupations, as well as job descriptions for hot career markets.

HireVetsFirst
www.hirevetsfirst.gov
This site is a government-sponsored employment portal designed for use by veterans and the companies seeking to hire them.

Army Career and Alumni Program
www.acap.army.mil
This site was created as part of the Army Career and Alumni Program to help veterans.

Ideal Military Hire
www.idealhire.com
Ideal Military Hire works with existing veterans, transitioning servicepersons, and their families in finding civilian jobs. It also includes access to a free military skills translator for turning military job titles into civilian job language.

Career Opportunities
www.career-opportunities.net
Provides information on schools and careers.

U.S. Office of Personnel Management
www.opm.gov/veterans
This government site features the VetsInfo Guide, offers a brief explanation on how the federal employment system works, and how veterans' preference and the special appointing authorities operate within that system.

10 Minute Resume
www.10minuteresume.com

This site offers free access to intelligent expert-software that helps resume writers frame their qualifications in the best possible way by using a series of steps. It guides users with tips and phrases to make the most of their credentials. As an additional service, 10 Minute Resume will post resumes to some of the best job sites on the Internet for free.

The Army Civilian Resume Builder and ANSWER
https://cpolst.belvoir.army.mil/public/resumebuilder/builder/index.jsp

The Resume Builder is designed to assist users in entering their resume into the Army's centralized Resumix system. Users can enter their resume, as well as provide supplemental data, to indicate their qualifications and preferences. Once a resume is entered using this system, the record is integrated with the other staffing tools used by the Army to recruit and place applicants.

Resume Templates
www.resume-templates.com

The website has downloadable products with over 250 sample resumes and a resource section with tips for resume writing.

ResumeDeliver
www.resumedeliver.com

Offers free, targeted resume delivery for job seekers. Users can select up to five regions and five industries to blast their resumes to thousands of interested recruiters.

Professional-Resume
www.professional-resume.org

A low cost resume and cover letter development service, that also offers free resume samples.

Employment Sites

AviaNation
www.avianation.com

Features aviation jobs and employment opportunities worldwide.

Veterans Resource Network Association
www.vrna.org.

This site's stated goal is to educate veterans about the benefits and programs they are entitled to and provide a network through which veterans can support one another.

Career Command Post
www.careercommandpost.com

This site specializes in bringing transitioning active duty military personnel and armed forces veterans together with civilian employers that are hiring for executive, managerial, professional, technical, skilled and semi-skilled positions.

Federal Jobs Net
http://federaljobs.net

This career center was created to help federal government job hunters find, apply for, and land government jobs. It was expanded to assist federal employees seeking upward mobility, career progression, and retirement planning assistance. Federal Jobs Net also includes comprehensive information on postal employment, overseas jobs, law enforcement opportunities, veteran's benefits, handicapped employment options, and special emphasis hiring programs.

Post Office Jobs
http://postofficejobs.info

This site assists with your job search and it provides valuable post office employment information that can help you land a high-paying and secure job. You will find a vast array information including a description of the postal exam and study guide, test dates in your area, job opportunities, qualification requirements, civil service application assistance, and employee benefits and salaries.

Healthcare Jobs
http://healthcarejobs.org

Healthcare Jobs helps locate and explore all medical, hospital, and nursing jobs. Users can also find jobs with the Veterans Administration.

Quintessential Careers
www.quintcareers.com

Site contains more than 3,500 pages of free college, career, and job search content.

Corporate Gray
www.corporategrayonline.com

A site for former military personnel to post resumes and search for jobs. It also includes articles and resources of interest for veterans.

Landmark Destiny Group
www.destinygrp.com

Site features a variety of resources for former military personnel, including job-hunting tips, resume writing, and job postings.

Military Candidates
www.militarycandidates.com

A site where active duty military personnel transitioning to the civilian workforce can search job listings by industry and submit resumes. Free to job seekers. Military candidates also includes basic job-search resources.

Recruit Military
www.recruitmilitary.com

A free service, Recruit Military matches military veterans and their spouses with military-friendly employers around the world. The website is targeted to military veterans, including enlisted transitioning military personnel, as well as senior officers and junior military officers.

Military Hire
www.militaryhire.com

Operated by veterans for veterans, Military Hire is about helping service veterans (active duty, reserve, and national guard) and their immediate family members transition to civilian employment. Job seekers can conduct a detailed job search, post resumes, and take advantage of career resources. Free to job seekers.

Military Job Zone
www.militaryjobzone.com

The site provides veteran users with the transition assistance needed to start a civilian career. The service is open to all veterans seeking employment: enlisted technicians, enlisted leaders, junior military officers, retired military, and ex-military personnel. Military Job Zone also contains information about military veteran jobs, military job placement, and general military to civilian career transition assistance.

Power Careers
www.power-careers.com

A veteran-owned service providing free transition assistance to active duty military members, as well as industry experienced ex-military leaders and technicians seeking to launch their careers in a new direction within the power generation and industrial manufacturing industries.

Military Spot
www.militaryspot.com

A private military web portal offering an array of resources for military people: military news, daily photos and videos, interactive features (forums, photo and video uploads, and a military social networking community) where users actively participate, contribute, and share.

Military Job Hunts
www.militaryjobhunts.com

Website for ex-military and veterans with technical, supervisory, and middle- management experience. Consists of targeted websites with quality job-listing sources and inexpensive career transition counseling and services for troublesome job hunts.

Nurse Universe
www.nurseuniverse.com

Job postings by state, as well as an array of information regarding a career in nursing.

Placement USA
www.placementusa.com

An online career resource for job seekers, employers, and recruiters.

Employment for Physicians
www.employmentforphysicians.com

A complete resource of physician employment (seekers and recruiters), physician jobs, and different varieties of medical, cardiology, and medicine jobs.

Biohealthmatics
www.biohealthmatics.com

A career networking site for biotechnology and healthcare IT careers.

Seltek Consultants
www.seltekconsultants.co.uk

U.K. science sales recruitment specialists for the recruitment of scientific sales people at all levels from graduate to sales director. Areas of concentration are life sciences, biotechnology, molecular biology, chemistry, diagnostics, immunology, and instrumentation.

Transition Assistance Online
www.taonline.com

In this transition assistance website, both prior and current servicemembers can find resources needed to transition from their military service to a desired civilian career. The site is open to employers and advertisers seeking ex-military and military candidates and to veterans who wish to search job ads, post resumes, and explore business and educational opportunities.

Vet Jobs
www.vetjobs.com

Owned and operated by veterans for veterans, Vet Jobs matches veteran-friendly employers with veterans seeking jobs in the civilian sector.

GI Jobs Online
www.gijobs.net

A civilian career guide for ex-military job seekers. Releases an annual list of the nation's Top 50 Most Military-Friendly Employers.

Hire a Hero
www.hireahero.org

Hire a Hero is a non-profit initiative founded by the Armed Forces Support Foundation. The site brings together military job seekers and military-friendly employers.

Military Spouse
www.milspouse.com

An online resource library for military spouse employment, education, and relocation information. It features links to employment-related information and other resources for military spouses and military families.

REALifelines (U.S. Department of Labor)
www.dol.gov/vets

Provides valuable information and access to contact information for one-on-one employment assistance and online resources to assist wounded and injured transitioning servicemembers and veterans in their reintegration into the civilian workforce. Intended for use by wounded and injured transitioning servicemembers, the site offers extensive information and resources that can benefit all veterans.

American Legion Federal Jobs
www.vetjobs.us

This site is an employment portal sponsored by the American Legion, in partnership with Avue. Through this site, you will be able to search for federal jobs by geographic location, have exclusive access to Avue's career choice advisor, get useful information on special hiring authorities for veterans, learn how veterans' preference is used in the federal hiring process, get tips on marketing your military experience, and a host of other information designed to address the special information needs of our country's veterans. The free membership includes access to military skill translation software.

Employer Assistance and Recruiting Network (EARN)
www.earnworks.com

EARN can connect you with employers in your area by linking you with local employment service providers in their network. Although EARN does not provide direct jobseeker placement, it works with its network to find you employment opportunities.

TechExpoUSA
www.techexpousa.com

This technology industry career center site and home of TECHEXPO Career Fairs seeks to bring qualified professionals together with the nation's leading employers from commercial and government sectors.

Soar Consulting, Inc.
www.soarcareers.com

SOAR Consulting specializes in military transition jobs, matching transitioning junior military officers, and enlisted leaders and technicians with some of America's top companies interested in recruiting candidates with developmental potential.

Link Up
www.linkup.com

An employment opportunity search engine that allows relevant searches using a variety of criteria, including geography, company, job description, keywords, and company size.

Career Voyages
www.careervoyages.gov

This website is a collaborative effort between the U.S. Department of Labor and the U.S. Department of Education. It is designed to provide information on high growth, in-demand occupations along with the skills and education needed to attain those jobs.

Career One Stop
www.careeronestop.org

The site, sponsored by the U.S. Department of Labor, features tools to help job seekers, students, businesses, and career professionals.

America's Job Bank
www.ajb.dni.us

A free service of the U.S. Department of Labor and the Public Employment Agency (unemployment office). Approximately 95% of the jobs listed are in the private sector, while 5% are in government.

Bigwigs.net
www.bigwigs.net

An executive employment resource for $100,000-plus compensated candidates to confidentially post their resumes and search jobs. Companies and recruiters can search resumes and post employment opportunities.

Career Bank
www.careerbank.com

This national job bank site focuses on careers in accounting and finance. Career Bank is a national site that provides career resources, as well as job listings.

Career Builder
www.careerbuilder.com

Career Builder boasts over 900,000 available jobs and includes helpful utilities like salary and resume tools and valuable tips on how to conduct interviews.

My Career Guide
www.mycareerguide.com

A career information site to help users make the right career choice. My Career Guide includes a number of career-related resources.

Career Magazine
www.careermag.com

This site offers job openings, employer profiles, news and articles, resume banks, career forums, job fairs, recruiter and consultant directories, relocation resources, and career links.

Career Manage
www.careermanage.com

Career Manage is an automated job search and career management service that promotes a design around the individual, rather than a traditional focus on the hiring company.

Career Net
www.careers.org

Career Net features over 11,000 links to jobs, employers, and education and career service professionals on the Internet. The site includes over 6,000 career resource references.

Computer Work
http://computerwork.com

This site features computer jobs and technical employment opportunities (VIS computer programming professionals, including programmers, DBAs, analysts, etc.) in the United States and Canada.

Corporation for Public Broadcasting
www.cpb.org

The Corporation for Public Broadcasting website features information and leads on public radio and television job announcements.

Developers
www.developers.net

A free employment service for software developers. The new searchable database has over 30,000 software development positions.

Dice Consultants Data Base
www.dice.com

A job search database for computer consultants and high tech professionals.

Elite Farmer
www.elitefarmer.com

Elite Farmer aims to disseminate information to people with small farms or rural property and career development resources to educate and prepare workforce-ready graduates.

For Farmers
www.forfarmers.com

A career site for workers seeking positions involved in the field of agriculture, featuring agricultural-related positions from around the world.

Garments Only
www.garmentsonly.com

A jobs portal focused on fashion and garment/apparel industry positions and the employers and recruiters searching for professionals in the field.

Help Wanted
www.helpwanted.com

A free job search website.

Hireability
www.hireability.com

Connecting technology job seekers with employers and recruiters.

Hotel Travel Jobs
www.hoteltraveljobs.com

Search for hotel, travel, restaurant, and other hospitality sector jobs from entry-level to management positions. The site is free for job seekers.

Mobile Marketing Job List
www.mobilemarketingjoblist.com

A job search portal for promotional, mobile marketing, special events, and experiential marketing job seekers, employers, and recruiters.

Monster
Monster.com

Monster offers free resume posting services with access to thousands of jobs and career/employment resources.

Netshare
www.netshare.com

This job posting service provides a means for staffing agencies, human resource professionals, and small business executives to take advantage of electronic recruiting.

iHire Publishing
www.ihirepublishing.com

A fee-based site that offers leads to jobs in the publishing industry.

Programming Services
www.programming-services.com

Users can post resumes for free, delete postings when required, as well as receive e-mails when a job or resume is posted.

Resume Coaches
www.resumecoaches.com

Resume Coaches will help you get the right job. Their unique service goes beyond traditional resume preparation and includes phone consultations, interview speakers' notes, and other services such as coaching.

Resume Rabbit
www.resumerabit.com

The service will instantly post your resume to Monster.com, Job.com, Headhunter.net, Dice.com, and other top jobs sites.

Resume Mailman
www.resumemailman.com

E-mail your resume to thousands of recruiters instantly.

TechReq
www.techreq.net

A technical staffing agency that offers temporary staffing and direct full-time placement of engineers, programmers, and IT professionals in California.

Tech Vibes
www.techvibes.com/job

Jobs listings in the field of technology that also includes a broader community of resources.

Television Jobs
www.tvjobs.com

An Internet-based employment service dedicated to helping job seekers find employment in the highly competitive broadcast marketplace.

Travel Jobs
www.traveljobz.net

An online job and resume posting board for employment in the U.S. travel and tourism industries.

The Riley Guide
www.rileyguide.com

The Riley Guide introduces users to the online job search, listing useful online sites and services related to conducting a job search. The site does not post jobs or resumes, but instead points users to sites that do.

Jobs For Programmers
www.prgjobs.com

Employment site for programmers. Search for jobs in C++, Visual Basic, Java, Oracle, WWW, Cobol, and Telecommute.

The Job Resource
www.thejobresource.com

A free site to connect recent college graduates and students to relevant employment and internships.

Tech Job Bank
www.techjobbank.com

The site focuses on listing job openings in the high-tech fields of computer/IT, electronics, and semiconductors.

LearningExpress's Top Test Prep Titles and Career Guides for Vets

Civil Service Test Prep: 9 Steps to a Great Federal Job
978-1-57685-509-6
$19.95

Becoming a Caseworker
978-1-57685-614-7
$14.95

Becoming a Firefighter
978-1-57685-655-0
$14.95

Border Patrol Exam, 4th Edition
978-1-57685-672-7
$24.95

California Police Officer Exam, 2nd Edition
978-1-57685-588-1
$35.00

Civil Service Exams
978-1-57685-592-8
$14.95

Corrections Officer Exam, 3rd Edition
978-1-57685-652-9
$14.95

Court Officer Exam
978-1-57685-580-5
$18.95

Firefighter Exam, 4th Edition
978-1-57685-671-0
$16.95

Math and Vocabulary for Civil Service Exams
978-1-57685-606-2
$19.95

Police Officer Exam, 3rd Edition
978-1-57685-576-8
$14.95

Police Sergeant Exam, 2nd Edition
978-1-57685-572-0
$18.95

Postal Worker Exam, 4th Edition
978-1-57685-525-6
$16.95

Probation Officer/Parole Officer Exam
978-1-57685-582-9
$18.95

State Trooper Exam
978-1-57685-583-6
$18.95

Treasury Enforcement Agent Exam, 2nd Edition
978-1-57685-537-9
$18.95

Professional Licensing Test Prep
CDL: Commercial Driver's License Test Prep
978-1-57685-659-8
$26.95

EMS Essentials
978-1-57685-385-6
$14.95

EMT-Basic Exam, 4th Edition
978-1-57685-620-8
$19.95

Healthcare Essentials

978-1-57685-419-8

$17.95

Health Occupations Entrance Exam

978-1-57685-478-5

$24.95

Nursing Assistant/Nurse Aide Exam, 3rd Edition

978-1-57685-547-8

$19.95

Nursing School Entrance Exam

978-1-57685-481-5

$19.95

Paramedic Exam, 3rd Edition

978-1-57685-544-7

$19.95

Workplace Skills: Business Writing Clear and Simple

978-1-57685-414-3

$15.95

The Complete Professional

978-1-57685-344-3

$14.95

Job Interviews That Get You Hired

978-1-57685-549-2

$12.95

Math for the Trades

978-1-57685-515-7

$15.95

Resumes That Get You Hired

978-1-57685-550-8

$12.95

Search Smart and Get Ahead

978-1-57685-202-6

$14.95

NOTES

NOTES

NOTES

NOTES

NOTES

NOTES

NOTES

NOTES

NOTES